Competitive Positioning

The key to market success

Competitive Positioning
The key to market success

GRAHAM J. HOOLEY

Aston Business School
Aston University

and

JOHN SAUNDERS

Loughborough University
Business School

Prentice Hall
New York ■ *London* ■ *Toronto* ■ *Sydney* ■ *Tokyo* ■ *Singapore*

First published 1993 by
Prentice Hall International (UK) Ltd
Campus 400, Maylands Avenue
Hemel Hempstead
Hertfordshire, HP2 7EZ
A division of
Simon & Schuster International Group

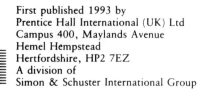

Typeset in 10/12pt Sabon
by MHL Typesetting Limited, Coventry

Printed and bound in Great Britain by
Redwood Books, Trowbridge, Wiltshire.

Library of Congress Cataloging-in-Publication Data

Hooley, Graham, J.
    Competitive positioning: the key to market success by
Graham Hooley and John Saunders.
       p.   cm.
    Includes bibliographical references and index.
    ISBN 0-13-155599-5 (pbk.)
    1. Marketing—Management.   2. Strategic planning.   3. Competition.
I. Saunders, John A., 1946–   II. Title.
HF5415.13.H668   1993
658.8'02—dc20   92-32732
                                       CIP

British Library Cataloging-in-Publication Data

A catalogue record for this book is available from the British

ISBN 0-13-155599-5 (pbk)

---

3 4 5 96 95 94 93

For
Jackie, Tom and Katy
Veronica, Carolyne and Paul

Contents

Preface

This book is about creating and sustaining superior performance in the market place. It deals with the two central issues in marketing strategy formulation:

- The identification of target market or markets — the customers that the organisation will seek to serve.
- The creation of a differential advantage, or competitive edge, that will enable the organisation to serve that target market more effectively than the competition.

Taken together decisions on these two issues create the *competitive positioning* of the organisation, from which implementation of the marketing programme, and hence elements of the marketing mix, are dictated.

PART ONE is concerned with strategy development and the role of marketing in strategy formulation. Important issues for marketing in the 1990s are identified and a framework for developing marketing strategy is presented that is then used in the rest of the book.

PART TWO deals with the competitive environment in which the company operates. Different types of strategic environment are first considered together with the critical success factors for dealing with each type. Discussion then focuses on the 'strategic triangle' of customers, competitors and company. Ways of analysing each in turn are explored to help identify the options open to the company. The emphasis is on matching corporate capabilities to market opportunities.

PART THREE examines in more detail the techniques available for identifying market segments (or potential targets) and current (and potential) positions. Alternative bases for segmenting both consumer and industrial markets are considered in detail as are the data collection and analysis techniques available.

PART FOUR returns to strategy formulation. Selection of market target through consideration of market attractiveness and business strength is followed by discussion of how to create a defensible position in the market place. Strategies for both defending own, and attacking competitor, positions are explored in detail.

The book is intended for two markets. It will be of interest to marketing practitioners who wish to explore new ways of looking at their markets with a view to gaining an edge over their competitors. It will also be of interest to students of marketing and business strategy on both undergraduate and postgraduate (MBA) programmes as a second level, specialist text.

Marketing strategy

The first part of the book is concerned with strategy development and in particular the role of marketing in leading strategy.

Chapter 1 discusses the need for organisations, both in the profit and non-profit sectors, to adopt the *marketing concept*, to put customers at the centre of their operations and to operationalise their goals in terms of *creating customer satisfaction*. Major changes in the marketing environment (political, economic, social, cultural and technological) are discussed and their implications for marketing management identified. The chapter then goes on to outline a set of *fundamental marketing principles* that should guide the actions of all organisations operating in competitive markets. Finally, the *role of marketing in leading strategic management* is discussed.

Chapter 2 presents a framework for developing a marketing strategy that is then adopted throughout the remainder of the book. A three-stage process is suggested. First is the establishment of the *core strategy*. This involves defining the business purpose, assessing the alternatives open to the organisation through an analysis of *customers*, *competition* and the *competencies* of the organisation, and deciding on the *strategic focus* that will be adopted. Second is the creation of the *competitive positioning* for the company. This boils down to the selection of *target market/s* (which dictates where the organisation will compete) and the establishment of a *differential advantage* (which spells out how it will compete). Third, *implementation* issues are discussed: the achievement of the positioning through the use of the *marketing mix*, *organisation* and *control* of the marketing effort.

Chapter 3 examines *portfolio planning* in a multibusiness organisation. Different product types are considered together with various techniques for modelling portfolio balance (in terms of today and tomorrow, cash use and generation, and risk and return).

The ideas and frameworks presented in Part One are used to structure the remainder of the book, leading into a more detailed discussion of market analysis in Part Two, segmentation and positioning analysis in Part Three and implementation of positioning strategies in Part Four.

ONE

Market-led strategic management

The purpose of business is to create and keep a customer.

Levitt (1986)

Introduction

Marketing, as an approach to doing business, has come of age. While a decade ago marketing was misunderstood by many senior managers, and typically thought to be just a fancy new name for good old-fashioned selling, nowadays most chief executives could offer passably accurate textbook definitions of marketing, centring on identifying and satisfying customer requirements at a profit.

As Piercy (1991) notes, however, while 'marketing' is on the lips of many managers in both private and public sector organisations, the critical issues have shifted from understanding what marketing is to actually implementing it. As organisations strive to become 'market focused' or 'customer led' so it becomes clear that marketing is a beguilingly simple philosophy, or approach to business, but often somewhat harder to put into practice.

This chapter sets the scene for the remainder of the book by examining what is meant by being 'market led' in the development of strategy for an organisation. It starts by briefly reviewing the marketing concept as an approach for businesses in assessing the main components of marketing orientation, relates these to the realities of the market in the 1990s and concludes by defining the role of marketing in leading strategic direction.

1.1 Marketing as a business philosophy

There has been much debate in recent years as to what marketing is all about (see, for example, Kotler and Levy, 1969; Hunt, 1976; and Lusch and Laczniak, 1987). In 1985 the American Marketing Association sought to clarify the situation. It reviewed over 25 marketing definitions before arriving at its own, now more or less universally accepted definition (see Ferrell and Lucas, 1987): 'Marketing is the process of planning and executing the conception, pricing, planning and distribution of ideas, goods and services to create exchanges that satisfy individual and organisational objectives.'

The above definition clearly places marketing as a process that is performed within an organisation. Within most western organisations of any size this process is managed by a marketing department or function. Bernard (1987) and Brown (1987), among others, however, have argued that in addition to being a process or function marketing is also an organisational philosophy, an approach to doing business. In addition, King (1985) has criticised too narrow a perspective on marketing — confining it to what a 'bolt on' marketing department does — and recommends a broader interpretation of what constitutes applying marketing.

Marketing in reality is both a management process (the activities conducted to ensure a fit between what the organisation supplies and what its customers want) and a business philosophy (often called the 'marketing concept') that should guide the approach of the entire organisation.

1.1.1   Approaches to marketing

A large-scale survey of marketing approaches and practices in the UK (see Hooley, Lynch and Shepherd, 1990) categorised respondent companies' approaches to marketing on the basis of how they viewed marketing and what was done by way of marketing activities. The analysis resulted in four categories of company shown in Figure 1.1.

The 'sales supporters' viewed marketing from a functional perspective. It was seen by them as a sales and promotional support activity. Marketing was confined to what the marketing or sales departments did and was not seen as particularly relevant to other parts of the organisation.

The 'departmental marketers' had a more up-to-date view of the functions performed

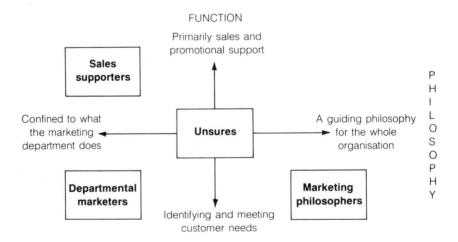

Source: Hooley, Lynch and Shepherd (1990).

Figure 1.1 Marketing approaches

by marketing — identifying customer needs and ensuring the organisation gears itself to meeting them. They still, however, saw marketing as a set of activities (now including marketing research) that were done by marketing specialists.

The 'marketing philosophers' recognised the same functional activities for marketing as the departmental marketers. In addition, and here is the crucial difference, they recognised that marketing is more than just what the marketing people do. They see marketing as a guiding philosophy, or approach to business, for the whole organisation.

The final group identified were termed the 'unsures'. These organisations did not seem to have any clear ideas about what marketing is, either in functional or philosophical terms.

1.1.2   The marketing concept

Put simply, the marketing concept holds that, in increasingly dynamic and competitive markets, the companies or organisations that are most likely to succeed are those that take notice of customer expectations, wants and needs and gear themselves to satisfying them better than their competitors. It recognises that there is no reason why customers should buy one organisation's offerings unless they are in some way better at serving their wants and needs than those offered by competing organisations.

Levitt (1986) has long argued that the purpose of business is not to make profits (profits, he argues, are merely necessary for survival) but rather to create and keep customers. To Levitt the old profit motive is immoral and outdated, and its course is now run.

Most executives with a real commercial company to run, however, would argue that their goal must be profit — that, after all, is what the owners of the company own it for, and why in harsh economic trading times the banks continue to support it. But what is crucial is how, in the increasingly competitive markets of the 1990s and beyond, long-term survival and profits can be assured (or at least made more likely).

The problems in the non-profit sector are no less acute. Churches, charities and other non-profit organisations such as Greenpeace and CND have their own long-term objectives to change attitudes, increase environmental awareness or abolish nuclear weapons. They also, however, compete for the scarce disposable income of potential donors and the active support of volunteers. Public services too compete with each other for central or local government funding to ensure their continued survival and their ability to put their cherished programmes into operation. For each to fulfil its long-term objectives, it must satisfy its more immediate 'customers' (donors, government, society at large, etc.), though it might not be completely comfortable with thinking of them as customers.

Logically there is only one sustainable route both for commercial and non-profit organisations both to survive and to pursue their other long-term objectives, and that is through serving their customers so well that the customers will continue to support

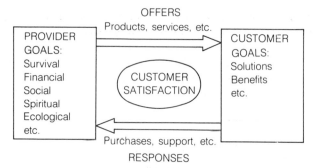

OFFERS
Products, services, etc.

PROVIDER
GOALS:
Survival
Financial
Social
Spiritual
Ecological
etc.

CUSTOMER
SATISFACTION

CUSTOMER
GOALS:
Solutions
Benefits
etc.

Purchases, support, etc.
RESPONSES

Figure 1.2   Mutually beneficial exchanges·

the organisation. In other words, the crucial operating goal should be to achieve customer satisfaction so as to enable other goals, such as survival, profit or the attainment of other social objectives, to be met in the longer term.

In essence, then, marketing is about facilitating mutually beneficial exchanges that create value for both the organisation and its customer (see Figure 1.2). The customer and the organisation producing the service or product must both get benefit from the exchange for it to continue into the future.

1.1.3   Who is involved in marketing?

The simple answer to the above question is: *everybody* in the organisation. The marketing concept is an approach to business that should not be confined to marketing people alone but should permeate the whole of the organisation's operations.

■   A national UK newspaper in the early 1980s reported a problem with EPOS (electronic point of sale) equipment in a branch of a well-known national supermarket chain. The branch was one of the first to be fitted with the new technology that basically removed the need for individual item pricing on the pack but enabled the price to be detected and charged through use of a light pen at the checkout from a bar coding. In addition to the obvious advantage of more rapid, and error-free, checking of customer goods the computerised system allowed for monitoring of stock levels and automatic reordering when stocks were sufficiently depleted.

Unfortunately, late one Saturday afternoon soon after installation, the computer system failed. Around 200 customers were in the store with trolleys full of food for the weekend but the checkouts were unable to add their bills due to the lack of individually marked prices. The assistant manager was called but he failed to make the system work again, and no immediate help was available from the computer system supplier. The manager was faced with increasingly irate customers and no real prospect of the technology responding.

There were, of course, several options the manager could have taken. He could have asked his staff to price items individually (this would probably have taken too long). He could have asked the customers to go back and note down the prices (at the risk of a riot!). He could also have asked each customer to estimate the value of his or her trolley and accepted the possible losses from selling cheaper than the marked price.

Perhaps with more marketing philosophy inside him he could even have given away the food free with the supermarket's compliments and gained customer goodwill and valuable good publicity for the store (200 shoppers at, say, £50 each would only have cost around £10,000 — a fraction of the store's daily turnover and peanuts in relation to its corporate advertising and promotional budget). Instead he asked the customers to leave without their food, offering to keep the trolleys as they were until Monday when they could be claimed and checked out on the repaired equipment.

The customers were enraged by this alternative (their Sunday meals were in the trolleys!) and refused to go without the food they had spent around an hour collecting from the shelves. The manager insisted they leave and eventually called the police to evict them. Needless to say a great deal of bad publicity ensued. (Example courtesy of Rick Brown, Bradford Management Centre.) ■

This story illustrates a distinct lack of marketing orientation on the part of the assistant manager. To be fair to him, however, the management system which led to the solution he chose was probably more to blame. His authority would not have extended to giving away £10,000 worth of groceries! Far from encouraging a marketing orientation many retail stores in practice train their managers to beware the customer, to ensure that items are not stolen from the shelves and to avoid losses at all costs. The customer is seen almost as a necessary inconvenience to an efficiently run operation. Any customer orientation that may have existed at marketing director level fails to filter through to the individuals responsible for dealing at the sharp end with the ultimate customers.

Beyond current costs and benefits, however, each existing customer should be seen as a future customer. An average weekly expenditure of £50 represents an annual spend of around £2,500 (or £500,000 for all 200). It is likely that much of this potential business was turned away through the actions taken. Contrast the attitude of the manager above with Stew Leonard, founder and chief executive of Stew Leonard's Dairy in the USA (reported in Peters, 1988), who sees every customer at his dairy as a potential $50,000 account over a successful ten-year shopping relationship.

Similar, though less dramatic, problems can be encountered when advertising of one sort or another induces customer action that the company is not fully geared up to respond to, or creates expectations that cannot easily be met. Clearing banks, for example, send information about new services available to customers with promises to 'listen', take 'action' or 'say yes'. Often the reality of the branch outlet, however, is a cashier under pressure from a queue of customers and without the information at his or her fingertips to respond immediately in the advertised way.

1.1.4   The need for a marketing orientation throughout the entire organisation

A marketing philosophy is needed not only at a senior executive level, or even only in the marketing department, but throughout the entire organisation.

To a production director being marketing oriented may mean that scarce financial resources should be spent on quality control checking rather than super-sophisticated robotic production lines if quality is of more concern to the customer. It may mean that production efficiency demands to standardise the products on offer have to be balanced by customer-led demands for variety and choice.

To the salesperson it may mean being prepared to listen to what the customer says he or she wants rather than using the elegant sales pitch worked out back at the office. To the R & D controller it may mean solving technically low-level problems which create customer dissatisfaction rather than inventing a state-of-the-art new product. To the finance department it may mean being prepared to invest in new ventures without immediate financial returns to build a stronger future in the market place.

Each department will have its own interests, often its own goals and reward structures. Ultimately, however, the way each department works should be geared to creating customer satisfaction rather than satisfying its own, often myopic, interests. It is a major task of the chief executive officer (CEO) to ensure that the total operations of the company add up in this way. Crucial to fulfilling that task is that the CEO personally recognise the centrality of marketing in the organisation. The better managers recognise this instinctively.

1.1.5   The need for senior executive commitment

The danger of becoming too remote from customers and what they want increases with the size, complexity and bureaucracy of the organisation. Even in large organisations, however, it is still possible to keep in touch.

■ When a new CEO took over at one of the UK's largest building societies he surprised colleagues by insisting that he spend one day per month behind a cash till in a branch office so as to keep him in touch both with the society's day-to-day operations and with its customers.

Similarly, the chairman of a speciality carpet manufacturing company spent a week working as a hospital porter to see the conditions under which his range of hospital carpets had to perform. He later declared that he had learnt more in that week than any amount of formal marketing research could have told him.

The bulk of the first six weeks of Peter Troughton's term as managing director of Telecom New Zealand were spent travelling round to customer locations with service engineers to see first hand customers' problems and requirements.   ■

Commitment to placing the customer at the centre of the firm's operations must come from the top of the organisation if it is to have much hope of filtering through to all aspects of the business. Adopting a marketing philosophy and seeing that it pervades the whole organisation is one of the prime characteristics of the most successful CEOs.

1.2 The changing marketing environment

Of high importance in developing and implementing a marketing orientation is being aware of how the environment in which marketing takes place is changing. The marketing environment can be divided into the competitive environment (including the company, its immediate competitors and customers) and the macro-environment (the wider social, political and economic setting). Understanding and analysing the competitive environment is dealt with in detail in Part Two of this book. Here we deal briefly with changes in the macro-environment that affect all marketers.

A number of important changes are taking place in the environment in which marketing operates and these are summarised briefly below. For these purposes change is discussed under four main headings: economic and political change, social/cultural change, technological change and the resulting marketing change.

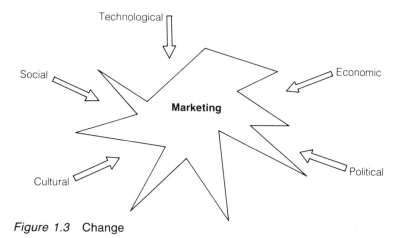

Figure 1.3 Change

1.2.1 Economic and political change

The slowing of economic growth experienced in most of the developed economies over the past two decades has brought with it many consequences. The debate is still current as to whether this slow-down is temporary or more structural. While growth undoubtedly goes in cycles, the indications are that the developed economies are unlikely to see again the rates of growth experienced in the years after the Second World War. The consequence will be that many organisations will have to learn to live with low growth in their once buoyant markets. Whereas in the past growth objectives dominated management thinking, other criteria are now becoming more important.

At the same time as developing economies are coming to terms with slower rates of growth, broader issues concerning both international economics and its political implications have been raised. The Brandt Commission (1980, 1983) has drawn attention to the inequalities of resources and wealth distribution throughout the world.

The Commission has pointed to the 'North—South' divide between the rich and poor nations, the developed and the underdeveloped.

One particular change in the last decade has been the recognition by Third World raw materials producers of the power they hold over the western, developed economies. This was sharply demonstrated by the formation of OPEC in the early 1970s and the immediate effect on world energy prices. At that time energy costs soared and other Third World countries with valuable raw materials realised the power their resources gave them.

More recently, the start of the final decade of the twentieth century has seen dramatic changes in East/West relationships. The dismantling of the Berlin Wall, the liberalisation of the economies of central Europe (Poland, Hungary, Czechoslovakia, Bulgaria) and the break-up of the Soviet Union into the new Commonwealth of Independent States, signal many potential changes in trading patterns.

While the political barriers have been coming down in Europe there is some concern that the emergence of regional trading blocs ('free-trade areas') will have a dramatic impact on the future of free world trade. The single European market after 1993, closer economic relations in the Asia-Pacific region (Australia, Singapore, Thailand, South Korea, etc.) and the North American free-trade zone (USA, Canada and Mexico) are emerging as massive internal markets where domestic 'international' trade will become freer.

At the same time, however, trade between trading blocs or nations outside them may become more restricted. Major trading partners such as the United States and Japan are increasingly entering into bilateral trade deals (e.g. the US—Japan deal on semiconductors). While most politicians espouse the goals of free international trade — see, for example, Sir Leon Brittan (1990), EC Competition Commissioner, speaking at the EC/Japan Journalists' Conference — the realities of the 1990s could be a concentration of trade within blocs and reduced trade between them.

The major economic and political changes of the last decade have been a slowing of rates of growth in the developed countries, the emergence of trading blocs and a growing gulf between the developed 'North' and the underdeveloped 'South'. The business challenges and opportunities of the 1990s are likely to centre around the changes in political relationships between East and West and the new trading patterns emerging between and within regional trading blocs.

1.2.2   Social and cultural change

Coupled with the changing economic environment has been a continuous change in social attitudes and values (in the developed West at least) that is likely to have important implications for marketing management.

There has been a questioning of the industrial profit motive as the main objective for commercial enterprises. More stakeholders are being recognised as having a legitimate input into the setting of organisational objectives. Stakeholders include the owners of the organisation (usually shareholders), the managers who run the business (management and ownership are increasingly being divorced as more professional managers move from one company to another during their careers), the people who work for the organisation, the customers of the organisation, the suppliers who depend on the organisation for their livelihoods, and the wider society on which the organisation has an impact. There are changing expectations from work both by managers and workers as standards of living increase.

Society in general has expectations from industry, primarily that it will provide jobs. This has led John Harvey-Jones, then chairman of ICI, to say: 'In this country [Great Britain], uniquely, industry is looked upon as a means of providing jobs, and that actually isn't the job of industry. The job of industry is to create wealth' (Pagnamenta and Overy, 1984).

A further social/cultural change has been in attitudes to, and concern for, the environment. Environmental pressure groups are beginning to have an impact on businesses, so much so that major oil multinationals and others spend large amounts on corporate advertising each year to demonstrate their concern and care for the environment.

The activities of Greenpeace have begun to have a major impact on public opinion and to affect policymaking at national and international levels. In November 1986 the British Labour Party, in what was seen as an early move in the run-up to the 1987 general election, appointed a spokesperson with specific responsibility for 'green' issues and promised ministerial appointments in that area if elected. The area was seen as a potential votewinner. By early 1989 the then British Prime Minister, Margaret Thatcher, had announced her concern for the ozone layer and the greenhouse effect, introducing measures to curb the use of harmful CFC gases in aerosols, refrigerators and production processes. It is to be expected that concern for the environment will increase and hence will be a major factor in managing that prime marketing asset — company reputation.

Coupled with greater concern for the environment is greater concern for individual health. There has been a dramatic movement in the grocery industry, for example, towards healthier food products, such as wholemeal bread and bran-based cereals. This movement, originally dismissed by many food manufacturers as a passing fad among a minority of the population, has accelerated in the recent past with the marketing of low-sugar products, free from additives, colourings and preservatives. Fitness products in general, such as jogging suits and exercise machines, have enjoyed very buoyant markets recently.

There have been many other trends in society which have a direct impact on business in general and marketing in particular. The age profile of many developed nations is undergoing change. With generally better standards of living, life expectancy has increased. For males in Britain life expectation has risen from 48 years in 1901, to 68 years in 1961 and to 73 years in 1991. For females it has risen from 52 years in 1901, to 74 years in 1961 and to 78 years in 1991. Death rates have declined in all age groups, but most significantly in the older age categories. In 1961 there were 259 deaths per 1,000 men aged 85 or over. By 1984 that figure had dropped to 213. For women in the age group deaths per thousand had fallen from 216 to 170. By 1985 15 per cent of the population were over the age of 65.

■   Barratt Developments in Britain were particularly quick to capitalise on this change in the demographic profile of the population and specialised in providing retirement homes for the elderly. ■

At the other end of the spectrum, the youth market has recently become more affluent and poses new opportunities for marketers appealing directly to it. Fashion and music industries have been quick to recognise this new-found affluence. Much of the success of Virgin Records (sold to Thorn EMI for over £500m in early 1992) was based on understanding and catering for this market. Clothes stores too, such as Now and Next, built their early successes on catering to the teenager market.

There has also been an increase in single person households, so much so that the BBC launched a television series on cooking for one. Barratt Developments have complemented their success in the retirement homes market by successfully developing 'studio solos', housing accommodation for the young, single but more affluent individual.

Even during a period of increasing unemployment there has been a significant growth in the number of women in employment, be it full- or part-time. This has led to changes in household eating patterns, added emphasis on convenience foods and cooking. It has, in turn, led to increased markets for products to make cooking and meal preparation easier and quicker, such as the deep freeze, the food processor and the microwave oven.

1.2.3   Technological change

The microprocessor has been attributed with heralding the post-industrial age and it is probably this invention above all others that has had the most profound effect on our lives today. Microprocessors have revolutionised data collection, processing and dissemination. They have caused major changes in production technology and have essentially served to increase the rate of technological change.

As Kotler (1991) points out, around 90 per cent of all scientists who ever lived are alive and working today, contributing to this increased rate of change in the technologies and processes available to us. This has led to a shortening of the commercialisation times of new inventions (Ansoff, 1979). Photography, for example, took over 100 years from initial invention to commercial viability. The telephone took 56 years, radio 35 years, television 12 years and the transistor only three years.

This shortening of commercialisation times has, in turn, led to a shortening of product life cycles with products becoming obsolete and out of date much more quickly than previously. Foster (1986c) points to the Japanese electronics industry, where the time between perception of a need or demand for a new product and shipment of large quantities of that product can be less than five months (Matsushita colour TVs).

Computer integration of manufacturing and design is helping to shorten product development times. It has been estimated that in automobiles the shortening has been in the order of 25 per cent.

> ■ Consider the case of the ballpoint pen. Earlier technology (a stick on a clay tablet) enjoyed a long product life which effectively only ended when the quill and ink became available as alternatives. The quill itself enjoyed a long product life until the end of the nineteenth century when the fountain pen was invented. This was found to have major problems of use in the aeroplanes of the Second World War (fountain pens do not work well under low atmospheric pressure) and the need to develop a new writing implement led to the ballpoint pen. The ballpoint, however, only really established itself in the consumer market during the 1950s and 1960s.
>
> Close on its heels came the felt-tip pen, offering better quality writing at a similar, throw-away price. The life of felt-tip pens was effectively even shorter (although they and ballpoint pens can still be bought and still enjoy a healthy market) as it was replaced by the superior 'technology' of the roller ball pen. This is currently a best-selling solution to the original writing problem but no doubt other solutions (such as the fineliner, or even cheap, pocket-sized word processors) will take over. At each stage in development the previous solution to the problem has been eclipsed more quickly than it eclipsed its predecessor. ■

Through technological changes whole industries or applications have been wiped out almost overnight. In 1977/8 cross-ply tyre manufacturers in the USA lost 50 per cent of the tyre market to radials in just 18 months (Foster, 1986c).

Newer technology has a major impact on particular aspects of marketing. The advent of the microcomputer and its wide availability to management has led to increased interest in sophisticated market modelling and decision support systems. Increased amounts of information can now be stored, analysed and retrieved very much more quickly than in the past. Innovative marketing research companies have been quick to seize on the possibilities afforded by the new technology for getting information to their clients more quickly than competitors.

Suppliers of retail audits (see Chapter 6) can now present their clients with on-line results of the audits completed only 24 hours previously. In a rapidly changing market place the ability to respond quickly afforded by almost instantaneous information can mean the difference between success and failure.

> ■ The new media, cable and satellite TV and the video recorder, have posed new problems and opportunities for advertisers. In the United States of America, for example, cable TV is widely available and an established advertising medium. As a consequence video recorders have not been as successful as in the UK.
>
> In Britain, the rapid penetration of the domestic market by video recorders (encouraged to a large extent by the unique British love of rental as opposed to outright purchase) has caused major difficulty for cable operators in locating a viable market. Video recorders are primarily used in the UK for time shift (i.e. watching broadcast programmes at different, more convenient times) and hence advertisers cannot be sure when their advertisements are likely to be seen, or indeed whether they will be edited out by the viewer. ■

Further changes are currently taking place in the high street. Electronic point of sale (EPOS) and electronic funds transfer at point of sale (EFTPOS) devices, used increasingly at supermarket, petroleum and other retail checkouts, offer the possibilities of almost instantaneous feedback on sales of products. This up-to-date information can be particularly valuable for tracking advertising effectiveness and in new product test marketing.

1.2.4   Marketing changes

In addition to the changes noted above, there are several important changes taking place in the general marketing environment and in marketing practices.

We are currently experiencing, in many markets, increased levels of competition, both domestic and international. In the decade from 1975 to 1985 exports from the UK to the rest of the world increased from £19 billion to £78 billion, while imports rose from £23 billion to £80 billion. In real terms, after allowing for inflation, exports have risen 46 per cent and imports 28 per cent in that decade.

Some writers, such as Levitt (1986), have argued that many markets are becoming increasingly global in nature, and that no business, however big or small, is exempt from global competition. The reasoning centres around the impact of technology on people throughout the world. Technology has made products more available and potential consumers more aware of them. Levitt believes we are currently experiencing a move towards gigantic, world-scale markets where economies of scale in production, marketing and distribution can be vigorously pursued. The result will be significantly lower costs, creating major problems for competitors that do not operate on a global scale. Many of these cost advantages are being realised as companies operating within the single market of the European Community rationalise their production and distribution facilities.

The counter argument to the globalisation thesis is that markets are in fact becoming more fragmented, with consumers more concerned to express their individuality (King, 1985) than to buy mass-produced, mass-marketed products. In addition, there is little evidence of the existence of widespread preference for the cheapest products available. The demand for low prices, relative to other product benefits and extras, is not proven in many markets. Each market should be examined individually and the factors likely to affect it explored.

Whether or not one subscribes to the globalisation argument, one factor is clear — that organisations ignore international competition at their peril. The British motorcycle industry is now a classic textbook example of a once supreme industry now virtually non-existent because of its failure to recognise and respond to the threat posed by cheap, good quality, Japanese bikes.

At a seminar conducted by the authors in the mid-1980s on Japanese marketing strategies one executive from a building society remarked: 'This is all very interesting but we don't compete with the Japanese in our markets.' The reality of international competition is now being felt by that executive as by others before him.

As of the end of 1989 nine out of the top ten banks in the world were Japanese owned.

At the same time as markets are becoming more global, the existence of distinct market segments is becoming clearer. The most successful firms are those that have recognised the increasing importance of segmentation and positioned their companies so as to take best advantage of it. Van den Berghs is a prime example in the UK 'yellow fats' market (butter and margarine). It has clearly identified several main segments of the market and positioned individual brands to meet the needs of those segments (see Chapter 11). The company now commands in excess of 60 per cent of the margarine market through a policy of domination of each distinct market segment.

A further development has emerged in recent years. This is the increasing importance placed on marketing by many companies, which has been found to be a major consequence of the tough economic conditions of the 1980s (see, for example, Hooley, Lynch and Shepherd, 1990). As companies have found their very survival threatened, they have increasingly recognised the need to adopt a marketing orientation.

Conversely, those that have not survived have often failed because of a lack of marketing expertise. In a study of corporate failure, Rothwell (1981) concluded that there is never a single factor for failure, nor for success, but in all the cases he examined it was the firm's failure to look for user needs and embody them in product design that contributed to, if not directly caused, failure. Almost a decade earlier, Argenti (1974) came to a similar conclusion in his studies of corporate collapse. He found that companies which fail almost always do so because they have been left behind by the modern world.

The marketing function clearly has a major role to play in keeping the company up to date with changes in both the broader environment and the competitive environment. As change accelerates, this role becomes even more vital to the very survival of the organisation.

1.2.5   The impact of change

Several broad conclusions can be drawn from the above, and their implications for marketing management identified.

First, in many industries the days of fast growth are gone for ever. In those where high rates of growth are still possible, competition is likely to be increasingly fierce and of an international nature. It is no longer sufficient for companies to become 'marketing oriented'. That is taken for granted. The key to success will be the effective implementation of the marketing concept through clearly defined positioning strategies.

Second, change creates opportunities for innovative organisations and threats for those who, Canute like, attempt to hold them back. It is probable that there will be a redefinition of 'work' and 'leisure' providing significant new opportunities to those companies ready and able to seize them. The changing demographic profile, particularly in terms of age, marital status and income distribution, also poses many opportunities for marketing management.

Third, the speed of change in the environment is accelerating, leading to greater complexity and added 'turbulence', or discontinuity. Technological developments are combining to shorten product life cycles and speed up commercialisation times. The increasing turbulence in the market makes it particularly difficult to predict: who would have predicted in 1970 that a major market for personal computers in the early 1980s would be as home games machines, or in 1982 that by Christmas 1984 the market would be saturated? As a result planning horizons have been shortened. Where long-range plans in relatively predictable markets could span 10 to 15 years, very few companies today are able to plan beyond the next few years in any but the most general terms.

Fourth, successful strategies erode over time. What has been successful at one point in time, in one market, cannot guarantee success in the future in the same or other markets.

■   Woolworth was the most successful UK retailer of the 1950s, trading on a 'cheap and cheerful', value-for-money positioning. By 1990 the retailing sector had changed out of all recognition, but Woolworth (now owned by Kingfisher), through the development of the B&Q do-it-yourself stores and the Comet discount electrical appliances chain, had stayed ahead of the game. The more traditional Woolworth stores, however, were facing more severe trading conditions, largely through not moving quickly enough from the 1950s positioning.

In contrast a major competitor from the 1950s, Marks & Spencer, had continuously adapted to changing customer expectations and more affluent and discerning customers, and had carved a more substantial niche in the market. Both M&S and Woolworth have conformed to the dictum of Napoleon Bonaparte, 'One must change one's tactics every ten years if one wishes to maintain one's superiority', though it is likely that tactics will have to be changed much more frequently in the future!   ■

The above factors all combine to make corporate planning in general, and marketing planning in particular, more difficult now than they have ever been before. They also make them more vital activities than ever. Strategic marketing planning today attempts to build flexibility into the organisation to enable it to cope with this increased level of complexity and uncertainty and to take full advantage of the changing environment. At the heart of that planning process is the creation of a strong competitive position, the subject of the remainder of this book.

1.3   Marketing fundamentals

From the underlying marketing concept outlined above, and the changes identified in the context in which marketing takes place, emerge a set of basic marketing principles which serve to guide both marketing thought and action. Each of these principles seems so obvious as not to require stating. However, recognition of these principles and their application has revolutionised how organisations respond to, and interact with, their customers.

1.3.1   Principle 1: The customer is king

The first principle of marketing is the marketing concept itself. This recognises that the long-run objectives of the organisation, be they financial or social, are best served through achieving a high degree of customer satisfaction. From that recognition flows the need for a close investigation of customer wants and needs followed by a clear definition of how the company can best serve them.

It also follows that the only arbiters of how well the organisation satisfies its customers are the customers themselves. The quality of the goods or services offered to the market will be judged by the customers on the basis of how well their requirements are satisfied. A quality product or service, from the customers' perspective, is one that satisfies or is 'fit for purpose' rather than one that provides unrequired luxury.

As Levitt (1986) demonstrates, adopting a market-led approach poses some very basic questions. The most important include:

● What business are we in?
● What business could we be in?
● What business do we want to be in?
● What must we do to get into or consolidate in that business?

The answers to these fundamental questions can often change a company's whole outlook and perspective. In Chapter 2 we discuss business definition more fully, and show how it is fundamental to setting strategic direction for the organisation.

1.3.2   Principle 2: Customers do not buy products

The second basic marketing principle is that customers do not buy products; they buy what the product can do for them. In other words, customers are less interested in the technical features of a product or service than in what benefits they get from buying, using or consuming the product or service.

■ The handyman does not want a quarter-inch drill bit, he wants a quarter-inch hole. The drill bit is merely a way of delivering that benefit (the hole) and will be the solution to the basic need only until a better method or solution is invented (Kotler, 1991).

Similarly, the gardener does not want a lawnmower. What he or she wants is grass only one inch high. Hence a new strain of grass seed, which is hardwearing and only grows to one inch in height could provide very substantial competition to lawnmower manufacturers. ■

Marketers view products and services as 'bundles of benefits', or a combination of attractions that all give something of value to the customer. Any product enhancements need to be assessed on the basis of the extra benefits they give. Some may be substantial, others minor.

The organisation should gear itself up to solving customers' problems, not exclusively promoting its own current (and often transitory) solution. An example of a company doing just this is shown in Exhibit 1.1.

1.3.3   Principle 3: Marketing is too important to leave to the marketing department

Marketing is the job of everyone in the organisation. The actions of all can have an impact on the final customers and the satisfactions the customers derive.

King (1985) has pointed to a number of misconceptions as to what marketing is. One of the most insidious misconceptions he terms 'marketing department marketing', where an organisation employs marketing professionals who may be very good at analysing marketing data and calculating market shares to three decimal places, but who have very little real impact on the products and services the organisation offers to its customers. The marketing department is seen as the only department where marketing is 'done', so that the other departments can get on with their own agenda and pursue their own goals.

As organisations become flatter, reducing layers of bureaucracy, and continue to break down the spurious functional barriers between departments, so it becomes increasingly obvious that marketing is the job of everyone. It is equally obvious that marketing is so central to both survival and prosperity that it is far too important to leave only to the marketing department.

1.3.4   Principle 4: Markets are heterogeneous

It is becoming increasingly evident that most markets are not homogeneous, but are made up of different individual customers, sub-markets or segments. While some customers, for example, may buy a car for cheap transport from A to B, others may buy for comfortable or safe travel, and still others may buy for status reasons or to satisfy and project their self-image. Products and services that attempt to satisfy a segmented market through a standardised product almost invariably fall between two or more stools and become vulnerable to more clearly targeted competitors.

Relating back to Principle 2 above, it is evident that one way of segmenting markets is on the basis of the benefits customers get in buying or consuming the product or service. Benefit segmentation (see Chapter 9) has proved to be one of the most useful ways of segmenting markets for the simple reason that it relates the segmentation back to the real reasons for the existence of the segments in the first place — different benefit requirements.

At IBM, the last thing we'll offer you is a computer.

Think about why you buy a computer.
Is it because you want one? Or feel you need one?

No, in all probability you're buying a computer because you have some sort of problem which you feel having a computer would solve.

So what you're really looking for is a solution. That's the way we approach computers at IBM.

When you come to us we won't immediately leap in and try to sell you a computer.

Firstly, we'll see what the problem is.
We'll study your needs. Analyse your whole business if need be.

And then we'll offer you a solution. One that's best for you.

It may not even involve a new computer. Perhaps it's simply updating software.

But if it does, we'll only be selling it to you because we believe it's the best solution.

And that, after all, is really what you're looking for.

NEW ZEALAND

If we can be of service please write to either: Chris Thodey, P.O. Box 6840, Auckland. Murray Jurgeleit, P.O. Box 3313, Wellington. Michelle van der Westhuysen, P.O. Box 1219, Christchurch.

Exhibit 1.1

1.3.5   Principle 5: Markets and customers are constantly changing

It is a truism to say that the only constant is change. Markets are dynamic and virtually all products have a limited life until a new or better way of satisfying the underlying want or need is found: in other words, until another solution or benefit provider comes along.

The fate of the slide rule, and before it logarithmic tables, at the hands of the pocket calculator is a classic example of where the problem (the need for rapid and easy calculation) was better solved through a newer technology. The benefits offered by calculators far outstripped the slide rule in speed and ease of use.

This recognition that products are not omnipotent, that they follow a product life cycle (PLC) pattern of introduction, growth, maturity and decline, has led companies to look and plan more long term, to ensure that when the current breadwinners die there are new products available in the company's portfolio to take over. The development of product portfolio planning has been one of the most far-reaching contributions of marketing to strategic management in recent years. These developments are discussed in Chapter 3.

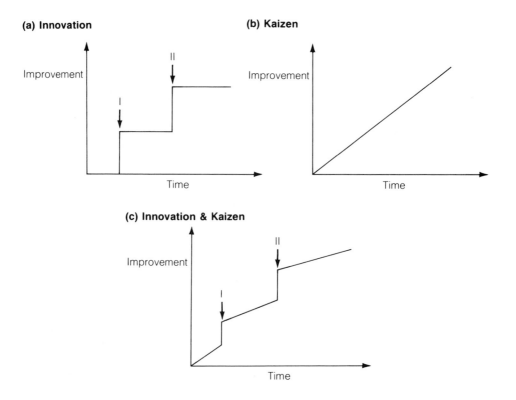

Figure 1.4 Product and process improvement

Also evident is the need for constant product and service improvement. As customer expectations change, usually becoming more demanding in the benefits they expect from a given product or service, so organisations need to upgrade their offerings continuously to retain, let alone improve position.

There are two main processes of improvement. The first is through innovation, where a relatively large step is taken at one point in time. The advent of the pocket calculator was a significant innovation that virtually wiped out the slide rule industry overnight. Other step changes in technology, such as the advent of colour television and the compact disc, have served to change whole industries in a similarly short period of time.

The second approach to improvement, however, is a more continuous process whereby smaller changes are made but on an insistent basis. This approach has been identified by a number of writers (see, for example, Imai, 1986) as a major contributor to the success of Japanese businesses in world markets since the early 1950s. The Japanese call continuous improvement 'Kaizen' and see it as an integral part of business life. Increasingly, organisations are attempting to marry the benefits of step change innovation with continuous (Kaizen) improvement. Figure 1.4 illustrates this process diagramatically.

The impact of technological change has been felt most, perhaps, in the computer industry. It is sometimes hard to remember that computers were only invented after the Second World War because they are now such a pervasive part of both business and home life. Toffler (1981) cites *Computer World* magazine: 'If the auto industry had done what the computer industry has done over the last thirty years, a Rolls-Royce would cost $2.50, get around 2,000,000 miles to the gallon and six of them would fit on the head of a pin!'

1.4 The role of marketing in leading strategic management

In order for strategic management to cope with the changing marketing environment there is a need for it to become increasingly market led. In taking a leading role in the development and the implementation of strategy, the role of marketing can be defined. It is threefold.

1.4.1   Identification of customer requirements

The first critical task of marketing is to identify the requirements of customers and to communicate them effectively throughout the organisation. This involves conducting or commissioning relevant customer research to uncover, first, who the customers are, and second, what will give them satisfaction.

Who the customers are is not always as obvious as it may seem. In some circumstances buyers may be different to users or consumers; specifiers and influencers may also be different. Where services are funded by central government, for example,

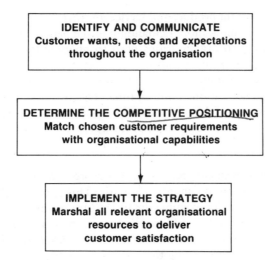

Figure 1.5   The role of marketing in leading strategic management

the suppliers may be forgiven for the (mistaken) view that government is their customer.

Customers may expect a degree of benefit from purchasing or using a product or service. They may actually want something more but believe they have to settle for second best because of budget or other constraints. The organisation that can give customers something closer to what they want than what they expect has an opportunity to go beyond customer satisfaction and create 'customer delight'.

Customer expectations, wants and needs must all be understood and clearly communicated to those responsible for designing the product or service in the first place, those responsible for creating or producing it, and those responsible for delivering it.

Identifying what customers require is dealt with in Chapter 6.

1.4.2   Deciding on the competitive positioning to be adopted

Recognising that markets are heterogeneous and typically made up of various market segments, each having different requirements from essentially similar offerings, leads to the need to decide clearly which target market or markets the organisation will seek to serve.

This decision is made on the basis of two main sets of factors: first, how attractive the alternative potential targets are; and second, how well the company can hope to serve each potential target relative to the competition — in other words, the relative strengths or competencies it can bring into play in serving the market. These two related issues are discussed at length in Part Four of this book.

1.4.3 Implementing the marketing strategy

The third key task of marketing is to marshal all the relevant organisational resources to plan and execute the delivery of customer satisfaction. This involves ensuring that all members of the organisation are co-ordinated in their efforts to satisfy customers and that no actual or potential gaps exist between offer design, production and delivery.

In the field of services marketing there has been a great deal of recent work aimed at identifying the factors that can create gaps in the process from design through to delivery of offer to customers. Parasuraman, Zeithaml and Berry (1985), for example, have studied each of the potential gaps and concluded that a central role of marketing is to guide design so as to minimise the gaps and hence help to ensure customer satisfaction through the delivery of high-quality (fit-for-purpose) services.

Chapters 12 and 13 address implementation and co-ordination issues more fully.

1.5 Conclusions

This chapter has sought to review the marketing concept and demonstrate its importance in providing a guiding approach to doing business in the face of increasingly competitive and less predictable marketing environments. This approach we term 'market-led strategic management'. A number of marketing principles were discussed together with the role of marketing in strategic management. The remainder of Part One of the book will present a framework for developing a market-led approach.

TWO

Strategic marketing planning

Strategy is the matching of the activities of an organisation to the environment in which it operates and to its own resource capabilities.

Johnson and Scholes (1988)

Introduction

The essence of developing a marketing strategy for a company is to ensure that the company's capabilities are matched to the competitive market environment in which it operates not just for today, but into the foreseeable future. This involves assessing the company's strengths and weaknesses, and the opportunities and threats facing it.

Strategic planning attempts to answer three basic questions:

- What is the business doing now?
- What is happening in the environment?
- What should the business be doing?

Strategy is concerned primarily with effectiveness (doing the right things) rather than with efficiency (doing what you do, well). The vast bulk of management time is, of necessity, concerned with day-to-day operations management. A time audit for even senior management will often reveal a disproportionate amount of time spent on routine daily tasks, with the more difficult and demanding task of planning further into the future relegated to a weekend or one-week conference once per year. In the most successful companies, however, thinking strategically, sitting back from the present concerns of improving what you do now and questioning what it is you are doing, is a constant process.

As with the adoption of a marketing philosophy throughout the organisation, the adoption of strategic thinking goes beyond the brief of marketing management alone. All senior executives in the company or organisation have a responsibility for developing the strategic profile of the company and giving it a strategic focus. Marketing management, however, with its specific responsibility for managing the interface between the organisation and its environment (both customers and competitors), has an increasingly important role to play in overall strategy development.

2.1 The marketing strategy process

The development of a marketing strategy can be viewed at three main levels: the

24

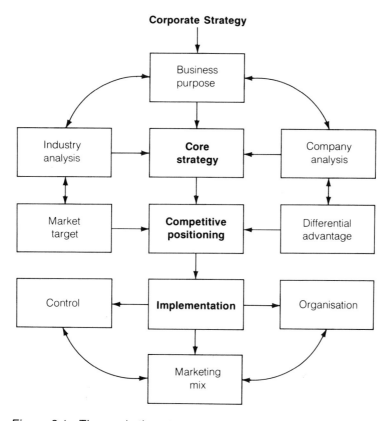

Figure 2.1 The marketing strategy process

establishment of a core strategy, the creation of the company's competitive positioning and the implementation of the strategy (see Figure 2.1).

The establishment of an effective marketing strategy starts with a detailed, and creative, assessment both of the company's capabilities — its strengths and weaknesses relative to the competition — and of the opportunities and threats posed by the environment. On the basis of this analysis the core strategy of the company will be selected, identifying marketing objectives and the broad focus for achieving them.

At the next level, market targets (both customers and competitors) are selected and/or identified. At the same time the company's differential advantage, or competitive edge, in serving the customer targets better than the competition is defined. Taken together the identification of targets and the definition of differential advantage constitute the creation of the competitive positioning of the organisation and its offerings.

At the implementation level, a marketing organisation capable of putting the strategy into practice must be created. The design of the marketing organisation can be crucial to the success of the strategy. Implementation is also concerned with establishing a mix of products, price, promotion and distribution that can convey both the positioning and the products and services themselves to the target market. Finally, methods of control must be designed to ensure that the strategy implementation is successful. Control concerns both the efficiency with which the strategy is put into operation and the ultimate effectiveness of that strategy. Each of the three main levels of strategy is now considered in more detail.

2.2 Establishing the core strategy

The core strategy is a statement of both the company's objectives and the broad strategies it will use to achieve them. The three main ingredients for establishing the core strategy are as follows:

- Defining the business purpose or mission.
- Analysing the company's capability profile, or strengths and weaknesses.
- Examining the industry (customers and competitors) in which the company operates or wishes to operate.

2.2.1   Defining the business purpose

Defining the business purpose or mission requires the company to ask the fundamental questions first posed by Levitt more than a quarter of a century ago (see Levitt, 1960):

- What business are we in?
- What business do we want to be in?

■ Several years ago, so marketing folklore has it, a new managing director took over at Parker Pens. One of his first actions was to assemble the board of directors, stand before them holding the top-of-the-range Parker of the day and ask, 'Who is our greatest competitor?'

The first answer to emerge from the board was Shaeffer. Shaeffer produced a pen very similar to the Parker. It had a good reputation for quality, had a similar stylish finish and was similarly priced at the top end of the market. The new managing director was not, however, impressed with this answer. 'We certainly compete to some extent with Shaeffer, but they are by no means our major competitor.'

A newer member of the board then suggested that the major competitor may be Biro-Swan, the manufacturers and marketers of a range of ballpoint pens. While these retailed considerably cheaper than the Parker, he reasoned that they were used for the same purpose (writing) and hence competed directly with Parker. The business definition was now changing from 'quality fountain pens' to 'writing implements' and under this definition pencils could also be considered as competitors, as could the more recent developments in the market of fibre-tip pens and roller ball pens. 'Your thinking is getting better,' said the MD, 'but you're still not there.'

Another board member then suggested that perhaps the major competitor was the telephone, which had been gaining more widespread use in recent years. Under this view of the market they were in 'communications' and competing with other forms of communication including the written word (perhaps competing here with typewriters and, more recently, word processors) and other (verbal) means of communication. 'More creative thinking,' said the MD, 'but you still haven't identified the main competitor.'

Eventually the MD gave his view of the major competitor. To an astonished board he announced, 'Our major competitor is the Ronson cigarette lighter!' When asked to explain his reasoning he defined the market that the company was in as the 'quality gift market'. Analysis of sales of Parker Pens showed that the majority of purchases were made by individuals buying them as gifts for other people. When they considered what to buy, a major alternative was often a quality cigarette lighter, hence the definition of the market. (Example courtesy of Graham Kenwright, Birmingham Chamber of Commerce.) ∎

This definition has widespread implications for the marketing of the product. Packaging assumes a more important role, as does the development and maintenance of a superior quality image. Price is perhaps less important than might have been thought under alternative market definitions. Distribution (through the outlets where potential customers buy gifts) also becomes more important.

The example above serves to illustrate how the asking of a basic question, such as 'who is our major competitor?' or 'what market are we in?', can affect the whole of the strategic direction of the company.

Mission formulation and statement

Hooley, Cox and Adams (1992) discuss the elements that go to make up an effective statement of mission. These are shown in Figure 2.2. Mission needs to spell out:

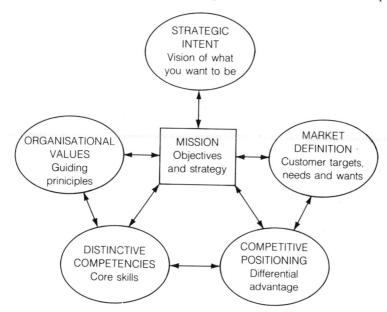

Source: Developed from Hooley, Cox and Adams (1992).

Figure 2.2 Components of mission

- The *strategic intent* (see Hamel and Prahalad, 1989), or vision of where the organisation wants to be in the foreseeable future. Hamel and Prahalad cite examples of strategic intent for Komatsu (earth-moving equipment manufacturers) as to 'encircle Caterpillar', and for the American Apollo space programme as 'landing a man on the moon ahead of the Soviets'. Vision need not be as competitive as these examples. The vision of an organisation such as a university might be the achievement of a set of worthy social goals.
- The *values* of the organisation should be spelled out to set the ethical and moral tone of operations. Fletcher Challenge, the New Zealand-based multinational, sets down its values in its statement of purpose (company report, 1991) as follows: 'Fletcher Challenge will operate with integrity and a people oriented management style which stresses openness, communication, commitment, innovation and decentralisation of authority, responsibility and accountability.'
- The *distinctive competencies* of the organisation should be articulated, stating clearly what differentiates the organisation from others of its kind; what is the distinctive essence of the organisation.
- *Market definition* concerns the major customer targets that the organisation seeks to serve, and the functions or needs of those customers that will be served. The retail store Mothercare has clearly focused on the needs of a well-defined market target as exemplified by its slogan, 'Everything for the mother-to-be and baby'. Many successful entrepreneurs, such as Richard Branson of Virgin, have built their businesses around a clear definition of customer targets and their needs.
- Finally, the mission should spell out where the organisation is, or intends to be, *positioned* in the market place. This is the result of bringing together market definition and distinctive skills and competencies.

Stonich (1982) has warned against business definitions that are too narrow in scope. He concludes that business definition should include definition of both target market and function served. As he points out, a carbon paper manufacturer who defines the function of his products in a way that includes only other carbon paper manufacturers ignores at his peril the fact that photocopying machines have virtually eliminated his product in many markets. The key to definition by function is not to be blinded by the company's perception of the function, but to allow the customer view to come through.

Levitt (1960) provided many examples of companies adopting a myopic view in defining their businesses. The railroads believed they were in the railroad business, not transportation, and failed to take note of alternative means of transport. The oil industry believed it was in the business of producing oil, not in the business of producing and marketing energy.

In defining the business, it is necessary to understand the total product or service that the customer is buying, and to avoid the trap of concentrating overmuch on the physical product being offered. In many markets the augmented or extended product (see Chapter 12) can be as important as the core product, if not more important.

There are several techniques that can be used to help define the current business

ITEM	USE	ITEM
POTATO CRISPS	'Elevenses'	Biscuits Piece of cake Bar of chocolate Toast and jam
	When friends drop in for a drink	Peanuts Olives Cocktail biscuits Cheese and biscuits
	In a pub	Sandwich Peanuts Cocktail biscuits Pork scratchings
	When watching TV	Sweets/chocolates Cup of soup Peanuts

Figure 2.3   Item-by-use analysis

that the company is in. Perhaps one of the simplest to use is Item-by-use analysis (see Frost, 1973). Under this marketing research technique consumers are shown a product, for example a packet of potato crisps (see Figure 2.3), and asked on what occasions they have used that product. The various responses are recorded: for elevenses, when friends drop round for a drink, to keep the kids quiet, in a pub, etc. For each of the uses given, the respondent is then asked what other products would be considered as alternatives if the original product were not available.

These alternatives may be general alternatives that could be used on all the occasions listed (e.g. peanuts) or specific to a particular occasion (e.g. biscuits with elevenses, but not when in a pub). Respondents can also be asked to gauge the proportion of uses associated with each occasion, and, using a large enough sample, a clear picture can be built up of the current market and competition. This approach combines business definition both by market (identifying who existing and potential customers are) and by function (the use or uses to which the product is put).

The second question posed at the start of this section, 'what business do we want to be in?' is often more difficult to answer. It requires a thorough analysis of the options open to the company and an understanding of how the world in general, and the company's markets in particular, are changing.

2.2.2   Company analysis

In deciding on core strategy, full regard must be taken of the skills and distinctive competencies of the company, defining what the company is good at, be that a technologically-based or a market-based definition. This can help to set the bounds on what options are open to the organisation and to identify where its strengths can be utilised to the full. Core competencies or core skills may result from any aspect of the operation. They may stem from the skills of the workforce in assembling the product effectively or efficiently, from the skills of management in marketing or financial planning, or from the skills of the R & D department in initiating new product ideas or creating new products on the basis of customer research.

■ One of the core skills of Royal Doulton was identified in its thorough understanding of porcelain technology. Traditionally, this skill has been put to use in producing tableware and ornamental porcelain, but more recently the skills have also been exploited in a totally new area — dealing with rising damp! The Doulton Wallguard system offered a relatively cheap and, importantly, less disruptive solution to the problems of rising damp through exploiting the properties of porcelain in attracting and expelling moisture.   ■

The distinctive competencies of the company may be its marketing assets of image and market presence or its distribution network or after-sales service. The crucial issue in identifying distinctive competence is that it be something exploitable in the market place. Having distinctive technological skills in producing a product are of little value if there is no demand for that product. Hence an important role of marketing management is to assess the potential distinctive competencies of the organisation in the light of exploitability in the market.

The counterbalance to distinctive competencies, or exploitable strengths, is weaknesses relative to the competition. Where, for example, competitors have a more favourable or protected supply of raw materials, or a stronger customer loyalty, the company must be fully aware of its limitations and generate strategies to overcome, or circumvent, them. Structural weaknesses, those inherent in the firm's operations, brought about by its very mode of doing business, may be difficult or even impossible to eliminate. Strategies should be developed to shift competition away from these factors, to make them less important to competitive success. Other weaknesses may be more easily avoided once they have been identified, or even changed to strengths by exploiting them in a different way.

Strengths and weaknesses can be effectively determined only through a systematic and comprehensive audit of the firm's resources and their utilisation relative to the competition. Chapter 5 describes in more detail how this can be accomplished.

2.2.3   Industry analysis

An analysis of the industry or industries in which the company operates can serve to throw into focus the opportunities and threats facing the company. Those opportunities and threats stem from two main areas — the customers (both current and potential) of the company, and its competitors (again both current and potential).

Most markets are segmented in one way or another. They consist of heterogeneous customers, or customers with varying needs and wants. Asking 'how is the market segmented?' can provide valuable insights into customer requirements and help in focusing on specific market targets.

■   In computers, for example, there are several ways in which the total market could be segmented. A simple, product-based segmentation is between mainframes, minicomputers and micros. The mainframe market has long been dominated by IBM. Recognising the difficulties in tackling such a giant head on, Hewlett Packard sensibly focused its efforts on the minicomputer market, for smaller users with different requirements, and established dominance of that market. Similarly, in the microcomputer market Apple were very successful in leading the market prior to the entry of IBM. The danger confronting HP now is that the growing sophistication and power of micros is squeezing the mini market and some observers believe that this segment of the market may soon disappear completely.

Epson, operating also in the computer market, have taken a different tack. They have recognised that computer users do not just need computers; they also need peripheral devices to enable them to use the computer to the best advantage. Epson carved a strong niche in the market as suppliers of good quality printers to enable hard copy output to be obtained. Still other companies, such as Microsoft and Ashton Tate, have specialised in the provision of software (computer programs) rather than competing in the hardware (machines) side of the market.

Even within these broad product-based definitions of the market, however, further segmentation exists. Consider, for example, the microcomputer segment. Users of micros are now many and varied, from the home games players using Atari and Commodore computers to the business user adopting Apple, IBM or IBM-compatible products. The requirements of these users vary enormously, both in terms of the computing power they need and the software and peripherals they require.

During the late 1980s a new market started to emerge — that for the 'home professional user' — and many companies are attempting to capitalise on the opportunities this segment affords. For example, the launch by Amstrad of a complete word-processing package including computer, printer and software at under £400 in the late 1980s was designed to take advantage both of this and the small business market.   ■

Having examined the current and potential segmentation of the market, the next step in assessing alternatives is to search for untapped, or undertapped, opportunities in the market. In the food market, for example, fundamental changes in eating habits are currently taking place. Two of the most important are the increased emphasis on convenience foods and the trend towards healthier eating. Both changes have opened up new opportunities to those companies willing and able to take advantage of them.

■   Yeoman instant mashed potato has, for example, been promoted with added emphasis on fibre content and vitamin C. Interestingly, the claim that the instant product contains more fibre and vitamin C than 'real' potatoes is based on the normal method of preparation of real potatoes. The peeling of the outer skin prior to cooking takes with it much of the fibre and vitamin C, which is located just below the surface of the skin. The instant product, however, utilises all of the original product in its manufacture.The marketers of Cadbury's Marvel dried milk have similarly attempted to take advantage of increasing health awareness by adding extra vitamins to their product.   ■

Opportunities are created through fundamental changes taking place in the market (as with increased health awareness and its impact on eating habits) or through competitor inability to serve existing needs. Apple's initial success in the micro-computer market was, in part, due to the fact that IBM originally chose not to enter the market. Market gaps can exist because existing companies cannot fill them (they do not have the skills and competencies to do so), or because they choose not to fill them for one reason or another.

Abell (1978) has discussed the importance of timing in recognising and capitalising on opportunities. His concept of strategic windows focuses attention on the fact that there are only limited periods during which the fit between the requirements of the market and the capabilities of the firm is at an optimum. Investment should be timed to coincide with periods when such strategic windows are open, and conversely disinvestment should be considered once a good fit has been eroded. A good deal of the success of Japanese companies in world markets has been attributed to an ability to time their entry such that their competencies and the market requirements are closely in tune.

■ An example of the concept of strategic windows at work in the UK was the spotting of an opportunity to break into the educational computing market by the microcomputer manufacturer Acorn. This Acorn did by securing a contract with the British Broadcasting Corporation (BBC) to produce what became known as the BBC microcomputer in the early 1980s. In the longer term, however, Acorn suffered from not having the 'Acorn' name on the product, and the company's subsequent attempts to launch its own brands into the home computer market (the Acorn Electron) were less successful. ■

In addition to considering the opportunities open to the organisation, it is important to examine the threats facing it. These threats stem from two main sources — a changing market place that the firm is not aware of, or capable of keeping up with; and competitive activity designed to change the balance of power within the market.

A changing world requires constant intelligence gathering on the part of the organisation to ensure that it can keep abreast of customer requirements. Keeping up with technological developments can be particularly important in many markets. The pocket calculator destroyed the slide rule market in the early 1970s and the digital watch caused severe problems for Swiss watch manufacturers in the mid-1970s. Changes also occur in customer tastes. Fashions come and go, many of them encouraged by marketers, but in markets where fashion is important keeping up is crucial. Chapter 6 deals in more detail with customer analysis.

The second major type of threat an organisation may face is from its competition. Increasing competition, from both domestic and international sources, is the name of the game in most markets. As competitors become more sophisticated in seeking out market opportunities and designing marketing programmes to exploit them, so the company itself needs to improve its marketing activities. In the UK many industries have failed or been unable to respond adequately to increased international competition and have suffered the consequences. In the more sophisticated marketing companies competitor analysis commands almost as much time as customer and self-evaluation. Effort is geared to identifying competitors' strengths and weaknesses and their likely strategies (see Chapter 7).

2.2.4   Core strategy

On the basis of the above anlaysis the company seeks to define the *key factors for success* (KFS, sometimes termed *critical success factors*, or CSF) in its particular markets. Key factors for success in the industry are those factors that are crucial to doing business (see Morrison and Lee, 1979; Ohmae, 1982). The KFS are identified through examining the differences between winners and losers, or leaders and also-rans in the industry. They often represent the factors where the greatest leverage can be exerted: that is, where the most effect can be obtained for a given amount of effort.

In the grocery industry, for example, the KFS can centre around the relationships built up between the manufacturer and the retailer. The power of the major multiples (less than a dozen major food retail chains now account for around 80 per cent of food sales in the UK) is such that, if a new food product does not obtain distribution through the major outlets, a substantial sector of the potential market is denied. In commodity markets the KFS often lie in production process efficiency, enabling costs to be kept down, where pricing is considered the only real means of product differentiation. As Ohmae (1982) points out, for the Japanese elevator business the KFS centre around service — it is essential that breakdown is rectified immediately as the Japanese hate to be stuck in lifts!

A further consideration when setting the core strategy for a multiproduct or multidivisional company is how the various corporate activities add up: that is, the role of each activity in the company's overall business portfolio (see Chapter 3).

Having identified corporate capabilities, market opportunities and threats, the key factors for success in the industry in which the firm operates and the role of the particular product or business in the company's overall portfolio, the company sets its marketing objectives. The objectives should be both long and short term. Long-term objectives indicate the future overall destination of the company, its long-term goals. To achieve those long-term goals, however, it is usually necessary to translate them into shorter-term objectives, a series of which will add up to the longer-term goal. Long-term objectives are often set in terms of profit or market domination for a firm operating in the commercial sector. Non-profit-making organisations too set long- and short-term goals. The long-term goal of CND, for example, is the removal of all nuclear weapons from the world. Shorter-term goals in the mid-1980s centred around removing Cruise missiles or preventing their further deployment in one country (the UK).

Often short-term and long-term goals can become confused and there is always the danger that setting them in isolation can result in a situation where the attainment of the short-term goals does nothing to further the long-term objectives and may, in some instances, hinder them. For example a commercial company setting long-term market domination goals will often find short-term profit maximisation at odds with this. Many of the managers, however, will be judged on yearly, not long-term performance, and hence will be more likely to follow short-term profit objectives at the expense of building a stronger market position.

The core strategy of the organisation is a statement of how the organisation intends to achieve its objectives. If, for example, the long-term objective is to be market leader in market X with a share of market at least twice that of the nearest competitors, the core strategy may centre around using superior technology to achieve this, or

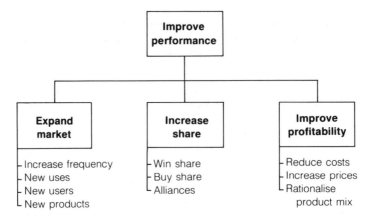

Figure 2.4 Strategic focus

it may centre around lower prices, or better service or quality. The core strategy will take advantage of the firm's core competencies and bring them to bear wherever possible on the KFS to achieve the corporate objectives of the company.

The core strategy to be pursued may vary at different stages of the product or service's life cycle. Figure 2.4 shows alternative ways in which a company may go about improving the performance of its products or services.

A basic choice is made between attempting to increase sales or improve the level of profitability achieved from existing sales (or even reduced sales in a declining market). When the objectives are to increase sales, again two fundamental approaches may be taken: to expand the total market (most easily, though not exclusively, achieved during the early, growth stages of the life cycle) or to increase share of the existing market (most often pursued during the late growth/maturity phases).

Market expansion

Market expansion can be achieved through attracting new users to the product or service, increasing the usage rate of existing users, identifying new uses for the product, or developing new products and services to stimulate the market. New users can be found through geographical expansion of the company's operations, both domestically and internationally. Asda, for example, pursued new customers for its grocery products by moving south from its home base in Yorkshire, while Sainsbury attacked new markets in its march north from the south-east.

Entering new markets

Alternatively, new segments with an existing or latent need for the product may be identifiable. Repositioning of Lucozade as a drink for healthy sportsmen and -women (as promoted through the use of decathlete Daley Thompson) found a new segment for a product once sold exclusively to parents for sick children. In the 1960s Hirondelle wines enjoyed success by appealing to non-wine connoisseurs as an affordable, everyday drink.

Increasing usage rate

Increasing usage rate may be a viable approach to expanding the market for some products. An advertising campaign for Guinness (the 'Guinnless' campaign devised by Ogilvy and Mather advertising agency) sought to convert irregular users (around one bottle per month) to regular use (at least one bottle per week). Similarly, Coleman has attempted to encourage more frequent use of mustard, and Hellmann more varied use of mayonnaise.

Pursue new uses

For some products it may be possible to identify new uses. An example is the use of the condom (largely abandoned as a contraceptive in favour of the more popular pill and IUD in the 1960s and 1970s) as a defence against contracting AIDS during sexual intercourse. In household cleaners Flash was originally marketed as a product for cleaning floors, but now it is also promoted as an all-purpose product for cleaning baths and wash basins.

Increase market share

Increasing market share, especially in mature markets, usually comes at the expense of existing competition. The main routes to increasing share include winning competitors' customers, merging with (or acquiring) the competitors, and entering into strategic alliances with competitors, suppliers and/or distributors. Winning competitors' customers requires that the company serve them better than the competition. This may come about through identification of competitor weaknesses, or through better exploitation of the company's own strengths and competencies. Each of the elements of the marketing mix — products, price, promotion and distribution — could be used to offer the customer added value, or something extra, to induce switching.

Improving profitability

Profitability of existing or even reduced levels of sales can be improved through improving margins. This is usually achieved through increasing price, reducing costs or both. In the multiproduct firm it may also be possible through weeding of the product line, removing poorly performing products and concentrating effort on the more financially viable. The longer-term positioning implications of this weeding should, however, be carefully considered prior to wielding the axe. It may be, for example, that maintenance of seemingly unprofitable lines is essential to allow the company to continue to operate in the market as a whole or its own specifically chosen niches of that market. They may be viewed as essential in the strategic game to reserve a seat at the competitive table.

Once the broad objectives and routes to achieving them have been defined, the specific competitive positioning of the company and its offerings can be created.

2.3   Creation of the competitive positioning

The competitive positioning of the company is a statement of market targets, i.e. where the company will compete, and differential advantage, or how the company will compete. The positioning is developed to achieve the objectives laid down under the core strategy. For a company whose objective is to gain market share and whose broad approach to that is to win competitors' customers, the competitive positioning will be a statement of exactly how and where in the market that will be achieved.

2.3.1   Market targets

While the discussion of core strategy above required an analysis of both customers and competitors to identify potential opportunities and threats, competitive positioning selects those targets most suited to utilising the company's strengths and minimising vulnerability due to weaknesses.

A number of factors should be considered in choosing market targets. Broadly they fall into two categories — assessing market attractiveness, and evaluating the company's current or potential strengths in serving that market (see Robinson, Hitchins and Wade, 1978; Porter, 1987).

Market attractiveness is made up of many factors, often conflicting with each other. Other things being equal, however, a market will generally be more attractive if the following conditions are fulfilled:

- The market is large.
- The market is growing.
- Contribution margins are high.
- Competitive intensity and rivalry are low.
- There are high entry and low exit barriers.
- The market is not vulnerable to uncontrollable events.

Markets which possess all of the above features do not exist for long, if at all. They are, almost by definition, bound to attract high levels of competition and hence to become less attractive to other entrants over time. For small- or medium-sized companies, small and/or static markets, which do not attract more powerful competitors, may be more attractive. In a market where high entry barriers (such as proprietory technology and high switching costs) can be erected, the company will be better able to defend its position against competitive attack (see Chapter 12).

All markets are to some extent vulnerable to external, uncontrollable factors such as general economic conditions, government legislation and political change. Some markets, however, are more vulnerable than others. This is especially true when selecting among international market alternatives. In the international context, one way in which companies assess vulnerability to external political events is through the British Overseas Trade Board (BOTB) and its Export Credit Guarantee Scheme

(ECGS). Under the scheme, advice is freely available about the risks involved in entering a particular market and insurance against default in payments is made available. Domestically, the company must weigh up the power of various pressure groups in determining market vulnerability.

The company's strengths and potential strengths in serving a particular market must be considered relative both to customer requirements and to competitor strengths in serving the market. Other things being equal, the company's existing strength in a market will be greater where (relative to the competition):

- It commands a high market share.
- It is growing faster than the market.
- It has unique and valued products or services.
- It has superior quality products.
- It has better margins.
- It has exploitable marketing assets.
- It can achieve production and marketing efficiencies.
- It has protected technological leadership.

As with assessing market attractiveness, it is unlikely that in any market a particular company will enjoy all of the above favourable characteristics. In any situation the management will have to assess the relative importance of each aspect of strength in evaluating overall strength in serving that market. (Target market selection is covered in more detail in Chapter 11.)

Having selected the market target or targets on the basis of market attractiveness and current, or potential, business strength in serving the market, the company creates its differential advantage, or competitive edge, in serving the market.

2.3.2   Differential advantage

A differential advantage can be created out of any of the company's strengths, or distinctive competencies, relative to the competition. The essential factors in choosing how to create the advantage are that it must be on a basis of value to the customer (e.g. lower prices, superior quality, better service) and should be using a skill of the company that competitors will find hard to copy.

Porter (1980) has argued that a competitive advantage can be created in two main, though not exclusive, ways: through cost leadership or differentiation (see Figure 2.5).

Cost leadership

The first type of advantage involves pursuing a cost leadership position in the industry. Under this strategy the company seeks to obtain a cost structure significantly below that of competitors, while retaining products on the market that are in close proximity to competitors' offerings. With a low-cost structure, above average returns are possible despite heavy competition.

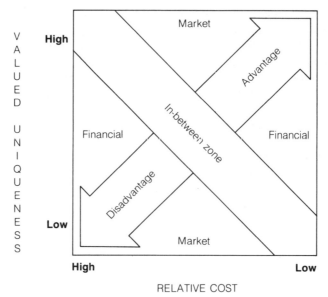

Figure 2.5 Competitive advantage

Cost leadership is attained through aggressive construction of efficient scale economies, the pursuit of cost reductions through experience effects, tight cost and overhead control, and cost minimisation in R & D, services, sales force, advertising, etc. The cost leadership route is that followed aggressively by Casio in the calculator market and Seiko in watches.

Cost leaders typically need high market shares to achieve the above economies, and favourable access to raw materials. If, for example, efficient production processes, or superior production technology enabling cheaper production, were identified as company strengths, or distinctive competencies, they could be effectively translated into a competitive advantage through cost leadership. Similarly, if backwards integration (merger with, or acquisition of, suppliers) has secured relatively cheaper supply of raw materials, that asset could also be converted into a competitive advantage.

This strategy is particularly suitable in commodity markets where there is little or no differentiation between the physical products offered. Where products are highly differentiated, however, the strategy has the major disadvantage that it does not create a reason why the customer should buy the company's offering. Low costs could be translated into lower price, but this would effectively be a differentiation strategy (using price as the basis on which to differentiate).

Differentiation

The second approach to creating a differential advantage is differentiation: that is, creating something that is seen as unique in the market. Under this strategy, company strengths and skills are used to differentiate the company's offerings from those of its competitors along some criteria that are valued by consumers.

Differentiation can be achieved on a variety of bases: for example, by design, style, product or service features, price and image. The major advantage of a differentiation strategy, as opposed to a cost leadership strategy, is that it creates, or emphasises, a reason why the customer should buy from the company rather than from its competitors. While cost leadership creates an essentially financially-based advantage for the company, differentiation creates a market-based advantage (see Hall, 1980; and Figure 2.5). Products or services that are differentiated in a valued way can command higher prices and margins, and thus avoid competing on price alone. An example of this in the market for blue jeans would be designer jeans. In the same market, Levi Strauss and Co.'s offerings are differentiated from the competition by the 'Levi' name.

Fulmer and Goodwin (1988) point out that the two strategies are not mutually exclusive, but could be pursued simultaneously. Buzzell and Gale (1987) demonstrate that differentiation, especially through superior quality, can often result in lower unit costs through achieved gains in market share and attendant economies of scale and/or experience effects.

Each of the two basic approaches to creating a diffential advantage has its attendant risks. Cost leadership may be impossible to sustain due to competitor imitation (using, for example, similar technology and processes), technological change occurring that may make it cheaper for newer entrants to produce the products or services, or competitors finding and exploiting alternative bases for cost leadership (see the discussion of cost drivers in Chapter 12). Cost leadership is also a risky strategy where there is a high degree of differentiation between competitive offerings. Differentiation creates reasons for purchase which cost leadership does not. In addition, cost leadership typically requires minimal spending on R & D, product improvements and image creation, all of which can leave the product vulnerable to competitively superior products.

Differentiation as a strategy is also open to a variety of risks. If differentiation is not based on distinctive marketing assets, it is possible that it will be imitated by competitors. This risk can be minimised by building the differentiation on the basis of skills or marketing assets that the company alone possesses and which cannot be copied by competitors. In addition, the basis for differentiation may become less important to customers, or new bases may become more important. These latter points should be guarded against by constant customer and competitor monitoring. A further danger of the differentiation strategy is that the costs of differentiating may outweigh the value placed on it by customers.

For both the cost leadership and differentiation approaches which seek to appeal industry-wide there is the added risk that focusers or nichers in the market (those competitors that focus their activities at a selected segment) may achieve lower costs or more valued differentiation in specific segments. Thus in markets where segmentation is pronounced, both of the basic approaches carry high risks. Chapter 12 explores further these approaches to creating a defensible position in the market place.

2.4 Implementation

Once the core strategy and the competitive positioning have been selected, the task of marketing management is to implement those decisions through marketing effort. The three basic elements of implementation — marketing mix, organisation and control — are discussed below.

2.4.1   Marketing mix

The marketing mix of products, price, promotion and distribution are the means by which the company translates its strategy from a statement of intent to effort in the market place. Each of the elements of the mix should be designed so as to add up to the positioning required.

Viewed in this light it is evident that decisions on elements of the mix, such as pricing or advertising campaigns, cannot be considered in isolation from the strategy being pursued. A premium positioning, for example, differentiating the company's offerings from the competition in terms of high product quality, could be destroyed through charging too low a price. Similarly, for such a positioning to be achieved the product itself will have to deliver the quality claimed and the promotions used communicate its quality. The distribution channels selected, and the physical distribution systems used or created, must ensure that the products or services get to the target customers.

Where elements of the mix do not pull in the same direction but contradict each other, the positioning achieved will be confused and confusing to customers.

2.4.2   Organisation

How the marketing effort and the marketing department are organised will have an effect on how well the strategy can be carried through.

At a very basic level, it is essential for the required labour, as well as financial resources, to be made available. Given the resources, however, the organisation of them can also affect the company's ability to implement the strategy effectively.

Kotler (1991) has identified three main types of marketing organisation: functional, product management and product/market management.

Under a functional organisation, the marketing department consists of specialists in the various marketing activities reporting to a marketing co-ordinator (manager or director). Typical functions include sales management, advertising and promotions management, market research and new product development. An extension of the functional design is geographic organisation where, within the functions (such as sales management), managers have a responsibility for specific geographic markets. Functional designs offer simplicity of structure and foster a high level of expertise in each function. They are often the first step in a company adopting a higher profile for the marketing function as a whole. They are most applicable where the number and complexity of products or services the company has on the market are limited.

Product management, pioneered in 1927 by the American multinational Procter and Gamble for its ailing Camay soap brand, vests responsibility for all the marketing activities of a particular product in one product manager. In diversified companies with many different products, the system has the major advantage of co-ordinating under one individual the entire mix of marketing activities, and hence making it more likely that they will all pull in the same direction. In the larger companies, product managers are able to call on the talents of functional specialists as and when necessary.

A potential disadvantage of the product management structure, however, is that products, along with their managers, are often made into profit centres. When this happens the danger is that immediate profit accountability will take over from longer-term marketing goals. It is, therefore, a structure particularly suited to companies with short-term profit goals, and less so to those intent on creating a longer-term market position.

The third, and increasingly used, organisational form is along product/market lines. Here managers are responsible either for specific markets or for specific products — or, when an individual product/market is sufficiently important, for both. The advantage of this organisational design is its added emphasis on the market, in addition to retaining the benefits of strong product co-ordination. New products are more likely to emerge from such a structure.

Whichever structure or organisation is adopted by the company, individuals are needed with the skills necessary to carry out the various marketing tasks. Two sources of personnel emerge, internal to the company or brought in from outside. When entering new markets, bringing in external expertise can be a short cut to creating the knowledge needed in-house. Skills can be improved and extended through training programmes held within the company or through outside training agencies.

2.4.3   Control

As the marketing strategy is being executed, an important role of the marketing department is to monitor and control the effort.

Performance can be monitored in two main ways: on the basis of either market performance or financial performance. Market performance measures, such as sales, market share, customer attitudes and loyalty, and the changes in them over time, can be related back to the original objectives of the strategy being pursued. Performance measures should, however, include factors other than those used to set objectives in order to ensure that pursuit of those objectives has not lost sight of the wider implications.

Financial performance is measured through a monitoring of product contribution relative to the resources employed to achieve it. Often a basic conflict between marketing and financial performance may arise. Where the marketing objective is long-term market domination, short-term financial performance may suffer. Where managers are rewarded (i.e. promoted or paid more) on the basis of short-term financial performance, it is likely that long-term marketing objectives will be sacrificed to short-term profit. In comparing the strategies pursued in a number of UK markets by Japanese firms and their UK competitors, Doyle, Saunders and Wong (1986) found that the Japanese were more prepared to take a longer view of market performance, compared to the short-term profit orientation pursued by many of the British firms.

The efficiency with which the strategy is being executed can be monitored through a detailed evaluation of each of the elements of the marketing mix. Many companies benefit from regular, independent marketing audits (Kotler, Gregor and Rogers, 1977). These are designed to offer an objective, external evaluation of both the effectiveness and the efficiency of marketing operations.

A final important element in implementation is contingency planning: that is, answering the question, 'what will we do if?'. Contingency planning requires a degree of forecasting competitive reaction to the plans developed, should they be implemented, and an estimation of the likely competitive moves. Forecasting a range of likely futures and making plans to deal with whichever occurs is termed *scenario planning*.

2.5 Conclusions

Strategic marketing planning involves deciding on the core strategy, creating the competitive positioning of both the company and its offerings, and implementing that strategy.

The above is as true of the one-product firm as it is of the large conglomerate containing many different businesses. For the conglomerate, however, there is an added dimension to planning. That extra dimension consists of portfolio planning — ensuring that the mix of businesses within the total corporation is suitable for achieving overall corporate objectives. Portfolio planning is discussed in Chapter 3.

THREE

Portfolio planning

A goat cannot be cooked with a hyena.

Saying of the African Hausa tribe

Introduction

Being 'one or two in all we do' is the driving philosophy of GE, the American power station to electric light bulb conglomerate. The businesses of GE are amazingly diverse. One of its most successful subsidiaries is market leader in America for electric light bulbs, a mature, high-volume, low-priced commodity. Other divisions make domestic electrical appliances of all types, another makes medical equipment including body scanners, and one of the most successful parts of the company is market leader in the military and commercial aero engine markets. It is clear that the different businesses within the company are operating in different markets, with different opportunities and threats, and utilising different corporate skills and resources. It is therefore important to ensure that appropriate objectives and strategies are formulated for each business unit and that these objectives and strategies support each other. The process of balancing the activities across this variety of business units involves *portfolio planning* and is the subject of this chapter.

Drucker (1973) has identified seven types of business to be found in many portfolios:

- *Today's breadwinners* — the products and services that are earning healthy profits and contributing positively to both cash flow and profits.
- *Tomorrow's breadwinners* — investments in the company's future: products and services that may not yet be making a strong financial contribution to the company but that are in growth or otherwise attractive markets and are expected to take over the breadwinning role in the future, when today's breadwinners eventually fade.
- *Yesterday's breadwinners* — the products and services that have supported the company in the past but that are not now contributing significantly either to cash flow or profits. Many companies have a predominance of businesses of this type, indicating that they have been slow to invest in future developments.
- *Developments* — the products and services recently developed that may have some future but where greater investment is needed to achieve that future.
- *Sleepers* — the products and services that have been around for some time but that have so far failed to establish themselves in their markets, or where, indeed,

their expected markets have failed to materialise. These are allowed to remain in the portfolio in the hope that one day they will take off.

- *Investments in managerial ego* — the products and services that have strong product champions among influential managers, but for which there is little proven demand in the market place. The company, because of the involvement of powerful managers, continues to put resources into these products in the hope of eventually coming good.
- *Failures* — the products and services that have failed to play a significant role in the company's portfolio and that have no realistic chance of doing so. These are kept on the company's books largely through inertia. It is easier to do so than admit defeat and withdraw or divest them.

The product life cycle, or death cycle, provides a link between the businesses identified by Drucker (see Figure 3.1). As they stand, developments, sleepers or ego trips contribute little to the company but it is hoped that they may one day do so. The markets they are in may be highly attractive, but because of underinvestment the company has little ability to serve them. If left alone, with no extra investment being made in them, the businesses will follow the death cycle and become failures.

Strategically, a company is facing a dilemma with these businesses. If left alone they are unlikely to succeed, so a choice has to be made between investing in them or getting out. In even the largest companies it is impossible to pursue all attractive markets, so the first portfolio decision is one of double or quits. If the choice is to invest, then the aim is to build the business strength until it is strong enough to become one of tomorrow's breadwinners. This usually means achieving some degree of market dominance in a growth sector. If successfully managed, the product will mature to become one of today's breadwinners and, as it ages, one of yesterday's. As with all things, the difficulty in the portfolio is not starting ventures, but knowing when to kill them and when to concentrate resources where success can be achieved.

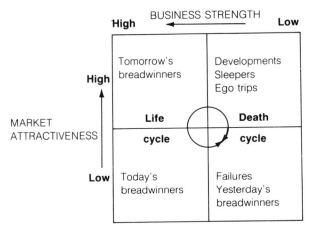

Figure 3.1 The product portfolio

3.1 The Boston Box

In the 1960s many companies, including GE, were looking for ways of balancing their portfolio of activities. Some companies called in the newly started Boston Consulting Group who, through their work with the Mead Paper Corporation, developed a way of classifying their acquisitions into four categories (*Business Week*, 1972). By 1970 this had developed into what was then called their *growth share matrix* (Henderson, 1970) or the *Boston Box*. Figure 3.2 explains the two dimensions which underlie the Boston Consulting Group's approach. The first dimension, along the vertical axis, recognises the impact of growth on cash flow. Early in the life cycle, a product is likely to be profitable but may be cash hungry because of the need to make capital investments or to defend market share. This problem is increased by the disequilibrium which occurs in growth markets where sales are at a lower level than production, and production is at a lower level than purchases. As the life cycle is followed from growth to maturity, profits decline as know-how becomes more available and differentiation diminishes. But, at the same time, capital investments are lower and companies become cash rich. This cash generation potential in companies in mature markets provides the strength of many blue-chip companies such as Unilever, Marks & Spencer, Sainsbury, etc. In Figure 3.2 the change is shown as a negative cash flow when the growth rate is high and a positive cash flow when the growth rate is low.

The horizontal axis through the Boston Box shows market share going from low to high. Negative cash flows are associated with low market share and positive ones with higher market share. The Boston Consulting Group poses this relationship on the basis of experience effects. These show a company's operating costs decreasing

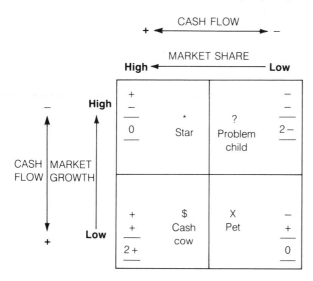

Figure 3.2 Boston Box: cash flow

as it gains experience in the market. Some of this is due to the learning curve as a company finds a task easier to do. But there are also other returns from scale economies and capital investment. Experience curves are linked to market share through a cycle of virtue where:

- A company with high market share gains more experience than its competitors.
- The experience results in lower costs.
- The lower costs mean that, at a given market price, the company with the highest market share has the highest profits.
- The company with the highest profits or contributions from sales has more to spend on research and development or marketing, which allow it to maintain its high market share.

The Boston Box received fresh impetus from the PIMS study (Buzzell and Gale, 1987), which showed a very strong relationship between market share and return on investment. Figure 3.3 shows a variation on these results, where the variation in the return on investments doubles for manufacturing-intensive companies as their market share rank increases from fifth to first, and more than trebles for R & D and marketing-intensive companies as they improve. These very powerful empirical results lend credibility to GE's strategy of being number one or two in everything they do.

The portfolio implications of the Boston Box follow from adding the cash flow implications for market growth rate and market share. The lower left-hand quadrant of Figure 3.2 looks particularly attractive where the positive cash flow from a

Return on investment

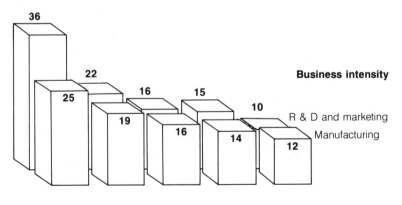

Market share rank

Source: Buzzell and Gale (1987), p. 98.

Figure 3.3 PIMS analysis: market share effect

low-growth market and high market share are added. These businesses have the benefit of experience effects from high market share and, because they are in mature markets, they have a limited need for investment. They have become cash generators and potentially a source of funds to be invested elsewhere in a business's portfolio.

Several companies can be identified which have many of their activities in this sector. In the UK GEC is renowned for the cash mountain which it has generated from its mature businesses. RTZ is another British company which has used the funds generated from its mineral extraction to good effect in diversifying into other sectors where it is a market leader. These cash cows are clearly today's breadwinners, but the danger is that they are milked to excess and therefore lose their competitiveness, or become indulgent consumers of their own surpluses. At a corporate level there is a danger of complacency, since companies which have a preponderance of cash cows may fail to develop tomorrow's breadwinners.

The beneficial qualities of the cash cows can be contrasted with the pets, which have low market share in low-growth markets. Maturity of the market means little investment needs to be made, but low market share means that profit margins and cash flows are well below those of the market leaders. The simple summation shown in Figure 3.2 indicates a cash flow of zero. More realistically, there is a modest cash flow which can be either positive or negative. Businesses in this quadrant are called pets because they do not cost much to keep and give a little pleasure. They are, however, of little financial significance to the company. The danger is the distraction of managerial time and resources which are out of proportion to their worth. Here may lie once profitable businesses which, because of competition from new technologies or global competitors, are no longer what they used to be — one-time breadwinners, which have fallen on bad times.

ICI Fertiliser Division falls into this category. Over many years, while it dominated the UK market and the Common Agricultural Policy was generous, it was a great and stable cash generator for ICI. In the 1980s and 1990s it became sick as farming became less profitable and the Europeanisation of the fertiliser market made ICI Fertilisers a small European player rather than a dominant British one. After a few years of trying to turn round the business unit, ICI was faced with a clear choice: close down the division, run it down, or sell it off. As yesterday's breadwinners in mature markets with low market share, the pets (or 'dogs', as they are often called in connection with the Boston Box) tend to make little money now and have little prospect of making money in the future.

Hedley (1977) noticed that many companies have a predominance of dogs in their portfolio. For them it is clearly impossible to follow GE's strategy of being first or second in the markets in which they compete. There are also many examples of companies with relatively low market share in mature markets which are making good returns. To reflect the value in these companies, the term 'cash dog' is used to refer to businesses which are close to the border between cash cows and pets. Strategies for these will be discussed later.

Business units with a high market share and high market growth tend to have a cash flow which is similar to that of pets. This is a case where static analysis of the company's accounts could be very dangerous in categorising these companies and the pets together. Companies in this quadrant have a business strength because of their market share, but are not generators of large volumes of cash because of the need to invest in their growth. They may not be making money now, but they are tomorrow's breadwinners. Failure to distinguish between these and the pets is one of the most important lessons of portfolio analysis. Whereas the poor cash flow of the pets suggests that they should be divested or milked and that a company should be wary of investing in them, a similar result for businesses with high market share in growth markets suggests that there could be good reasons for investing in them in order to gain or hold share. Not surprisingly, these companies are called the stars. They are tomorrow's breadwinners. They are in the growth markets in which a business unit can grow with the market.

The last quadrant suggests that businesses with low market share in high-growth markets could show a negative cash flow. They lack the experience or economics to have a high margin and yet their presence in a growth market demands investments. The label 'problem children' reflects the dilemma which companies face with these business units. If they fail to invest in them they are likely to follow a death cycle and proceed from being a development, which is losing money at present, to a failure, which will not make any money in the future. The alternatives here are double or quits: to get out of that market, or to invest heavily to gain market share in order to achieve star status. Since the market is growing there are opportunities for this, as technologies shift, dominant designs emerge and new segments appear.

In the UK Amstrad did this in the PC market, when it launched late against established competition and succeeded by offering a cheap and simple word processor sold through electrical retailers. This initial success was followed by the launch of an inexpensive PC compatible with high service back-up, once again sold through low-cost retailers rather than more expensive computer retailers.

In America Compaq achieved the same thing against IBM for several years until the maturity of the mainframe market forced IBM to take the microcomputer market more seriously. So, as an alternative to the death cycle, the Boston Box proposes a life cycle where funds are invested in the problem children in order to make them stars (tomorrow's breadwinners) which will, one day, become cash cows (today's breadwinners). In the end these cash cows may decay to become pets. Figure 3.4 illustrates this sequence, cash being taken from the cash cows and invested in the problem children in order to make them stars.

The success sequence is closed by the stars one day themselves becoming cash cows. The alternative disaster sequence shows the danger which can occur if companies enter a market early and gain high market share which they fail to support. The star may then degenerate from being a reasonably profitable star into a loss-making problem child and from there into a pet or dog. Ironically, this progression covers the results of short-termism where a company fails to see the value of investing in a market and tries to take money out of it quickly. This partly explains the failure of EMI with its world-beating body scanner. The company failed to invest in product quality and technological development, and so lost its early lead to the large competitors

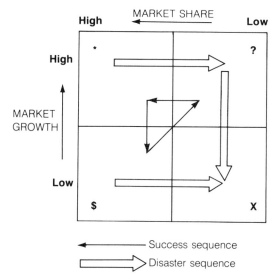

Figure 3.4   Boston Box: product sequence

attracted to the market. One of its early competitors, GE, eventually acquired EMI's ailing subsidiary. Another disaster sequence could occur if, in a desire to take profits, a cash cow is overmilked and therefore becomes vulnerable to competition. The British motor cycle industry fell foul of this when it became complacent in the world motor cycle market, which it dominated. The industry paid for its lack of investment in current development and production technology when Honda, Yamaha and Suzuki decimated such firms as BSA, Norton, Triumph and Royal Enfield.

3.2   The process of portfolio planning

The portfolio planning process has four stages: defining the unit of analysis; analysing the current position of each business unit; examining the interrelationships between the business units; and, finally, projecting the future portfolio. Later in this chapter other portfolio planning tools will be introduced and limitations of the Boston Box explained, but at present the Boston Box will be used to illustrate the portfolio planning process.

3.2.1   Define the unit of analysis

The definition of the unit of analysis for portfolio planning is a critical stage and one that is often poorly done in practice. It is intended for use at a strategic business unit (SBU) level, where SBUs are generally defined as subsidiaries which can operate independently as businesses in their own right. In reality, however, boundaries are seldom clear cut and the problems of definition can be substantial (see, for example, Haspeslagh, 1982; Gluck, 1986). Practitioners have often used the Boston Box to look at products rather than business units, or to provide a pictorial presentation of international markets. These applications do not strictly conform to those for which the Boston Box was intended, but its value as a means of presenting much information still remains and there is no danger if the limitations of the matrix are kept in mind.

3.2.2   Analyse the current position of each SBU

In Figure 3.5 the Boston Box has been calibrated to allow the position of individual SBUs to be plotted. The vertical axis is somewhat arbitrary but the central axis (which in this case is set at 10 per cent) would logically refer to the rate of growth which is necessary in order for a company to retain its current position in its overall industry. It should also show the rate of growth which reflects a switchover from the growth phase of the product life cycle to early maturity. The upper and lower limits of the axis are also changed to ranges which are typical of the industry concerned. Whereas the scale suggested may be quite adequate for an evolving industry, in some markets a 25 per cent rate of growth would be way below what was expected. Whatever scales are chosen, users should expect that sometimes business units will fly off the scale, or be congregated in markets with similar growth rates.

It is most important to note that the vertical axis refers to the market growth rate and not the growth rate achieved by business units. All competitors within a market

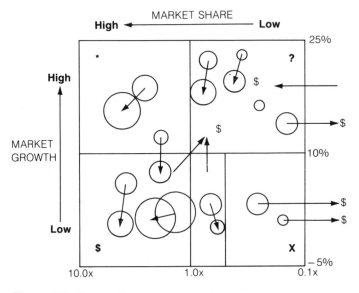

Figure 3.5   Boston Box: representation

should be in a horizontal line across the plot. This means that a company which gains market share and sales would be shown as moving across the Boston Box rather than down it.

The horizontal axis, market share, is much more rigidly defined. It is a log scale with the centre being at 1, the left-hand limit being at 10 and the right-hand limit being at 1/10. Here it must be remembered that the appropriate measure is not market share but relative market share. Two ways of measuring this have been suggested: (a) market share relative to the largest competitor, and (b) market share relative to the average size of the top three players in the market. Both these measures tend to be rather brutal since it is very difficult for anyone other than the market leader to be shown on the left-hand, high-rated market share side of the box.

As a final pictorial aid to representation, each SBU is represented as a circle with its centre corresponding to its market share and growth rates, and an area proportional to its sales. In Figure 3.5 the current positions of SBUs are represented by circles. The arrows emanate from the current position of the SBUs and point to their projected positions.

The impact of this summary presentation is a reason for the popularity of the Boston Box. It provides a clear portrayal of the business units of a company where their size and position have clear managerial implications.

3.2.3   Examine interrelationships

The proposed interrelationships between the SBUs have been suggested in the success sequence in Figure 3.4 and the life cycle and death cycle in Figure 3.1. These ideas are projected on to Figure 3.5 to show the sources and applications of funds. Two pets and a problem child are shown as being divested and therefore generating funds. Potential fund flows are also indicated from the cash dog which is being harvested, and from the cash cows. It is likely that most of the cash generated by the stars and the cash cows remains within their business units, but some of the cash taken from them and that from the divestments is shown as invested in the problem children, where it could be used in an attempt to shift them close to being stars or to start new ventures.

This rationale for the sources and applications of funds has been described by practitioners as one of the major values of the box. It is on call for headquarters to explain how the SBUs need to be managed and it can help SBU managers to argue for the cash they need.

3.2.4   Project the future for each SBU

The box can be used to represent the likely future of the SBUs and to help choose strategies appropriate for them. Problem children which are to be retained must break even, so as not to be a drain on cash, or grow aggressively before it is too late. Since the problem children are in growth markets, it is particularly important to see market share gain rather than sales improvement. If the assumptions of the Boston Consulting Group are correct, it would be wrong to anticipate that these problem children, which are set to grow, would be able to do so on the basis of internally generated funds.

Stars may be given growth objectives which are difficult to achieve for political or competitive reasons. It is not uncommon to see an early market leader slowly lose share as more companies enter the market. What is important is to retain market share and grow with the market, maybe taking market share gains as a shake-out occurs. This may appear to be a smooth process, but the shifts which occur are often the result of discontinuity in product, technological or market development; discontinuities which can be to the advantage of aggressive entrants.

Two dangers for a star business are excessive milking and satisfaction with sales growth levels which leave market share eroded. A company which is overstretched by trying to cultivate too many problem children or maintaining too many pets may find the bulk of its stars a temptation.

The main concern for cash cows is the generation of money now. There may occasionally be opportunities for market share gain, but experience shows that once markets are mature companies and brand shares remain stable for a long time. For these business units, appropriate strategies will focus on the maintenance of market share and the generation of adequate profit levels. Future funds for the company's development may depend on the continued success of the cash cows, but growth is likely to come from the growth markets occupied by the problem children or the stars.

The future for each SBU is represented by an arrow connecting its present and projected position. This direction is a function of the uncontrolled change in market growth and the market share strategy being pursued by the SBU. For a successful company, many of these improvements will show market share gain, but it may also be appropriate to show a decline in market share where competition is intensifying and an early lead is being lost or, as is the case in Figure 3.5, a cash dog is being milked to provide funds for SBUs with greater promise.

3.2.5   Project the future portfolio

If left to their own devices, SBUs will tend to drift down the Boston Box as markets mature and from left to right if neglected. This drift downwards will suggest the need for a company to view its future portfolio and seek out opportunities and markets which may create tomorrow's breadwinners. This has proved one of the most difficult tasks for large mature companies, which inevitably find it hard to find new growth industries to replace those on which they have depended for so long. Many of the blue-chip companies in retailing, groceries and the oil industry fall into this category. Global expansion provides some opportunities for growth, but when that has been achieved it is perhaps time to give the profits back to the shareholders.

3.3   The pros and cons of the Boston Box

The Boston Box, along with Peters and Waterman's view of excellence and Porter's more recent views on competitive strategy, is one of the few business ideas with the subtlety and attractiveness to become well known within business circles. The very success of these ideas means that they become controversial and that the simplicity which is such an important factor in their diffusion makes them vulnerable to accusations of lack of sophistication. So venomous has been this criticism that it is necessary to consider the limitations of the Boston Box along with its strengths.

The success of the Box has been lucidly explained by Morrison and Wensley (1991). On psychological grounds it fulfils a human desire for taxonomy, classifying a complex mix of different businesses. It is easy to grasp, has an attractive presentation and uses catch terms and phrases which are easy to memorise and have a link to strategy. These may be poor reasons for using a strategic tool, but they make it an effective means of communication in an area where little else is clear.

Research has provided some evidence to support the Boston Box. It embodies simple ideas with cash flow implications which are intuitively appealing to managers. The PIMS study has been a particularly fruitful source of support for the Boston Box. Figure 3.6 provides some evidence and shows the percentage of businesses with positive cash flows in each of the four categories. The difference is strong along the market share axis but certainly not strong along that for market growth. It is also noticeable that the much maligned dogs do provide a positive cash flow in most cases. These reflect a strategy which does not come within the remit of the Boston Box, where business units with low market share can find niche opportunities. For example, in the car market the BMW was a relatively small player but is often regarded as the most successful competitor. Its quality and sporting image allow the company to charge more than competitors with a similar car of a similar size.

Fashion has led to the Box being popular. This means it is an idea that is well

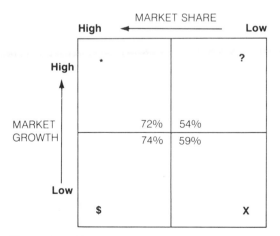

Figure 3.6   Boston Box: business showing positive cash flow

understood and liked by many managers and therefore one which allows communication with headquarters and SBUs. It has become part of the common business vocabulary, so its use and terminology have become symbols of membership of the informal executive club. Strategically, it allows companies to pursue a purposive strategy rather than to follow the vagaries of the market place. It gives the illusion of control to managers by suggesting that they could move SBUs around the chart like pieces around a chess board. But of course, it is not possible for a single player to decide where each of his or her SBUs should be moved to, no more than it is possible for a single player to decide where all the pieces on a chess board should be positioned. Simplicity is probably the Boston Box's greatest virtue. It brings together a number of very important strategic issues and allows them to be presented and understood quickly.

Perhaps the greatest disadvantage of the Boston Box is its excessive simplicity. It would be ridiculous for an organisation to follow it as the only guide to strategy, or not to question the dimensions upon which it is based. This is particularly true where the various business units represented are competing for funds.

It is as easy to enunciate the limitations of the Boston Box as it is to praise its elegance. There is no rigid definition of what an SBU is or how a market may be defined. For example, British Aerospace with its Harrier jump jet could easily define itself as being totally dominant in the market since there is no other vertical take-off fighter. Alternatively, it could be seen as a very small producer of tactical support aircraft, since the Harrier is one of many answers to general defence problems. This problem of definition of the product market leads to the difficulty of measuring market growth and market share. Although these can be difficult to measure, however, even if a company is not using the Boston Box it is hard to defend failure to gather information that is so vital to the company's operations. Moreover, the tool is concerned not so much with odd percentage points as with broad classifications and shifts.

The tool is certainly simple and so prone to overuse. But perhaps there is even more danger of misusing more complex tools when the underlying assumptions are difficult to grasp. Take, for example, regression analysis, which is often used to analyse markets but is understood by few marketers.

A major problem with the Boston Box is the euphoria with which it was first received and the exaggerated claims which were made for it. In 1973 Henderson claimed: 'Such a simple chart with a projected position for five years out, is sufficient alone to tell a company's profits ability, debt capacity, growth potential and competitive strength.' Would it were true. Nevertheless the Boston Box certainly has its advantages. It is clearly inadequate as a complete solution but is of undisputed value as a starting point in many analyses.

3.4   Multifactor approaches to portfolio modelling

Comparison of Figures 3.1 and 3.5 suggests that relative market share is just one business strength of a company. This is certainly true. There are other strengths that a company could have: maybe a brand name or exclusive access to distribution channels, unique product features or financial strengths. It is also quite possible that a company willing to commit vast resources to new technology could achieve lower costs than the market leader, thereby rendering the higher market share of no advantage at all. Toyota's success relative to the market-leading General Motors is a case in point. It is also clear that the British motor cycle industry's dominance of the motor cycle market did not help, and that British Leyland's strength in the UK market did the company very little good.

Just as market share is only one business strength, so market growth is only one dimension of market attractiveness. The low market growth rate of the UK grocery trade may not make it attractive in itself, but when its margins are compared across Europe it seems a very good one to exploit, hence the movement of the German grocery retailer Aldi against long-established and strong competitors like Sainsbury and Tesco. Stability may be another attractive feature. Although small, the market for academic journals is very attractive and has been exploited very successfully by MCB. Its two attractive features, beside the low fluctuation in demand, are the relatively low price sensitivity of subscribers, particularly in the supposedly hard-pressed libraries, and the mailing list associated with the publications. Certainly, if the desire is to generate a regular income, it is probably a better idea to invest in a company which occupies a dominant position in a mature market than to invest in one in a growth market of uncertain future. Note how long the leading brands in mature markets have survived and how short has been the life of companies in the electronics industry.

In order to understand its own portfolio, GE devised a matrix which was able to show business strength and market attractiveness across a multitude of dimensions. Figure 3.7 shows a typical example. The *GE market attractiveness—business position matrix* considers two sets of factors which appear to influence the relative attractiveness of investing in a business. 'Business' in this context could conceivably be defined as an individual product, a product line, a market segment, a business unit or even a division.

The first set of factors addresses the favourability of the market in which the business is located. The second refers to criteria by which the business or company's position in a market is judged to be weak or strong. All these criteria are then employed to construct scores of market attractiveness and of business position. These are plotted usually on a three-by-three matrix depicting the relative investment opportunity for a business. Normally, as in portfolio analysis, the business unit is represented on the chart by a circle whose diameter or area corresponds to the sales volumes of the business. Sometimes, the size of the circle represents the market size rather than the size of the company's business and parts of the circle are shaded to represent the business's absolute market share.

3.4.1   By any other name

The GE matrix is often known by other names, such as the General Electric multifactor

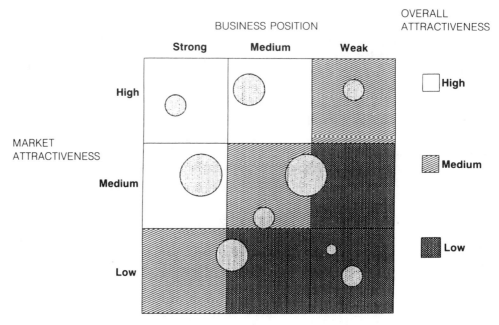

Figure 3.7 The GE matrix

portfolio matrix, or the business position—market attractiveness matrix. Another similar model, and a refinement on the GE matrix, which evaluates business sector prospects and the company's competitive position, is the *directional policy matrix*, developed by Shell (Hughes, 1981). Either technique is applicable to almost any diversified business with separately identifiable sectors: for example, an engineering company offering a range of products and services, or an electrical company where the separate business sectors might be different types of electrical appliance. The main issue is to measure the two variables forming the axes of the matrix. To do this, the factors underlying each dimension must be identified, measured and brought together to provide an index or value.

3.4.2   Identifying the factors

Each company has to decide on its list of factors which make a market 'attractive' or a business position in a market 'strong'. Experience suggests the factors listed in Table 3.1 to be among the most important. The importance of each factor depends primarily on the nature of the product, customer behaviour, the company itself and the industry it operates in. For example, for commodity products, low production costs and entry barriers may be important contributors to business position and industry attractiveness respectively. With more highly differentiated products (for example, precision measurement instruments, specialised machine tools, and so forth)

Table 3.1 *Factors contributing to market attractiveness and business position*

Attractiveness of your market	Status/position of your business
Market factors	
Size (sterling, units or both)	Your share (in equivalent terms)
Size of key segments	Your share of key segments
Growth rate per year:	Your annual growth rate:
Total	Total
Segments	Segments
Diversity of market	Diversity of your participation
Sensitivity to price, service features and external factors	Your influence on the market
Cyclicality	Lags or leads in your sales
Seasonality	
Bargaining power of upstream suppliers	Bargaining power of your suppliers
Bargaining power of downstream suppliers	Bargaining power of your customers
Competition	
Types of competitors	Where you fit, how you compare in terms of products, marketing capability
Degree of concentration	
Changes in type and mix	Service, production strength, financial strength, management
Entries and exits	Segments you have entered or left
Changes in share	Your relative share change
Substitution by new technology	Your vulnerability to new technology
Degrees and types of integration	Your own level of integration
Financial and economic factors	
Contribution margins	Your margins
Leveraging factors, such as economies of scale and experience	Your scale and experience
Barriers to entry or exit (both financial and non-financial)	Barriers to your entry or exit (both financial and non-financial)
Capacity utilisation	Your capacity utilisation
Technological factors	
Maturity and volatility	Your ability to cope with change
Complexity	Depths of your skills
Differentiation	Types of your technological skills
Patents and copyrights	Your patent protection
Manufacturing process technology required	Your manufacturing technology
Sociopolitical factors in your environment	
Social attitudes and trends	Your company's responsiveness and flexibility
Law and government agency regulations	Your company's ability to cope
Influence with pressure groups and government representatives	Your company's aggressiveness
Human factors, such as unionisation and community acceptance	Your company's relationships

Table 3.2 *Market attractiveness*

Factor	Score	Weighting	Ranking
1 Market size	0.5	15	7.5
2 Volume growth (units)	0.0	15	0.0
3 Concentration	1.0	30	30.0
4 Financial	0.5	25	12.5
5 Technology	0.5	15	7.5
		100	57.5

the customer seeks technical innovation, precision or other benefits. Relative technological status may be a prime contributor to business position and being 'first in' with new processes or technology having patent protection may be a major factor determining market attractiveness.

Identification of the relevant factors requires detailed examination of customers, competitors, market characteristics, the external environment and the organisation itself. It also relies on management judgement, experience and an appreciation of the technique's limitations. The latter, hopefully, avoids easy generalisations made by management.

3.4.3   Scoring the factors

Having identified the relevant factors, the analyst has to summarise them into measures of market attractiveness and business position. This can usually be done by assigning scores to each factor (0.0 = low; 0.5 = medium; 1.0 = high), then weighting each factor depending on its relative importance. Finally, the score and weighting for each factor are multiplied together to obtain the factor's ranking or value in respect of the two variables — market attractiveness and business position.

Tables 3.2 and 3.3 provide hypothetical examples of the scheme. The sum of ranks or values under each variable would then be used to plot the location of the business analysed in the matrix. Scores and weighting are a matter of managerial judgement and experience, but in practice the weightings have much less impact on the final outcome than one might expect.

3.4.4   Implications for marketing strategy

The GE model uses return on investment (ROI) as the criterion for assessing an investment opportunity. (Contrast this with the cash flow criterion used in the BCG growth—share analysis.) A business located in the upper left part of the matrix — that is, one showing high overall attractiveness — would be indicative of one showing good investment opportunity: the business shows a high ROI.

Table 3.3 *Business position*

Factor	Score	Weighting	Ranking
1 Product technology			
Current quality	0	20	0
New technology	0.5	20	10
2 Manufacturing			
Scale	0.5	10	5
Efficiency	0.5	10	5
Physical distribution	0.5	10	5
3 Marketing			
Expertise	0	10	0
Sales	0.5	10	5
Service	0.5	10	5
		100	35

The GE model has useful implications for marketing strategy. The analyst or planner can use it to plan in three stages. First, the model could be used to classify the present opportunity facing the business given the present business strategy, industry character and competitive structure. Second, an analysis of future market environment and position could be conducted assuming no major changes in strategy are made. Third, the latter process could be repeated several times but with new and alternative strategic options explored. Different assumptions can be made about objectives and investments to be put into the business each time the process is repeated.

The final choice of strategy requires estimation of the long-term costs and benefits of contemplated changes, as well as consideration of competitors' reaction to any strategic change. Several major strategic options are usually available in terms of changes in business position. These are as follows:

- Invest to hold or maintain the current business position. The investment has to be sufficient to keep up with market changes. This option is likely to make sense in a market of declining attractiveness.
- Invest to improve the market position of the business. Such a strategy requires sufficient investment to penetrate the market, thereby strengthening the business. It is usually undertaken in the early development or growth phase of the market.
- Invest to rebuild. This is a high-investment strategy aimed at restoring or revitalising business position in a maturing or declining market.
- Selectivity. This strategy aims at strengthening position in segments where the benefits of penetration or rebuilding exceed the costs: for example, building 'problem children' up to 'stars' or letting them turn into 'pets'.
- Low investment or harvest the business. This option is usually effected over a period of time. The business tends to be subject to selective investment over the short term and eventually 'cashed in' when the price is right. This strategy may

be appropriate for businesses holding strong positions in declining markets: 'cash cows', for example.

Other strategic options are also available, such as investing heavily to enter new markets, or withdrawing or diverting from the market because the business is not viable at all.

3.5   Limitations of the multifactor matrix

Market attractiveness—business position analysis focuses on the ROI potential of alternative business strategies. In a way it can be used to complement portfolio analysis, which looks at the cash flow implications of strategy. The technique does, however, contain practical limitations.

Many factors influencing the two major variables might have been considered. These are not specified but based on managers' subjective judgement. The problem is whether all relevant contributory factors are identified by planners. Weightings of the relative importance of factors are also decided subjectively, not specified by any objective procedure. Subjectivity can be a problem, especially if planners are inexperienced or incapable of exercising the judgement required.

Another limitation is the unproven relationship between influencing factors and the dimensions (market attractiveness and business position) themselves. For instance, management recognise that their company's technological innovativeness gives them a strong status in the market, but the form and direction of that relationship is not specified or easily quantifiable.

Despite the limitations and practical difficulties of assessing future changes and strategic choices to deal with them, the technique has useful implications for marketing strategy. The limitations may be somewhat minimised if management uses informed judgement throughout the assessment (that is, judgement based on detailed examination of information about customers, markets, competitors and so on). The model can be used to build up a qualitative picture of the product portfolios of other companies, hence providing useful insight into competitors' market positions and business strength.

3.6   Financial portfolio theory

The mean variant rule suggested by Markowitz (1952) has led financiers into developing an approach which is quite different from those already discussed. This is most frequently thought of as a way of examining a portfolio of investments in the Stock Exchange, but it has also been found to be fairly robust at the level of the firm (Rubinstein, 1973).

The *capital asset pricing model* (CAPM) applies Markowitz's portfolio theory to the resource allocation decision. It focuses on the rate of return that should be obtained from an investment with a certain risk level. The underlying principle is portrayed diagrammatically in Figure 3.8, where the line is used to portray the relationship between the risk of the investment and its appropriate rate of return. At zero risk, the rate of return expected is the lowest and is called the risk-free rate of return. This is akin to the safe but low rates of return that an individual can obtain by investing cash in a building society or a bank deposit account. A more risky investment would be to put some money into a wide spread of shares on the stock market. In this case, the investor suffers the uncertainty of dividends going up and down with economic cycles and incurring potential capital loss if share prices as a whole go down. To compensate the investor for this new level of risk (rm) the investor would expect a higher rate of return (Rm). Riskier still would be investing in a single firm, where it is to be expected that the share price will oscillate more than the market itself and there is much greater likelihood of fluctuation in dividends. Counted against this could be expectation of high capital gains if the investment performs well. There is clearly much higher risk in this investment (rc), so for this the investor would demand a much higher rate of return (Rc). In a sense, the line in Figure 3.8 relating the risk levels to the rates of return is an indifference curve where all investments with their appropriate levels of risk and return are of equal utility to an investor.

The level of risk of a particular investment can be represented using the CAPM formula:

$$b = (Rc - R0)/(rc - r0)$$

which gives the b coefficient for stock C. This is known as the *systematic risk* to the investor.

This has interesting implications for the portfolio manager. Clearly everyone is looking for an investment which is likely to perform above the line R^*, which has a higher rate of return than the level of risk implies; of course, these investments are very easy to identify after the event. A number of financial analysts have argued that there is a general relationship between increased market uncertainties and systematic

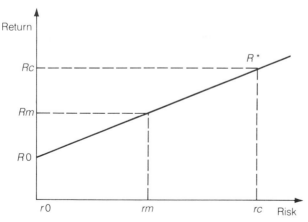

Figure 3.8 The capital asset pricing model

risk (*b*). This could imply, for instance, that an investment in a new venture may involve higher systematic risk than an investment associated with a mature product. On this basis, Franks and Boyles (1979) suggest that products should be grouped into Class A projects, which are lower-risk, cost-reducing products; Class B projects, which are average risk, skill expansion projects; and Class C projects, which are new projects with high risk. Using the Boston Box terminology this has interesting implications, for it suggests that the question marks and stars are likely to be in high-growth and uncertain markets where new projects in Class C and skill expansions in Class B are likely. This then overlays the cycle of cash investment from marketing portfolio theory with the expectation that this higher-risk investment in the question marks and stars should be expected to gain a higher return than the investments in cash cows. This requirement is realistic since there is a hope that increased market share in the early days of the product life cycle will be an investment which will allow the company to grow with the market and reap long-term cash benefits in the future.

At first sight it is easy to draw the conclusion from the CAPM model that it is the corporate manager's task to invest in a diversified portfolio of product markets and so reduce the risk of the overall investment. In particular, it looks like a good idea to invest in a number of investments with high specific risk (*b*) where the risks will tend to cancel out and the average returns will be high. In reality, analysis of the CAPM model suggests that stockholder wealth is maximised if the investor is allowed to diversify his or her portfolio rather than the firm making its own series of relatively restricted investments. The conclusion is therefore that the management should concentrate on achieving a return appropriate to the risk level involved, rather than diversifying in a portfolio.

Other evidence suggests that this is clearly the case, for to develop the portfolio product market investments which are sufficiently diverse to move independently means that a firm has to become a conglomerate of unrelated businesses. Although conglomerates of such businesses tend to form very quickly in periods of growth when firms are cash rich and share prices are high, evidence suggests that these firms rarely survive cyclical downturns in the economy and often end up performing poorly or being broken up by a more conservative and thoughtful predator.

Kellogg is a very good example of a company which avoided the temptation of diversifying out of trouble. In the late 1970s, 75 per cent of Kellogg's revenue and 80 per cent of its profits came from the cereal market, an environment which was becoming increasingly risky and hostile. The company's pre-sweetened cereals were being denounced by consumer groups; anti-trust legislation was being mounted against its dominant position in the market; and the proportion of children in the population (high consumers of cereals) was declining. Faced with this uncertainty, the competitors of Kellogg, General Mills and General Foods, diversified into other food and non-food products. In contrast, Kellogg stuck to the business it knew and has since outperformed the firms which tried to escape the rigours of the cereal market (*Business Week*, 1979).

Being based on financial theory, the CAPM approach to portfolio analysis is far better founded than the Boston Box or the multifactor matrix approach of portfolio analysis. Empirical evidence supports the descriptive validity of the CAPM, but in practice there is great difficulty in the prior determination of the b coefficient. Finally, as Wensley (1981) suggests, the actual investment decision goes beyond the estimation of the positive net value of an investment. The basic application of CAPM must be compared with the strategic analysis of competitive advantage in any resource allocation decision.

3.7 Conclusions

Portfolio theories provide a link between the wide activities of a company and appropriate strategies for individual product markets. They provide ways of viewing the pattern of all of a company's product market activities, drawing conclusions about their interactions and considering appropriate strategies for them.

Portfolio theories have certainly not provided the answers hoped for by the early pioneers, but they remain valuable tools which need to be used with some concern for their limitations. Table 3.4 provides an overview of them.

The Boston Box is the most seductive of the approaches. It is simple and intuitively appealing, and there is some moderate evidence in support of the underlying ideas. It is easy to use, although there can be some difficulty in determining the business units involved. The strategic implications of the Box are quite important, even though the tool is very simple. It is clearly important that the company seeks for tomorrow's breadwinners while benefiting from today's. The simplicity and ease of understanding of the BCG make it a useful operational tool.

Table 3.4 *Portfolio models*

Model	Focus	Measure	Complete-ness	Theoretical support	Empirical support	Ease of use	Strategic value	Operational value
Boston Box	Cash flow	Market share vs market growth	Low	Moderate	Moderate	Good	Moderate	Good
GE matrix	ROI	Business strength vs market attract.	High	Low	Low	Moderate	Moderate	Good
CAPM	Beta ratio	Risk vs return	Very low	High	High	Low	High	Low

The GE matrix recognises the need to take a broad view of business strengths and market attractiveness. The danger in its application is the tendency of the weightings and scorings used to push all the business units investigated towards the central, medium or overall attractiveness area. Theoretical and empirical support for the multifactor matrices is low, but the message is simple and companies should certainly consider very carefully investments in markets with low or medium overall attractiveness. The matrix is certainly more cumbersome to use than the Boston Box and depends upon far more subjective decisions, but it is easy to understand and operate. As a way of analysing the overall portfolio of a company's activities, the Boston Box and the GE matrix complement each other very well.

The CAPM approach has the elegance and simplicity of a great scientific discovery. It contains very important truths about portfolio investments and provides counter-intuitive implications about how firms should manage themselves. The strategic importance of the theory is very high, and this is backed by theoretical underpinning and empirical support of the descriptive ability of the model. Unfortunately, at a practical level it is not easy to use and, in a marketing sense, is of little operational value. One danger of the CAPM lies in its application without strategic vision. It is easy to see the risk of new ventures but much more difficult to calculate the high, long-term return that could exist. It may lead companies towards cost-cutting support of today's breadwinners rather than investing in the more risky ventures. These models do not provide a complete answer to analysing a company's portfolio but they do provide a very useful starting point.

PART TWO

Competitive market analysis

The second part of the book examines market analysis in finer detail. This is pursued through four chapters.

Chapter 4 examines *industry analysis*. The discussion commences with a review of *strategic groups* followed by analysis of *industry evolution*. *Environmental stability* is assessed together with *SPACE* analysis. Finally the *advantage matrix* is reviewed as a means of assessing the key characteristics of an industry when forming strategy.

Chapter 5 is concerned with internal analysis of the organisation's *strengths and weaknesses* — its capability profile. The discussion covers the identification of the organisation's *core competencies* and methods for identifying *marketing assets* — properties (often intangible) that can be employed to gain strategic advantage in the market place.

Chapter 6 considers *customer analysis*. *Information requirements* are discussed first, followed by sources of *customer information*. The variety of *marketing research techniques* available to aid customer analysis is examined. The discussion then turns to the *processes by which customer data are collected* and how that data can be turned into *information* to aid marketing decision making.

The final chapter in the section, Chapter 7, addresses *competitor analysis*. The dimensions of competitor analysis are discussed, together with *techniques for identifying competitor response profiles*. The chapter concludes with a review of *sources of competitor information*.

FOUR

Industry analysis

Success breeds failure . . . the historical success model becomes the major obstacle to the firm's adaptation to the new reality.

Ansoff (1984)

Introduction

Within the environment there are industries; within industries there are strategic groups; and it is within those strategic groups that firms compete to grow, survive or decline. Industry analysis, therefore, forms a link between the general environment which all industries face and the immediate competitive situation of firms. It depends on identifying strategic groups within an industry and ascertaining the particular environment they face. Central to this are the measurement of environmental stability and industry strength, which between them identify the competitive state within an industry, and the organisation which the situation demands.

This chapter provides a series of tools for identifying industrial environments and recognising the opportunities that they present. It can provide no simple rules to achieving competitive success but can explain the forms of industrial environment that exist, the competition within them, and when and why certain strategies succeed.

4.1 Strategic groups

A strategic group is composed of firms within an industry following the same or a similar strategy. Their identification is fundamental to industry analysis since, just as industries can rise or fall despite the state of the overall environment, so strategic groups with their distinctive competencies can defy the general fluctuations within an industry.

The separation of strategic groups within a market depends on the barriers to mobility within the industry. For instance, all the companies within the British ship-building industry tend to compete with each other for high-value-added defence contracts, but their lack of cheap labour and resources mean that they are not in the same strategic group as the Korean or Japanese suppliers or bulk carriers. Other barriers may be the degree of vertical integration of companies, as in the case of British Gypsum and its source of raw materials for making plasterboard within the UK, or Boots Pharmaceuticals with its access to the market via the Boots retailing chain. At a global level, geopolitical boundaries can also cause differences. For instance, the fragmented buying of the European military and the resultingly small production runs tend to position European defence contractors in a different strategic group from their American counterparts — as do the differences in technology, reliability and safety standards form barriers between the Russian and western aerospace manufacturers.

Besides the barriers surrounding them, strategic groups also share competitive pressures. Within the American defence industry firms share similar bargaining power with the Pentagon and similar influence through the political lobbying system. This can help protect them from non-American suppliers but does not give them an advantage within their home market. The threat from substitutes may also provide a unifying theme for strategic groups. Within the computer industry suppliers of low-cost products such as Amstrad, Apricot and Compaq are facing intense competition from inexpensively manufactured lap-tops or even palm-top machines, whereas the companies within the higher-value-added mainframe businesses are under less threat from low-cost manufacturers. Finally, strategic groups often share common competitors because they are often competing to fulfil similar market needs using similar technologies.

■ The map of strategic groups within the US automobile market shows their dynamics (Figure 4.1). The presentation dictates that two dimensions are used although, if necessary, an analysis may use more. In this case the strategic groups show their clear geographic and historic origins. The 'big three' of GM, Ford and Chrysler remain dominant in supplying a broad range of cars with high local content. In this they retain some technological and styling expertise in the supply of regular and luxury sedans, but until recently they had the common basic defence of promoting import restrictions.

Another group is the 'faded champions', which were once the major importers into the American market. Both are European companies whose American ventures have seen either better days, in the case of Volkswagen/Audi, or much better days, in the case of the Rover group. Once suppliers of a relatively broad range of vehicles, both these companies are retreating towards the luxury car sector where they appear to have little competitive edge. The demise of the faded champions is due not to the big three, but to the entry of the 'samurai' into the American market. Initially, the quality and low cost of the Japanese strategic group gave them an advantage over the European broad range suppliers. But now the Japanese are gaining even more power by becoming local manufacturers and therefore overcoming the local content barriers.

High European labour costs have meant that they operate in strategic groups selling high-added-value luxury cars or specialist cars: the luxury cars being supplied by relatively large-scale manufacturers with moderately wide product ranges, or by specialist manufacturers producing very expensive, small-volume products.

The strength of the barriers surrounding the industries is reflected by recent shifts that have taken place. Although the samurai have never attacked the hard core of the big three, they have continued to nibble away at the weaker imports, first of all the faded champions and now the luxury car makers. Even though they are very large, the big three have found it beyond their ability to defend their position by developing their own luxury cars, and so have been seeking to defend their flanks against the samurai by purchasing European manufacturers such as Jaguar, Saab, Lamborghini, Aston Martin and Lotus. After years of the big three and the samurai avoiding direct competition, the luxury car market has become the point where the two meet. Although the samurai have not found it

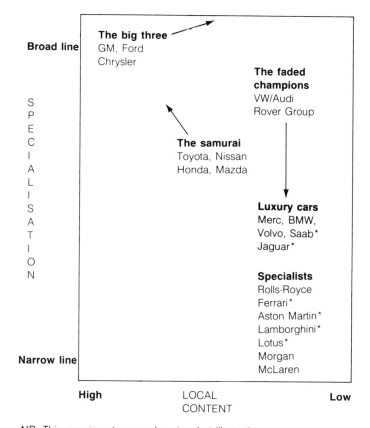

NB: This map is not comprehensive, but illustrative.
*Brands now owned by large-scale American or European automobile manufacturers.

Figure 4.1   Map of strategic groups in the US automobile market*

appropriate to purchase European companies in order to overcome entry barriers to those sectors (with the exception of Toyota, which has bought and sold Lotus), so distinct are the luxury car markets that both Toyota and Honda are launching totally new ranges with new brand names and distribution systems to attack the market (the Acura and the Lexus).

With the luxury car market already being fought over, the next stand-up battle between the big three and the samurai is in the specialist market, where the Americans have again been purchasing European brands and the Japanese have been aggressively developing 'Ferrari bashers'. Although the one-time distinct strategic groups are becoming blurred as the main protagonists enter new markets, it is to be noted that in all cases the strategy involves establishing distinct business units with the skills appropriate for the strategic groups being fought over. Examination of the US automobile market shows that even when markets are mature there can be areas of rapid growth and competition, such as the luxury car and specialist markets. And the different expertise and situation of the strategic groups mean that the protagonists from the different groups may well compete in different ways. ∎

The inability of companies to understand the differences in strategic groups is a cause of the frequent failures of companies entering new markets by acquisition. Although the broad business definition, products being sold and customers may be similar within the acquired and the acquiring company, where the two are in different strategic groups there can be major misunderstandings. Although having great expertise in the British market, many British retailers have found international expansion very difficult because of the competition they face in the new markets and their failure to understand the strategic groups they are entering.

Examples include Boots in Canada and Dixons in the United States where, although their international diversification was into the same industries as those with which they were familiar in the UK, those skills which allowed them to beat competition within their strategic groups at home did not transfer internationally. If the companies had faced the same competition within the European markets it is likely that their ventures would have been more successful. In a sense that is what the Japanese have been doing, as their industries have rolled from country to country across the world. Their major competitors are their own compatriots, whom they have faced in many markets in the past.

4.2   Industry evolution

The critical issue to be addressed within an industry depends on its evolutionary stage (Porter, 1980). This has industries emerging, transforming to maturity and declining in much the same way as the product life cycle (Figure 4.2). However, industry evolution is to the product, what the product life cycle is to the brand. For example, whereas in the music industry the product life cycle may relate to a vinyl record,

STAGE	ISSUES	STRATEGIES
Emergence	Technological uncertainty Commercial uncertainty Customer uncertainty Channel uncertainty	Establish standard Reduce switching cost/risk Cost leadership Finding customers Locating early adopters Encourage trials
Transition to maturity	Slow growth Falling profits Excessive capacity Intense competition Extended product Customer power	4P marketing Efficiency Better co-ordination Retaining customers Segmentation
Decline	Substitution Demographic shift	Divest Focus

Source: Based on O'Shaughnessy (1988), Table 8.1, p. 183. Reproduced by kind permission of Unwin Hyman Ltd.

Figure 4.2   Industry evolution

industry evolution embraces the transition from cylinders to 78s, the 45, vinyl albums, 8-track cartridges, cassettes, CD, CCD, DAT and MD. Uncertainty is the salient feature within emerging industries.

■ Recent developments in broadcasting show this most clearly. There is no technological uncertainty about the basic technologies involved in achieving the direct broadcasting of television programmes by cable or satellite, but there are vast uncertainties about the combination of technologies to be used and how they should be paid for. In the early 1980s the discussion was about cable and the terrific opportunities offered for industrial redevelopment by cabling declining cities such as Liverpool. In America, many cable channels emerged but with no particular standard and with numerous channels that had a short life. In only a few years the vast infrastructure requirements of cable have been replaced by the equally capital-intensive but more elegant solution of satellite television. Even there, however, there is uncertainty about whether to use high-, low- or medium-powered satellites and the means of getting revenue from the customers. In the United Kingdom, to that brawl has been added uncertainty concerning British regulations and those of the European Community and the activities of the broadcasting channels which were once the oligopolistic supplier. It is not surprising that with this uncertainty consumers have shown reluctance in adopting the new viewing opportunities open to them. ■

The high losses that can be associated with the emergent stage of an industry are shown by the losses incurred by the pioneers of the competing technologies within the video industry. Out of three competing video disc and video cassette recording technologies only one, VHS, has survived. Two of the losers in that round (Philips with the laser disc and V2000 VCRs, and Sony with BetaMax) managed the emergence of laser-based reproduction more carefully. The two industry leaders collaborated in the development of a CD standard and licensed the technology widely in order to accelerate its diffusion and reduce customer uncertainty. With the establishment of a single technology, the compact disc was less prone to the software shortages that made video discs so unattractive to customers. Customers still faced potentially high switching costs if they traded in their existing album collection for CDs, but the impact of this was reduced by focusing on segments which were very conscious of hi-fi quality and heavy users. The CD was also capable of being integrated into existing hi-fi systems and quickly became an established part of budget rack systems. The smooth and orchestrated emergence of the CD album market has to be compared with that of CD singles where Philips and Sony have failed to agree a single technology.

In the transition to maturity, uncertainty declines but competition intensifies. Typically, the rapid growth, high margins, little competition and apparent size of industries in the late stage of emergence attract many competitors. Those who sought to avoid the uncertainty in the early stages now feel the time is right for them to enter the market. This decision usually coincides with a transition towards maturity in a market place where competition increases, profits fall, growth slows and capacity is excessive as more producers come on stream. Also by now a dominant design has emerged, so competitors are forced to compete on a basis of price or the extended product. In technological terms, there is a switch to process technology; in marketing terms, a switch from entrepreneurship to the Four P marketing — that is, towards efficiency and the careful identification of market segments with a marketing mix to address them.

Not unexpectedly, companies which fail to notice this transition from entrepreneurial to bureaucratic management find things difficult. Take, for instance, Clive Sinclair who was still seeking to differentiate the market with his QL Microcomputer after the emergence of the IBM PC had established industry standards. Equally, examine the increasing difficulties which Amstrad faces once its entrepreneurial, cost-cutting and channel strategies have been followed by industry leaders such as IBM and Olivetti.

Industry evolution also shows that their very success can lead to failure for industries that have learnt to manage their maturity; the cost-cutting and efficient bureaucracies being totally inappropriate for managing in the entrepreneurial fashion necessary in emerging sectors. An industry's decline is usually caused by the emergence of a substitute or a demographic shift. Two strategies are appropriate: either divest or focus upon the efficient supply of a robust segment. Although the options are few, industries often find this decision a difficult one because of the vested interests within the declining sector. It is extraordinary that at this last stage there seem to be more organisational choices than at any other stage in an industry's evolution. At a clinical level there can be the decision to divest or milk a company in an erring sector. There is the option of carefully nurturing a long, lingering target market. For an opportunist with entrepreneurial zest, there is a possibility of taking advantage of shifting needs. There is certainly much money to be made in the remnants of industries, as AEM, a subsidiary of RTZ, has found. AEM specialises in the aviation engineering and maintenance of products which are no longer the main focus of the leading airframe and aero engine manufacturers.

Industry evolution shows the violent shifts which occur within an industry as it progresses from stage to stage. Not only do the major issues change, but the management tasks and styles appropriate are equally shifting. An analysis of industry evolution is essential if a company is to avoid managing in an environment with which it is unfamiliar, with an inappropriate management style.

4.3 Environmental stability

A limitation of Porter's industry evolution model is the rigid association of technological and marketing uncertainty with only the emerging stage of an industry. This may not be so. For instance, the UK grocery trade has certainly been mature for generations, but the growth of supermarkets and hypermarkets, the removal of retail price maintenance and the move towards out-of-town shopping have meant that the market has faced great turbulence, despite its being mature. Ansoff's (1984) theory is that environmental turbulence is fundamental to understanding industries, but that it should not be seen as relating only to industry life cycle.

A distinction is drawn between marketing and innovation turbulence (Table 4.1). The reason for this is apparent when one considers many industries, such as the

Table 4.1 *Determinants of environmental turbulence*

Association of high/marketing turbulence	Association of high/innovative turbulence
High % of sales spent on marketing	High % of sales spent on R & D
Novel market entrant	Frequent new products in the industry
Very aggressive leading competitor	Short PLCs
Threatening pressure by customers	Novel technologies emerging
Demand outstripping industry capacity	Many competing technologies
Emergence, decline or shifting stage of PLC	Emergence, decline or shifting stage of PLC
Low profitability	Low profitability
High product differentiation	Creativity is a critical success factor
Identification of latent needs a critical success factor	

automobile industry, where competition has been rapidly changing but for which the competing technologies have changed little. The determinants of environmental turbulence parallel industry evolution in relating uncertainty to the stage of the product life cycle: for both marketing and innovation turbulence. However, along with the emerging stage, decline and the transition from stage to stage can spell danger for the unwary company. And in some markets the antecedents of marketing and innovation turbulence are quite different.

Figure 4.3 provides a mechanism for combining two dimensions of turbulence and shows how two strategic groups in the same industry can be facing different environments. Within the UK food retailing trade, the environment for the leading grocers, such as Sainsbury and Tesco, is *developing* in terms of both marketing and innovation. The shift out of town is continuing as is the move towards larger establishments, but the pattern is well understood as is the position of the main protagonists within the industry. Similarly, major changes with EPOS and stock control have been absorbed by this sector and are now a well-established part of their activities. The intersection of the developing market turbulence and developing innovation turbulence not surprisingly indicates that the overall environmental turbulence is appropriately classified as *developing*.

The situation of the leading grocers contrasts with the convenience stores which form another strategic group within the same industry. Although their innovation turbulence is similar to leading grocers, convenience stores face *discontinuous marketing* turbulence. This is due to their not yet having faced the shift from in-town to out-of-town shopping, their existence within the emergent phase of an industry in which many new entrants are appearing, their dependence upon Sunday trading

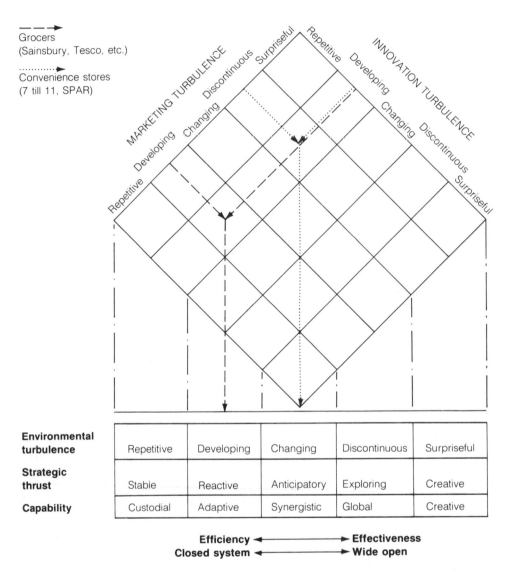

Source: Based on Ansoff (1984), Figure 3.4.5, p. 222.

Figure 4.3   Environmental turbulence

laws which keep the grocery chains closed for a large part of weekends, and the need for them to trade illegally at weekends with some of the goods they stock. Although in the same industry as the leading grocers, the convenience stores therefore face *changing environmental* turbulence.

Ansoff draws broad strategic and managerial conclusions from the differences in environmental turbulences that companies face. Whereas, he suggests, the leading retailers see the need to be *reactive* in terms of their strategic thrust and have the ability to adapt, he would suggest that the convenience stores need a more dynamic management style where they *anticipate* shifts in the environment and look for synergistic opportunities. Within that context the convenience stores have concentrated upon a series of goods for which their position is critical, such as alcoholic beverages, milk and soft drinks, which constitute a very large proportion of their sales. Many have also opened video libraries.

From a marketing point of view, there is great importance in correctly assessing environmental turbulence. A firm must try to match its capability to appropriate environments or develop capabilities which fit new ones. The Trustee Savings Bank and many other retailing banks in the UK have shown the dangers of believing that their resources can enable them to operate in unfamiliar style. The TSB, in particular, almost epitomised custodial management where for a long time it provided an efficient service in a standard way to a very stable market. This meant that, even more than other banks, the company was built around closed systems and operations where there was little need for entrepreneurship. The privatisation of the TSB gave it a dangerous combination of a large amount of money and wider opportunities, together with a massively changed banking environment. Two almost inevitable developments have occurred: (a) the bank has shown its inability to manage businesses with a more dynamic environment, and (b) it has found itself unable to work out what to do with its cash mountain. Similar examples within the British financial market are legion, where the very mentality paramount in providing security and correct balances at the end of each trading day left management with completely inappropriate skills to manage modern, fast-moving trading houses.

4.4 SPACE analysis

SPACE (Strategic Position and ACtion Evaluation) analysis (Rowe *et al.*, 1989) extends environmental analysis beyond the consideration of turbulence to look at industry strength, and relates this to the competitive advantage and financial strength of a company. Like Shell's directional policy matrix, and other multidimensional portfolio measuring devices, it is a method of combining a large number of strategic issues on a few dimensions. One of the dimensions is environmental stability (Table 4.2), which includes many of the facets of environmental turbulence. But with SPACE analysis environmental instability is seen as being counterbalanced by financial strength, a company with high liquidity or access to other reserves being able to withstand environmental volatility.

Industry strength is the second environmental dimension considered. This focuses upon the attractiveness of the industry in terms of growth potential, profitability and the ability to use its resources efficiently. For a company within the industry, these strengths are no virtue unless a company has a competitive advantage. SPACE

Table 4.2 *SPACE analysis: components*

Company dimensions	Industry dimensions
Financial strengths	*Environmental stability*
Return on investment	Technological changes
Leverage	Rate of inflation
Liquidity	Demand variability
Capital required/available	Price range of competing products
Cash flow	Fntry barriers
Exit barriers	Competitive pressures
Risk	Price elasticity of demand
Competitive advantage	*Industry strength*
Market share	Growth potential
Product quality	Profit potential
Product life cycle	Financial stability
Product replacement cycle	Technological know-how
Customer loyalty	Resource utilisation
Competition's capacity utilisation	Capital intensity
Technological know-how	Market entry ability
Vertical integration	Productivity

analysis, therefore, opposes industry strength by competitive advantage (Figure 4.4) to provide a gauge of a company's position relative to the industry.

Rating a company and the industry on each of the four dimensions gives the competitive profile *abAB* on Figure 4.4. The example clearly shows a company in a weak position: moderately high environmental instability is not balanced by financial strength, and the competitive advantage of the company is not great compared with the overall industry strength.

The relative size of the opposing dimension gives the guide to the appropriate strategic posture of a firm. For example, from Figure 4.4, $A + a$ and $B + b$ show the overall weight of the SPACE analysis to be towards the bottom right-hand quadrant. This indicates a *competitive* posture which is typical of a company with a competitive advantage in an attractive industry. However, the company's financial strength is insufficient to balance the environmental instability it faces. Such firms clearly need more financial resources to maintain their competitive position. In the long term this may be achieved by greater efficiency and productivity, but the firm is likely to need to raise capital or merge with a cash-rich company.

Firms which find their strategic posture within the *aggressive* quadrant are enjoying significant advantages yet are likely to face threats from new competition. The chief danger is complacency, which prevents them gaining further market dominance by developing products with a definite competitive edge. The excessive financial strength of these companies may also make it attractive for them to seek acquisition candidates in their own or related industries.

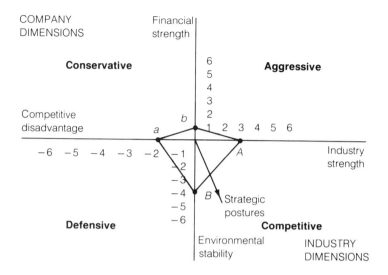

Source: Based on Rowe *et al.* (1989), Exhibit 6.10, p. 145.

Figure 4.4 SPACE analysis: map

A *conservative* posture is typical of companies in mature markets where the lack of need for investment has generated financial surpluses. The lack of investment can mean that these companies compete at a disadvantage, and lack of opportunities within their existing markets make them vulnerable in the long term. They must, therefore, defend their existing products to ensure a continued cash flow while they seek new market opportunities.

Companies with a *defensive* posture are clearly vulnerable. Having little residual strength to combat competition, they need to foster resources by operating efficiently and be prepared to retreat from competitive markets in order to concentrate on ones they have a chance of defending. For these it just appears to be a matter of time before either competition or the environment gets the better of them.

4.5 The advantage matrix

Once strategic groups within a market have been identified, it becomes apparent that the groups have differing levels of profitability. For instance, in the machine tool industry conventional lathes are almost a commodity and are frequently produced at low cost in the Third World. But in another part of the industry, say flexible manufacturing systems, profits can be quite high for those companies with special skills. Recognition of this pattern in the 1970s led the Boston Consulting Group (1979) to develop the *advantage matrix*, which helps to classify the competitive environments that can co-exist within an industry. The framework identifies two dimensions: the number of approaches to achieving advantage within a market and the potential size advantage. In Figure 4.5 the quadrants of the advantage matrix show how relationships between relative size and return on assets for companies can differ.

The *stalemate* quadrant represents markets with few ways of achieving advantage and where the potential size advantage is small. Companies in such a strategic group would therefore find trading akin to a commodity market. Theirs can be relatively complex products, as in the case of desk-top computers, where the technologies are well known, product designs are convergent and similar sources of supply are used by everyone. Both large and small manufacturers are using overseas suppliers, and consumers are well able to compare product with product. Attempts to differentiate the market, as tried by IBM with their PS_2, have failed. Therefore all competitors are forced to compete mainly on the basis of efficient manufacturing and distribution.

The *volume* quadrant represents markets where the opportunities for differentiation remain few, yet where potential size advantages remain great. This has occurred in some of the peripheral markets which support desk-top computers. In particular, the printer industry has come to be dominated by Epson, Canon, HP and IBM. The reason

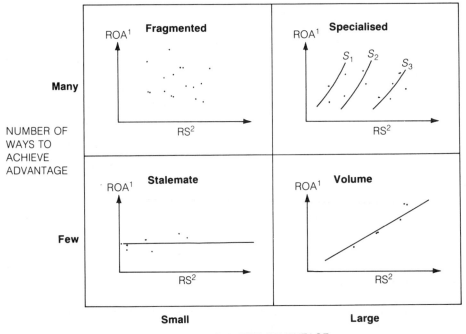

[1]Return on assets.
[2]Relative size.

Source: Based on unpublished material from The Boston Consulting Group. Reproduced with permissi

Figure 4.5 **The advantage matrix**

for this is the convergence in needs of users of printers and the mass production of the intrinsically mechanical printer units. Unlike microcomputers, where the manufacturing process is one of assembly of basically standard components in a very fixed fashion, as any user of printers will know there are numerous ways of solving the printing and paper-feed problems. This results in an industry where large economies of scale can be achieved by a few dominant suppliers. Where there are markets of this form, battles to achieve volume and economies of scale are paramount. Dominant companies are likely to remain dominant for some time once their cost advantage is achieved, although there is always a threat from a new technology emerging which will destroy the cost advantage they have fought to obtain. In this way, HP joined the band of leaders in the printer market by becoming the industry standard in the newly emerged market for laser printers.

Specialised markets occur when companies within the same market have differing returns on scale. This occurs most conspicuously among suppliers of software for microcomputers. In the overall market for software there are clear sub-sectors with dominant leaders. It is also apparent that the market leaders, because of their familiarity and proven reliability, are able to charge a price premium. Such a case is Lotus 1-2-3 and D-Base, which are priced well above competitive levels and yet remain frontrunners within the industry. In the games sector Atari is less able to command premium prices, although its dominance does mean it is reaping size advantages within its own segments. The result in these specialised markets is therefore a series of experience curves being followed by different companies. In these specialised markets the most successful companies will be those which dominate one or two segments. Within the market for microcomputer software this has often meant that they will be the companies creating a new generic class of product, as did SuperCalc for the original spreadsheet, Lotus 1-2-3 for the integrated business planning packages and Microsoft Windows 3 — making the IBM clone as 'friendly' as the Mac.

Fragmented markets occur when the market's requirements are less well defined than in the stalemate, volume or specialised cases. Several parts of the computer peripheral market conform to this pattern. In contrast to the demand for printers, the specialised users of plotters have a wide variety of requirements and the opportunity for colour and high resolution means that there is an unlimited variety of differentiated products that can be made. Similarly, in the provision of accounting software, alternative specifications are numerous and therefore many different prices and products co-exist in the same market. Where this fragmentation has occurred, success depends on finding niches where particular product specifications are needed. Each niche provides little opportunity for growth; therefore a company hoping to expand depends on finding a multiplicity of niches where, hopefully, some degree of commonality will allow economies to be achieved.

4.6 Conclusions

Industry analysis has three main components: (a) the recognition of the strategic groups within a market which can allow a company to address its efforts towards specific rather than general competitors; (b) the recognition of the different competitive environments and scale economies that can exist within the sub-markets in which the strategic clusters operate; and (c) the degree of turbulence within markets. Through understanding these a company can identify the sort of competition that is likely to exist within chosen segments and the types of strategy that are likely to lead to success. From the study of turbulence they can also find a guide to the necessary orientation of the company and the blend of custodial management and entrepreneurial flair which will be needed to manage the venture. Just as segmentation allows a company to direct its resources towards fulfilling a particular set of customer needs, so industrial analysis helps a company to build its defences oriented towards a specific group of competitors, and to build its strengths in accordance with the type of market it faces.

FIVE

Assessment of corporate capabilities

The most important assets a company has are its brand names. They should appear at the head of the assets list on the balance sheet.

Marketing Director, an international food marketing company

Introduction

To understand an organisation's marketing options, its capabilities and distinctive competencies need to be clearly understood. These help to define both organisational and marketing strengths and weaknesses.

A major aspect of identifying strengths and weaknesses for marketing purposes is to define and fully understand the marketing assets of the firm. An asset, as defined by Levitt (1986), 'consists of its ability to generate revenue, either directly by its sale or by the sale of what it helps, finally, to produce'. In this respect a company's reputation, if that helps lead to revenue generation, is as much an asset of the company as is the plant and machinery used for production purposes.

This chapter first discusses approaches to identifying corporate strengths and weaknesses with particular emphasis on how they relate to marketing activity. The discussion then turns more specifically to the identification and evaluation of marketing assets.

5.1 Assessing corporate strengths and weaknesses

Strengths and weaknesses of an organisation are of two distinct types. First, there are structural strengths or weaknesses that result from decisions that have been made in the past (such as plant location and its consequences for direct labour costs or the availability, cost and quality of raw materials). While these factors can be changed in the long term, they generally require major strategic decisions to alter and are generally taken as 'given' in the marketing strategy formulation process.

Second, there are created strengths and weaknesses which are the result of conscious decisions and actions. Examples include the strength of a brand name or corporate reputation. Strengths of this type may have taken many years to build and should be exploited to the full. Created weaknesses (often inadvertently created, or the result of creating other strengths), on the other hand, which put the organisation at a distinct disadvantage in the market place, should form the focus for remedial action.

Assessing the organisation's capabilities, its strengths and weaknesses, commences with a thorough audit of the resources of the organisation that can be brought to bear in the market place. The assessment needs to go beyond a mere listing of resources to identify those resources which make the organisation strategically distinct from its competitors.

For marketing purposes, the marketing audit (see Kotler, Gregor and Rogers, 1977) has been suggested as a systematic approach to assessing marketing resources and their utilisation within the organisation. Strengths and weaknesses exist, however, only in relation to the tasks the organisation is seeking to achieve and the capabilities of competitors (see Johnson and Scholes, 1988). A major aspect of strengths and weaknesses analysis is, then, drawing comparisons with other organisations. Finally, the analyses should lead directly to the identification of the distinctive competencies of the organisation and the core weaknesses inherent in its current operations and activities (see Prahalad and Hamel, 1990).

5.1.1   Resource auditing

The first stage in assessing strengths and weaknesses is to conduct an audit of the resources available to the company. There are several types of resources open to a company, including: the physical resources of its plant and machinery; the structural resources of its systems and organisation; and the less tangible resources of its people and their skills in one capacity or another.

Technical resources
A key resource in many organisations, and one becoming increasingly important in a world of rapidly changing technology, is technical skill. This involves the ability of the organisation to develop new processes and products through research and development (R & D) which can be utilised in the market place.

Technical skills go beyond, however, the ability to come up with new, innovative, ideas. They also involve putting existing ideas into action (see Frohman, 1982). Production skills are essential to producing goods effectively and efficiently. Similarly, increasing importance is being placed on the skills necessary to ensure adequate quality control.

Financial standing
A second important resource of the organisation is its financial standing. This will dictate, to a large extent, its scope for action and ability to put its strategies into operation. An organisation of sound financial standing can raise capital from outside to finance ventures. In deciding marketing strategy a major consideration is often what financial resources can be put into the programme.

Managerial skills
Managerial skills in the widest possible sense are a further resource of the organisation. The experience of managers and the way in which they discharge their duties and

motivate their staff have a major impact on corporate performance. This is an area in which international comparisons show British companies to be particularly weak, in terms of both professional training at all levels within organisations (NIESR, 1990) and the specific provision of management training (Handy *et al.*, 1989).

The very structure of the organisation can be a valuable asset or resource. Some structures, such as the matrix organisation, are designed to facilitate wide use of skills throughout the organisation.

For organising the marketing effort, product management, as pioneered by Procter and Gamble in the early years of this century, has proved particularly successful in developing brand champions. The system has proved useful in focusing control at the brand level, encouraging a co-ordinated marketing mix and facilitating a flexible, rapid response to changing circumstances. It is not without its drawbacks, however. The product management system can lead to responsibility without authority, conflicts between product managers within the same organisation and the 'galloping midget' syndrome (managers moving on to the next product management job having maximised short-term returns at the expense of longer-term market position).

Information systems

The information and planning systems in operation also provide a valuable resource. For example, those organisations such as banks dealing in foreign currency speculation rely heavily on up-to-the-minute and accurate information systems. New technological developments, such as electronic point of sale (EPOS) scanning, allow data to be collected and processed in a much shorter time than a few years ago. The companies with the systems to cope with the massive increases in data that such newer collection procedures are creating will be in a stronger position to take advantage of the opportunities afforded.

5.1.2   The marketing audit

More specifically, in the marketing activities of the firm the marketing audit has been developed as a systematic approach to identifying and evaluating marketing practices, resources and their utilisation (see Kotler, Gregor and Rogers, 1977). Often, especially in the major marketing textbooks (see, for example, Kotler, 1991) the marketing audit is presented as a means of controlling the marketing effort. While in its fullest and most comprehensive sense it is often used in this way, it also has great value in helping to define marketing capabilities.

A full marketing audit consists of an examination of the marketing environment, the marketing strategy currently being pursued and the organisation of the marketing function, an analysis of the marketing systems in use (e.g. decision support systems and new product development systems), an assessment of marketing productivity and a marketing functions audit covering the marketing mix.

• The marketing environment audit examines changes both in the broader economic, technical, social and cultural environment and in the more immediate task environment of markets, customers, competitors, suppliers and distributors. These latter are discussed more fully in Chapters 4, 6 and 7.

- A strategy audit examines the appropriateness and clarity of corporate and marketing objectives. In addition, it ensures that the resources needed to carry out the strategy are available and optimally allocated.
- The formal structure of the marketing department, its functional efficiency and its interface efficiency (with other departments such as finance, production and R & D) is examined in an organisation audit.
- A marketing systems audit examines the information systems, planning systems, control systems and new product development systems of the company.
- Productivity auditing involves profitability and contribution analysis of the organisation's various offerings together with a cost effectiveness analysis to identify areas where costs may be excessive in relation to returns.
- Finally, a marketing functions audit examines in more detail the elements of the marketing mix: the products and services on offer, the prices charged, the distribution system employed, the sales force effort, advertising, promotion and publicity.

5.1.3   Balance and flexibility

A company with many strengths over its competitors may not, necessarily, be in a healthy position. Crucial to diagnosing overall strength is assessing the balance of activities within the organisation. Product portfolio analysis techniques (see Chapter 3) can be useful here for assessing the balance of cash use and generation, today's and tomorrow's breadwinners and vulnerability to major changes in competitive action or the broader marketing environment.

A truly balanced organisation has a built-in flexibility to allow it to respond to uncertain events. In an effort to increase flexibility of response, some companies are buying in services that once were done in-house. An example is the use of contractors to handle distribution for companies that no longer wish to tie up resources with large-scale distribution fleets. Contracting offers the flexibility to expand or contract distribution capability without incurring substantial fixed costs or penalties.

There is evidence too that in other aspects of marketing there is greater use of specialised services rather than developing skills as fixed resources in-house. There have been a plethora of specialist marketing services agencies launched in recent years, covering aspects such as design, branding and public relations. The modern marketing organisation stays lean in its internal staff structures and buys in specialist expertise as and when needed.

A helpful technique, *flexibility analysis*, is explained by Johnson and Scholes (1988). Under this approach a company's flexibility to respond to uncertain events is assessed, and action to increase flexibility is suggested where necessary. For example, an area of uncertainty may be an expectation that a competitor could launch a new brand.

The flexibility required to respond to this event, should it occur, may be the requirement of a 'better' brand than the company's present offering (in terms, say, of quality or design features).

The actual flexibility in the company may not be adequate should the competitor go the anticipated route (i.e. there is currently no suitable brand available for launch by the company). It is clear that the action required is to do further R & D to improve on current brands offered or to develop new ones that will become available should the need arise. Thus an R & D programme would be set in train to increase the organisation's flexibility of response to the identified uncertain event.

5.1.4   Evaluating resources

Resources and their utilisation in isolation do not constitute the strengths and weaknesses of an organisation. Potentially useful resources may be underutilised and present scope for further development. Other resources may be stretched to breaking point and need additional support.

To assess whether the organisation has a strength or weakness requires comparisons to be made between the organisation's resource utilisation and that of its competitors. Stevenson (1976) suggests two main ways in which organisations can assess their relative strengths and weaknesses.

Historical comparison
Historical comparisons show corporate capabilities now relative to capabilities in the past. A reason for this basis for assessment given by Stevenson (1976) is that managers are constantly searching for improvements to problem areas. The base then becomes the standard by which current capabilities are judged. An improvement in productivity from one time period to another is seen as a corporate strength.

In multibusiness organisations, comparisons are often made intrabusiness. The resource utilisation of one SBU is compared to the resource utilisation of another. Both historical and intrabusiness assessments of strengths and weaknesses suffer from adopting a purely internal perspective. Of crucial importance is recognising strengths and weaknesses relative to competitors because, after all, it is performance relative to them that will dictate the fortunes of the organisation in the future, not performance relative to last year or other SBUs in the same organisation.

Competitor comparison
The second approach to assessing strengths and weaknesses compares the company's resources and their utilisation with major competitors. These may be direct competitors (those which produce the same goods and services for the same target markets) or indirect competitors (those which offer similar products and services to different target markets or other satisfactions to the same target market).

In addition, some companies assess their strengths and weaknesses relative to industry norms, or pars. The PIMS programme (see, for example, Gale, 1978) provides 'par reports' which an organisation can use to assess its performance relative to the par for organisations facing similar market and competitive circumstances.

Often perception of relative strengths and weaknesses differs depending on who is carrying out the analysis, and especially at what level in the organisation assessment is made. Many companies prefer the auditing of their own and their competitors' resources to be conducted by independent assessors such as management or marketing consultants.

Comparisons should give a clear indication of the relative pluses and minuses of the organisation and pinpoint areas for improved effort.

5.2   Identifying the core competencies of the organisation

Prahalad and Hamel (1990) have argued that the fundamental source of competitiveness lies in the *core competencies* of an organisation. Core competencies they define as the underlying skills, technologies and competencies that can be combined in different ways to create the next generation of products and services.

Canon's core competencies, for example, are its skills and technologies in optics, imaging and microprocessor controls that have enabled it to survive and thrive in markets as diverse as copiers, laser printers, cameras and image scanners.

Three tests are suggested by Prahalad and Hamel for identifying core competencies:

- A core competence provides potential access to a wide variety of markets. Competencies in display systems are needed, for example, to enable a company to compete in a number of different markets including miniature TV sets, calculators, lap-top or notebook computers.
- A core competence should make a significant contribution to the benefits the customer derives from using the ultimate product or service. In other words, the competence is important where it is a significant determinant of customer satisfaction and benefit.
- A core competence should be difficult for competitors to copy. Clearly, a competence that can be defended against competitors has greater value than one which other companies can share.

A major output from a strengths and weaknesses analysis of the organisation should be to articulate the core competencies that can be brought to bear in the market place. Options for further participation in existing markets and for development into new markets are often dictated by the array of core competencies the organisation has at its disposal. Investing in the building of new competencies and combining them with existing ones can be one of the most successful routes to new product development.

Finally, it is important to stress that strengths and weaknesses and the resulting core competencies are relative to the competition and require a clear understanding of both the company's and its competitors' capabilities. The distinctive competence of the organisation is a statement of what it does best or uniquely well. These factors form the basis for developing a competitive advantage in the market place.

Our discussion of strengths and weaknesses has so far looked at the organisation as a whole. Specifically marketing assets are examined in more detail below.

5.3   Itemising marketing assets

The term 'marketing assets' was first used by Davidson in a series of articles in *Marketing* magazine in 1983. Marketing assets are essentially properties that can be used to advantage in the market place. Davidson gives a good example of this:

In the early 80's the brand share of Kellogg's Corn Flakes, while still in the low 20's, was in long term decline. The company had spare capacity, but did not produce corn flakes for private label store brands.

Kellogg solved this problem by launching Crunchy Nut Corn Flakes which used the Kellogg name and the corn flakes plant. It was priced at a heavy premium, but it gained 2–3% market share, mainly incremental to the share of other Kellogg's brands, at very attractive margins.

The new product exploited the existing brand name, flake technology and plant, but did so in a way that attracted new customers at high margins.   (Davidson, 1983)

An asset-based approach to marketing attempts to match the assets of the organisation to the needs and wants of its chosen customers. In that sense it is different

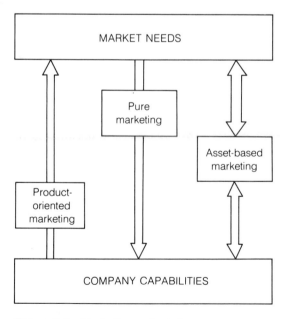

Figure 5.1 Marketing orientations

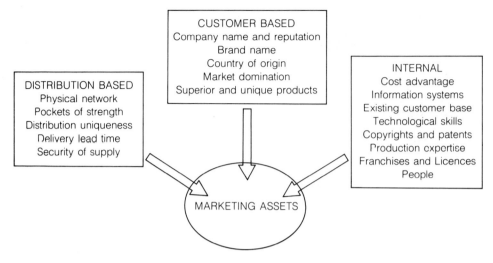

Figure 5.2 Marketing assets

from a product orientation (which starts from what the company is — or believes it is — good at producing, irrespective of market requirements) and from a pure marketing orientation (where markets are chased because they are attractive irrespective of the company's long-term ability to serve the market more effectively than its competitors. The distinction is shown in Figure 5.1.

A wide variety of company properties can be converted into marketing assets. They can be usefully grouped under customer-based, distribution-based and internal (or potential) assets (see Figure 5.2).

5.3.1   Customer-based assets

Customer-based assets are those assets of the company, either real or imaginary, valued by the customer or potential customer. Often they exist in the mind of the customer and are essentially intangible in nature.

Company name and reputation
One of the most important customer-based assets a company can possess is its reputation or image. Companies such as IBM and Rolls-Royce have a clear image of supplying a particular set of customer benefits (reliability, durability, prestige, overall quality) in the markets in which they operate.

■   IBM successfully carried over its image as the natural choice in the established mainframe computer market into the personal computer market. The name and reputation of IBM helped it to attack Apple, the well-established market leader in PCs. The IBM name is now being used to good effect on a range of computer peripherals including external drives and printers.

Ross Foods (a frozen-food processor and marketer in the UK) discovered through marketing research that it is perceived by its customers to be a small, friendly, family business in contrast to the more impersonal image held of its competitors such as Bird's Eye and Findus. Advertising campaigns were developed reinforcing this image and stressing how the company takes note of consumer views in new product development.

Thomas Cook, the travel company, was sold to the private sector by its then owner, the British government, in 1972. The purchasers, the Midland Bank Group, paid £22 million. This was following a period of decline in the fortunes of Thomas Cook which showed a profit of £2 million in 1965 reduced to a mere £200,000 in 1971. On paper the company was worth considerably less than was actually paid. What was of value, however, was the Thomas Cook name which had achieved world-wide recognition in a business where much depends on good faith and reputation. The company has gone on to establish itself as one of the leading travel companies in the world (Johnson and Scholes, 1988). ▪

Company name confers an asset on all products of the company where it is clearly identified. Indeed, in many cases where the company identity is a strong asset it has been converted into a brand name for use on a wide variety of products. For example, IBM, Kodak and Sainsbury are not only company names but also brands with strong customer franchises.

Image and reputation can also, however, be a negative asset or a liability.

▪ Austin Rover, for example, for a long time suffered from a poor image among some potential customers and a belief that its products were inferior to the competition. This image stemmed from problems experienced during the 1960s and 1970s. It is noticeable that the company has changed its name several times in the recent past, presumably in an attempt to put the unfavourable image behind it. The most recent change was to Rover Group plc, attempting to capitalise on the still good reputation of the Rover brand. ▪

Contrast the approaches to marketing assets of two of the major companies in the UK car market: Ford and Rover. Ford clearly believes the company identity to be a major asset. The various cars produced are clearly linked to the Ford name — Ford Fiesta, Ford Escort, Ford Sierra, Ford Granada. Advertising for the various models within the Ford brand is co-ordinated using such slogans as 'Have you driven a Ford lately?'. In contrast, Rover concentrated on building individual brand names such as Mini, Metro, Maestro, Montego and Rover, playing down the corporate identity.

Recent reports have attempted to list the ten most valuable company/brand names in the world and the UK. The results are presented in Table 5.1.

Brand name

For companies where corporate identity is a liability, or a non-existent asset, more emphasis is placed on building or acquiring individual brand names as assets. Beecham, for example, has deliberately set out to acquire brands with a marketable reputation. The Bovril brand was purchased to ease the company's launch into the stock cubes market (Bovril being an established brand property in the similar meat extracts market).

Table 5.1 *The top ten brand names*

World[1]	UK[2]
Coca-Cola	Marks & Spencer
IBM	Cadbury
Sony	Kellogg
Porsche	Heinz
McDonald's	Rolls-Royce
Disney	Boots
Honda	Nescafé
Toyota	BBC
Seiko	Rowntree
BMW	Sainsbury

Sources: [1] *The Economist*, 24 December 1988.
[2] *Guardian*, 17 November 1988.

Companies with little customer-based corporate identity, such as Rank Hovis MacDougal (RHM), have developed their various brands into major assets.

■ The Bisto brand, famous as the UK market leader in gravy making, has been used to good effect by RHM in its movement into the soups and sauces market. In late 1988 RHM decided to calculate a value for its brands and place them on its balance sheet. The company put a value of £678 million on the brands, overnight tripling the reported shareholders' funds. ■

As with company reputation, the value of brands has long been recognised as 'goodwill' in valuing companies. When the Rowntree confectionery company was purchased by Nestlé in 1988 the buyer paid six times the book value of the company's assets to acquire brands such as Kit Kat, Quality Street, Smarties, Rolo and Yorkie.

The British car industry is perhaps one of the best examples of assets based in brand names or marques. Over the years Rover Group and its predecessors have had valuable assets in marques such as Rover, Wolsey, MG, Austin Healey and Jaguar.

■ Rolls-Royce Cars, now part of Vickers (and completely independent of the Rolls-Royce Aero Engines company), rejuvenated the Bentley name. Bentley became part of Rolls-Royce in the 1930s as a successful, 'sporty' car but was never really developed to its full potential — it was used essentially as a different badge on the front of the same car.

Market research showed, however, that 'Bentley' and 'Rolls-Royce' meant very different things to customers and potential customers. While the Rolls was seen as the car in which those who have 'arrived' are driven, the Bentley was 'the sporty car you drive yourself'. Bentley stands for understated wealth rather than the blatant wealth of the Rolls owner. The Bentley has now been relaunched to take advantage of this with a sportier, turbo engine appealing directly to the younger, sportier, but still wealthy driver. In this market it is doing well in competition with Porsche and Mercedes. ■

Putting a value on brand names

A recent trend in the UK and USA, now being mirrored in other parts of the world, is to attempt to put a value on a company's brand names and then to enter them on the balance sheet as assets distinguished from goodwill.

While Saunders (1990) has questioned the case for valuing brands, it is clear that many companies are now adopting this policy. A survey in Australia (Arthur Young and Co., 1989), for example, showed that of the top 150 companies 25 per cent had included some amount for brand names or intellectual property in their accounts.

A number of factors are taken into account when valuing brands for accounting purposes (see Murphy, 1991). They are all, however, related to the ability of the brand to produce a better return than competitors now or in the future.

- *Current market position.* Brands that are market leaders are typically valued more highly than brands which may have good market shares but which operate in markets where another brand is dominant. This is because, particularly in consumer markets, buyers often have a strong tendency to purchase leading brands and this is not easily overcome by competitors or newcomers. Market leadership can, therefore, create a barrier to competitor entry or development.

- *Market type.* Brands are more valuable in established, high-volume markets with further potential for growth. They are more valuable also in markets where margins are high, rather than markets which are highly price competitive (indeed, valuable brands are those which enable the company to compete on grounds other than price), and in markets which are less prone to technological or fashion change (e.g. confectionery or beer).

- *Durability.* Brand names which have lasted for many years are likely to have developed stronger customer loyalty and become part of the 'fabric' of the market. IBM is a prime example in the computer hardware market. Brands which have become generically associated with the product (e.g. Formica in kitchen work surfaces and Hoover in carpet vacuum cleaners) also have higher value.

   While specific products may have increasingly short life cycles due to rapid technological or market change, durable brands can survive through product change and improvement. Persil has remained market leader (or thereabouts) in washing powders for nearly 50 years through continuous product improvement and adaptation to changing washing habits and conditions.

   Blackett (in Murphy, 1991) notes that Stork (margarine), Kellogg (cornflakes), Cadbury (chocolate), Gillette (razors), Schweppes (mixers), Brooke Bond (tea), Colgate (toothpaste), Kodak (film) and Hoover (vacuum cleaners) were all brands that led their product categories in 1931 and continued to do so in 1991, though few have survived in their original form.

   Brands which can remain contemporary and relevant to customers over an extended period constitute greater assets.

- *Global presence.* Those brands which are, or can be, exploited internationally are generally more valuable than those restricted to domestic markets. Recent developments in global media and global advertising have enhanced the value of international or global brands.

● *Extensibility*. Brands which can be extended and exploited in the same or new markets have greater value than brands which are more limited in their scope. The Gillette brand, for example, has been successfully extended across a number of 'disposable' markets, the Guinness name has been used to sell books and the Levi name has been extended to other garments and accessories over and above five-pocket blue jeans.

Fashion house names, such as Dunhill, Gucci and Yves Saint Laurent have proved particularly successful at extension beyond their original product fields.

● *Protection*. Brands which can be protected through registered trademarks, patents and/or registered designs can potentially offer greater value than those which can be easily copied.

> ■ In New Zealand a soap opera called *Gloss* was very popular in early 1989 and gave rise to a range of women's cosmetics marketed under licence using the Gloss brand name. An existing cosmetics manufacturer and marketer, Gloss Cosmetics Supplies Ltd, which had been using the Gloss name previously, had failed adequately to protect the name in law and was ruled in the High Court to have no rights to the name. Gloss Cosmetics Supplies was served with an injunction preventing it from manufacturing, distributing, advertising or selling cosmetics or personal care products under the name Gloss. ■

To date much of the interest in brand valuation has come from accountants and valuers attempting to get a truer picture of the value of companies for the purposes of takeovers and defences against takeovers. Hence much of the debate on valuation has centred around methods of putting a current value on the brand. Marketers are more concerned with the potential value of a brand and how it can be extended or better exploited in the market place.

Country of origin

For companies operating in international markets, the home country can constitute either an asset or a liability (see Hooley, Krieger and Shipley, 1988). Japanese firms, for example, collectively enjoy a good reputation for quality and value for money. Similarly 'made in Hong Kong' or 'made in Taiwan' still gives the impression, rightly or wrongly, of poor workmanship and cheap materials. British-made goods are currently enjoying something of a revival in the United States of America due to the currently favourable image of Britain.

The value of image of home country, company or brand should not be under-estimated. Image often takes a long time to build up, but it can be destroyed very quickly by mistakes. Conversely, it is often more difficult, though not impossible, for competitors to destroy a company's image-based assets, than, say, to copy its technology or imitate its products.

Market domination

In addition to image the domination or apparent domination of the market can constitute an asset. As discussed above, market presence or domination has been used as a criterion for valuing brands. Market leaders typically enjoy good coverage of the market, wide distribution and good shelf positions.

Moreover, market leaders are often believed by consumers to be better in some way than the rest of the market. Simply being there and highly visible confers an asset on the product. As Brown (1986) has pointed out: 'Visible advertising makes people believe the brand is popular nowadays . . . you have to have a good reason, if you are a young and inexperienced housewife, not to buy the brand everyone buys.'

There is, however, a counter argument to the above emerging. Some researchers (e.g. Hamil and O'Neill, 1986) present evidence of an increasing desire among more affluent consumers to demonstrate their independence and sophistication by not buying the same goods and services others buy. In some product areas this could lead to the situation where being popular and widely used actively discourages some customers who wish to feel they are different from the mass.

■ In Japan there has recently been a surge in the sales of unbranded goods in an attempt by conspicuous consumers to stand out from the mass in their Jean Paul Gaultier dresses, Hermes scarfs, Cartier gold watches and Chanel handbags. *The Economist* (14.3.92) reported the success of the clothes retail store Seibu in Tokyo which sells only *Mujirushi ryohin* ('no brand/good quality') products. Its labels say only what materials are used and the country of manufacture. The clothes have simple designs, plain colours, high quality and reasonable pricing. Seibu's parent group has also developed the no-brand idea for tinned food and household items in its Seiyu supermarkets. ■

Superior products and services

Having superior products and services on the market, products that are, or are believed to be, better in some way (e.g. cheaper, better quality, more stylish and up to date) than the competitors', can be a further marketing asset for the company. Unique products or services, until they are imitated, can provide marketing assets, so long as customers want them and are prepared to pay for them.

5.3.2 Distribution-based assets

Distribution-based assets are concerned with the manner in which the product or service is conveyed to the customer. They include the distribution network, its uniqueness and pockets of strength.

Distribution network

The physical distribution network itself can be a major asset. Hertz, for example, in the car hire business, owes much of its success to a very wide network of pick-up and drop-off centres, especially in the United States. This wide network ensures availability of the required services in the right place, increasing convenience of use for the customers. Similarly, in the UK the Post Office found its distribution system a major asset in offering new postal services to potential customers when deregulation permitted increased competition from other parcel carriers.

■ New Zealand Railways Corporation (NZRC) is different from railways in many other countries in that it carries primarily industrial goods rather than passengers. Indeed, over 85 per cent of revenue comes from the top 60 industrial customers and over 95 per cent from the top 200. Following Levitt's advice, NZRC has defined its business as 'freight transportation' and fully recognises that its major competition is from truckers and road hauliers.

The key marketing asset that NZRC has in competing with the seemingly more flexible road transporters is its rail network which, in the case of leading commercial customers, often goes right into their industrial plant. The CEO of NZRC describes the network as a 'moving warehouse' for these large customers, enabling them to put products from the factory directly on to the trains for immediate transportation nationally to the key markets (or to ports for international distribution), and hence to minimise the need for costly on-site warehouse storage.

Finally, a sophisticated computer-based customer information system, enabling the customers to keep in direct touch with and in control of their products at all stages in the distribution process completes a strong bond, or linkage, between NZRC and its most valuable customers. ■

Pockets of strength

Selective but close relationships between a company and its distribution outlets can lead to pockets of strength. Where a company is unable, through size or resource constraints, to serve a wide market, concentrating effort, either geographically on specific regions of the market (Morrison's supermarkets are particularly strong in Yorkshire) or on specific outlets can enable a pocket of strength to be developed.

Companies adopting the latter approach of building up a strong presence with selective distributors, or even end users in many industrial markets, often achieve that pocket of strength through key account marketing: that is, giving full responsibility for each key account development to a specific, normally quite senior executive.

Distribution uniqueness

Further distribution-based assets can be built through uniqueness, reaching the target market in a novel or innovative way. For instance, Rington sells tea and coffee door to door in the north of England and the Avon Cosmetics company has built a strong door-to-door business in cosmetics sales through the 'Avon Calling' campaign.

Similarly, in the early 1970s Hirondelle built an impressive share of the table wine market through achieving sales in a new and emerging outlet, namely supermarkets. Until that time the bulk of wines were sold through off-licences to men. Hirondelle secured the new outlets, selling more often to women, to great effect. Seeking and securing new or different outlets is becoming increasingly difficult as many products are becoming ever more widely available.

Delivery lead time and security of supply

Delivery lead time is a function of at least three main factors — physical location, order through production systems and company delivery policy. In an increasing number of situations the ability to respond quickly, at no compromise to quality, is becoming more important. Deliberately creating a rapid response capability can constitute a significant marketing asset (see Stalk, 1988).

Similarly, particularly in volatile markets where the supplier's offering is on the critical path of the customer company, the ability to guarantee supply can be a major asset. As with lead time that ability will be a function of several factors, but perhaps central is the desire on the part of the supplier to meet agreed targets.

5.3.3   Internal assets

Many of the factors discussed above under resource auditing can be converted into marketing assets. A resource becomes an asset when it is actively used to improve the organisation's performance in the market place.

Cost advantages

A cost advantage brought about by employing up-to-date technology, achieving better capacity utilisation than competitors, economies of scale or experience curve effects can be translated into lower prices in shops. Where the market is price sensitive — for example, with commodity items — lower price can be a major asset. In other markets where price is less important, cost advantages may not be translated into marketing assets; rather they are used to provide better margins.

Information systems and market intelligence

Information systems and systematic marketing research can be valuable assets in that they keep the company informed about both its customers and its competitors. Information is a major asset that many firms guard jealously, but until it is utilised to make better decisions it does not convert to a marketing asset. The example above of NZRC utilising information it already possessed to add value for its customers through keeping them in touch with their products during the entire distribution process shows how information can be used effectively as a marketing asset.

Existing customer base

A major asset for many companies is their existing customer base. Particularly where a company is dealing with repeat business, both consumer and industrial, the existence of a core of satisfied customers can offer significant opportunities for further development.

This has been especially noted in the recent development of the direct marketing industry (currently accounting for around half of all marketing expenditure in the USA), where it is recognised that the best customer prospects for a business are often its existing customers. Where customers have been satisfied with previous company offerings they are more likely to react positively to new offers. Where a relationship has been built with the customer this can be both capitalised on for market development and employed as a barrier to competitive entry.

The converse is, of course, also true. Where a customer has been dissatisfied with a product or service offering it may not only be negative towards new offers but may also act as a 'well poisoner' in relating its experiences to other potential customers.

There is an old marketing adage that goes: 'Each satisfied customer will tell 3 others, each dissatisfied customer will tell 33!'

Technological skills

The type and level of technology employed by the organisation can be a further asset. Technological superiority can aid in cost reduction or in improving product quality. A factor in the Golden Wonder gain of market share over Smiths Crisps in the 1960s was superior plant technology, producing a product of consistent quality, innovatively packed in an airtight film pack for longer shelf life, enabling the product to be sold through new outlets.

> ■ Davies and Brooks (1989) report a company manufacturing cigarette lighters being concerned at the downward trend in smoking. The company identified a key technological strength in the use of a novel crystal mechanism to produce a spark from mechanical contact. The business was redefined as 'the ignition business' and subsequently offered products in a variety of markets from gas appliances to car and jet engines. ■

Production expertise

Production know-how can be used to good effect as a marketing asset. Mars, for example, is particularly good at producing high-quality nougat (a great deal of effort has been put into quality control at Mars, developing its production processes as a core competence). This has been turned into a marketing asset in a number of leading products such as the Mars Bar, Milky Way, Topic and Snickers, all of which are nougat based.

Copyrights and patents

Copyright is a legal protection for musical, literary or other artistic property which prevents others using the work without payment of an agreed royalty. Patents grant persons the exclusive right to make, use and sell their inventions for a limited period. Copyright is particularly important in the film industry to protect films from illegal copying ('pirating'), and patents are important for exploiting new product inventions. The protection of copyrights and patents, in addition to offering the holder the opportunity to make and market the items protected, allows the holder to license or sell those rights to others. They therefore constitute potential marketing assets of the company.

Franchises and licences

The negotiation of franchises or licences to produce and/or market the inventions or protected properties of others can also be valuable assets. Retailers franchised to use the 'Mitre 10' name in hardware retailing in New Zealand, for example, benefit from the strong national image of the licenser and extensive national advertising campaigns.

Similarly, in many countries American Express cards and products are marketed under licence to the American Express Company of the USA. The licence agreement is a significant asset for the licensee.

5.4 Conclusions

Each company has its own unique strengths and weaknesses with respect to the competition and its own distinctive competence. A key factor for competing successfully in ever more competitive markets is to recognise these factors and utilise them to the full.

At a fundamental level, each organisation needs to be aware of its core competencies: those particular skills and processes that it is uniquely good at, that can produce the next generation of products or services.

At the next level, the organisation should be aware of its exploitable marketing assets. The asset-based marketing approach encourages organisations systematically to examine their current and potential assets in the market place and to select those for emphasis where they have, ideally, a defensible uniqueness. Assets built up in the market place with customers are less prone to attack by competitors than low prices or easily imitated technologies.

SIX

Customer analysis

... when the future becomes less visible, when the fog descends, the forecasting horizon that you can trust comes closer and closer to your nose. In those circumstances being receptive to new directions becomes important. You need to take account of opportunities and threats and enhance an organisation's responsiveness.

Igor Ansoff quoted by Hill (1979)

Introduction

Information is the raw material of decision making. Effective marketing decisions are based on sound information; the decisions themselves can be no better than the information on which they are based (Tull and Hawkins, 1984).

Marketing research is concerned with the provision of information that can be used to reduce the level of uncertainty in decision making. Uncertainty can never be eliminated completely in marketing decisions, but by the careful application of tried and tested research techniques it can be reduced.

The first part of this chapter looks at the information needed about customers to make effective marketing decisions. This is followed by a brief discussion of the various research techniques available for collecting data from the marketing environment. The use of these techniques in a typical marketing research study aimed at creatively segmenting a market and identifying current and potential product/service positions is then discussed. The chapter concludes with a discussion of how marketing-related information can be arranged within an organisation and the development of marketing decision support systems (MDSS).

6.1 What we need to know about customers

Information needs about customers can be broadly grouped into current and future information. The critical issues concerning current customers are: who the prime market targets are; what gives them value; how they can be brought closer; and how they can be better served.

For the future, however, we also need to know: how customers will change; which new customers to pursue; and how to pursue them.

6.1.1 Information on current customers

The starting point is to define who the current customers are. The answer is not always obvious as there may be many actors in the purchase and use of a particular product or service. Customers are not necessarily the same as consumers. A useful way to approach customer definition is to recognise five main roles that exist in many purchasing situations. Often several, or even all, of these roles may be conducted by the same individuals, but recognising each role separately can be a useful step in more accurately targeting marketing activity.

The initiator

This is the individual (or individuals) who initiates the search for a solution to the customer's problem. In the case of the purchase of a chocolate bar it could be a hungry child who recognises his or her own need for sustenance. In the case of a supermarket the reordering of a particular line of produce nearing sellout may be initiated by a stock controller, or even an automatic order-processing system.

The influencer

Influencers are all those individuals who may have some influence on the purchase decision. A child may have initiated the search for a chocolate bar, but the parents may have a strong influence (through holding the purse strings) on which product is actually bought. In the supermarket the ultimate customers will have a strong influence on the brands ordered — the brands they buy or request the store to stock are most likely to be ordered.

The decider

Taking into account the views of initiators and influencers, some individual will actually make the decision as to which product or service to purchase. This may be back to the initiator or the influencer in the case of the chocolate bar. In the supermarket the decider may be a merchandiser whose task it is to specify which brands to stock, what quantity to order and so on.

The purchaser

The purchaser is the individual who actually buys the product or service. He or she is, in effect, the individual who hands over the cash in exchange for the benefits. This may be the child or parent for the chocolate bar. In industrial purchasing it is often a professional buyer who, after taking account of the various influences on the decision, ultimately places the order, attempting to get the best value for money possible.

The user

Finally comes the end user of the product or service, the individual who consumes the offer. For the chocolate bar it will be the child. For the goods in the supermarket it will be the supermarket's customers.

What is important in any buying situation is to have a clear idea of the various actors likely to have an impact on the purchase and consumption decision. Where the various roles are undertaken by different individuals, it may be necessary to adopt a different marketing approach to each. Each may be looking for different benefits in the purchase and consumption process. Where different roles are undertaken by the same individuals, different approaches may be suitable depending on what stage of the buy/consume process the individual is in at the time.

A central theme of this book is that most markets are segmented: in other words, different identifiable groups of customers require different benefits when buying or using essentially similar products or services. Chapter 9 discusses methods for segmenting markets, while Chapter 11 explores ways of determining the value of alternative segments.

Identifying who the various customers are, and what role they play, then leads to the question of what gives them value. For each of the above members of a decision-making unit (DMU), different aspects of the purchase and use may give value.

For the child's purchase of a chocolate bar, a number of benefits may emerge. The child/initiator/decider/user gets a pleasant sensory experience and a filled stomach. The parent/influencer gets a feeling of having steered the child in the direction of a product that is nutritious and good value for money. In an industrial purchase such as a tractor the users (drivers) may be looking for comfort and ease of operation, the deciders (top management) may be looking for economical performance, while the purchaser (purchasing officer) may be looking for a bulk purchase deal to demonstrate his or her buying efficiency. Clearly, the importance of each actor in the decision needs to be assessed and the benefits each gets from the process understood.

Having identified the motivators for each actor, attention then shifts to how they can be brought closer to the supplier. Ways of offering increased benefits (better sensory experiences, enhanced nutritional value, better value for money) can be examined. This may involve extending the product service offering through the 'augmented' product (see Levitt, 1986; and Chapter 12).

For industrial purchases, a major route to bringing customers closer is to develop mutually beneficial alliances that enhance value for both customer and supplier. A characteristic of Japanese businesses is the closeness developed with suppliers so as to ensure the continuous supply of appropriate quality semi-finished material 'just in time' for production purposes.

Better service is at the heart of improving customer relations and making it difficult for customers to go elsewhere. Surveys in the USA have shown that less than 20 per cent of lost business is down to poor products and only 20 per cent down to high (relative) prices. The major reason for losing business is poor service (over 40 per cent of cases).

6.1.2   Information on future customers

The above issues have been concerned with today's customers. Of importance for the future, however, is how those customers will change. There are two main types of change essential to customer analysis.

The first is changes in existing customers, their wants, needs and expectations. As competition intensifies so the range of offerings open to customers increases. In addition, their experiences with various offers can lead to increased expectations and requirements. As pointed out in Chapter 1, a major way of dealing with this type of change is continuous improvement (or the Kaizen approach of the Japanese).

In the hi-fi market continuous product improvements, coupled with some significant innovations such as the CD player, have served to increase customer expectations of both the quality of sound reproduction and the portability of equipment. A manufacturer still offering the products of the 1970s or even 1980s in the 1990s would soon find its customers deserting in favour of competitors' offerings.

The second type of change comes from new customers emerging as potentially more attractive targets. Segments that may be less attractive at one point in time might become more attractive in the future. As social, cultural and economic change has affected living standards so has it affected the demand for goods and services. There is now increased demand for healthy foods, sports and leisure equipment and services, such that markets which might have been less attractive in the 1960s are now booming.

The main ways in which organisations go about analysing their customers is through marketing research (to collect relevant data on them) and market modelling (to make sense of those data). Each is discussed below.

6.2 Marketing research

The use of marketing research services by a variety of organisations, from commercial firms to political parties, has increased dramatically in recent years. In 1985 the turnover of the market research industry in the UK was around £150m and increasing annually. Estimates for 1991 put it at nearer £300m (see *Marketing*, 19.3.92).

Not only large companies and organisations benefit from marketing research. It is possible, through creative design of research studies, for organisations with smaller budgets to benefit from marketing research studies. Commercial research organisations will conduct studies for clients costing as little as £2,000, depending on the research being undertaken.

Figure 6.1 shows the range of marketing research activities engaged in by research agencies. In the UK there are currently around 200 agencies providing research services. Some companies, such as NOP (part of MAI Research) and AGB (restructured in March 1992 following the collapse of its parent Maxwell Communications Corporation, and incorporated into the Taylor Nelson Group), offer a wide variety of services. Others specialise in particular types of research (e.g. A.C. Nielsen specialises in retail audits). For a full listing of companies in the UK providing marketing research services, and where appropriate their specialisations, see the *Market Research Society Yearbook*. Each type of research is discussed below.

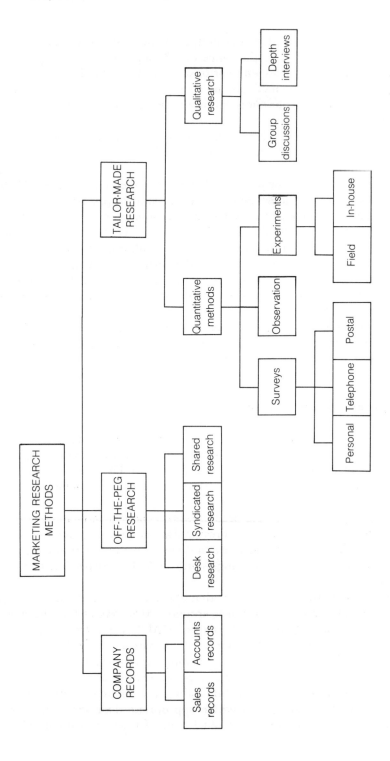

Figure 6.1 **Marketing research methods**

6.2.1 Company records

An obvious, but often underutilised, starting point for gathering marketing data is through the effective use of the company's own records. Often large amounts of data that can be used to aid marketing decisions, both strategic and tactical, are held in unlikely places within the company — for example, in the accounts department. Data on factors such as who purchases and how much they purchase may be obtained from invoice records. Similarly, purchase records may show customer loyalty patterns, identify gaps in customer purchasing and highlight the most valuable customers.

The value of internally collected data is dependent, however, on how it is collected in the first place. Unfortunately, sales data are often not collected or maintained in a manner that facilitates their use for marketing decision making. As a general rule it is desirable to collect routine data on as detailed a basis as possible to allow for unforeseen data analysis requirements. For example, sales records should be kept by customer, customer type, product, product line, sales territory, sales person and detailed time period. Data of this type would allow the isolation of profitable and unprofitable customers, territories and product lines, and the identification of trends in the market place.

In direct marketing it is said that the best customer prospects are often existing customers. Adequate sales records should reveal frequencies of purchase and latent and lapsed customers, and may suggest alternative products that could be of interest. In the mail order business, catalogue companies keep records of the types of product customers have bought from them. This enables additional catalogues, more specialist in nature, to be targeted at the most likely prospects.

6.2.2 Off-the-peg research

As the name implies, off-the-peg research consists of tapping into existing research services, often locating and using data that are already in existence but are held externally to the company. Much basic information, such as market sizes and growth rates, broad social and economic trends, customer firms and competitor firms, is already available in some form or another. Crouch (1984) classifies three main types of off-the-peg research:

- Research using the very large body of already published data, usually termed secondary or desk research.
- Research using data available from regular market surveys of syndicated research. Both the costs of the research and the data collected are shared by the syndicate of research buyers.
- Research in which the method of data collection is shared, but the data are not. Off-the-peg research instruments, such as omnibus surveys, are employed to collect client-specific data.

Secondary desk research

Secondary desk research uses data that have already been published by someone else. The researcher is a 'secondary' user of the research. Secondary data have the advantage of being relatively cheap and quick to obtain (when you know where to look!). They can also be reliable and accurate. Unfortunately, secondary data are often out of date and not specific enough to answer the majority of marketing questions. They will, for example, often tell you how many customers buy each competitor's offering, but will not tell you why.

In the UK there are very many sources of secondary data; the major problem facing the inexperienced researcher is finding them.

The government publishes a great deal of statistical information about industry, trade, commerce and social trends. Most of these data are free, or charged for at the cost of publishing only. The starting point for identifying relevant government statistics is the booklet, *Government Statistics: A brief guide to sources* (available free from HMSO).

Increasingly, it is possible to use on-line information services such as Harvest to search through alternative sources and to scan quickly what data are already available.

Secondary data vary dramatically in quality, both from country to country and from supplier to supplier within a particular country. In assessing the accuracy of secondary data the following questions should be borne in mind:

- Who collected the data and why? (Are they likely to be biased in their reporting?)
- How did they collect the data? (Sample or census? Sampling method? Research instruments?)
- What level of accuracy do they claim? (Does the methodology support the claim?)
- What use did they put the data to? (Is the use limited?)

Primary or field research is undertaken where the secondary sources cannot provide the detail of information required to solve a particular problem or to aid the decision making sufficiently. Primary research involves the collection of new data, often directly from customers or distribution intermediaries (such as retailers or wholesalers).

Syndicated research

Syndicated research occurs where a group of research buyers share the costs and the findings of research among themselves. The majority of such syndicated research services are conducted by the larger marketing research agencies and the results are sold to whoever will buy.

In the UK syndicated research is carried out in a wide variety of markets, though primarily consumer markets. The most widely used services are the Retail Audits of A. C. Nielsen, the Television Consumer Audit (TCA) (a consumer panel) of AGB, the Target Group Index of British Market Research Bureau Ltd (BMRB) and the various media research services including the National Readership Survey currently administered by Research Bureau Ltd (RBL), and the television viewing survey, BARB, researched and administered by AGB.

There are a great many sources of syndicated research covering a wide variety of markets. They have the major advantages that the methodology is usually tried and tested, the samples are often bigger than individual companies could afford to survey on their own and they are considerably cheaper than conducting the research for one company alone.

The disadvantages are that the data are limited in usefulness to monitoring sales over time, identifying trends in markets and competitors, and tracking advertising and other promotional activity. They do not allow further probing of motivations for purchase, nor indeed any additional, company-specific questioning.

Shared research

The final type of research to be classified as 'off the peg' is research where some of the costs and fieldwork are shared by a number of companies but the results are not. Omnibus surveys are regular research surveys which are being undertaken using a predetermined (off-the-peg) sampling frame and methodology. Individual clients then 'buy a seat' on the omnibus by adding their own questions. These are asked, along with the questions of other clients, and the results are tabulated against such factors as social class, ACORN category, age, etc.

Typical omnibus surveys in the UK are the NOP Random Omnibus of 2,000 adults per week, the RSGB Motoring Omnibus of 1,000 motorists monthly and the BMRB National Children's Survey of 1,100 7–17-year-olds monthly.

Omnibus research has the major advantages of low cost, as the fieldwork costs are shared by all participating companies, and added flexibility in that each client can ask his or her own questions of a typically large sample of respondents. The number of questions that can be added to an omnibus is, however, generally limited to between six and ten and, because the respondent will be asked questions about a variety of product fields in the same interview, questions are best kept short and factual to avoid respondent fatigue.

In summary there are a wide variety of off-the-peg sources from which the company or organisation wishing to conduct market or social research can choose. They have the advantages over conducting primary research that they have established methodologies and are relatively quick and cheap to tap into. The disadvantages lie in the scope and number of the questions that can be asked. Before undertaking costly primary research, however, marketing managers are well advised to examine the possibilities that off-the-peg research offers.

6.2.3   Tailor-made research

Tailor-made research, in contrast to off-the-peg, provides the organisation undertaking the research with the flexibility to design the research to match exactly the needs of the client company. Depending on those needs there are a variety of techniques available (see Figure 6.1). The techniques available are broadly categorised as qualitative and quantitative.

In qualitative research emphasis is placed on gaining understanding and depth in data that often cannot be quantified. It is concerned with meaning rather than numbers, usually involving small samples of respondents but probing them in depth for their opinions, motivations and attitudes. Quantitative research, on the other hand, involves larger samples and more structured research instruments (questionnaires and the like), and produces quantifiable outputs. In major studies both types of technique may be used hand in hand. Qualitative research is often used in the early, exploratory, stages of research and quantitative research then used to provide quantification of the broad qualitative findings.

Qualitative techniques

Qualitative techniques are essentially unstructured or semi-structured interviewing methods designed to encourage respondents to reply freely and express their real feelings, opinions and motivations. There are two main techniques used in qualitative research: the group discussion (variously termed the focus group or group depth interview) and the individual depth interview.

Group discussions usually take the form of a relaxed, informal discussion among between six and nine respondents with a group leader or moderator ensuring that the discussion covers areas relevant to the research brief. The discussions are typically held in the moderator's home (in the case of consumer studies) or in a hotel room (for industrial groups). The advantage of the group set-up is that it encourages interaction among the participants, which can generate broader discussion than a one-to-one interview and answer session. Its value as a research technique rests with the quality of the group moderator (usually a trained psychologist) and his or her ability to encourage wide-ranging but relevant discussion of the topics of interest. Products can be introduced into the group for trial and comment in an informal setting conducive to evaluation.

■   Group discussions were used effectively in the development of the advertising message 'naughty but nice' for fresh cream cakes (see Bradley, 1987). A series of group discussions discovered feelings of guilt associated with eating fresh cream cakes and that the advertising could capitalise on this by emphasising the sheer pleasure of cream cakes and the slightly naughty aspects of eating them. Feelings and emotions of this sort could not have been obtained from quantitative research. The relaxed, informal settings of the group discussion were essential to obtaining the clues that led to the advertising copy development.   ■

The depth interview takes place between one interviewer (again often a trained psychologist) and one respondent. It is used extensively for deeper probing of motivations, especially in areas of a confidential nature, or on delicate subjects where it is necessary that rapport and trust are built up between the interviewer and the respondent. Many of the techniques used in depth interviews have been developed from clinical psychology, including the use of projective techniques such as word associations and Kelly repertory grids.

Qualitative research is often used as preliminary research prior to a more quantitative investigation. In this context it can help in the wording of questions on a further questionnaire, indicate what questions to ask and elicit important product and brand features and image dimensions. Qualitative research is also used on its own in motivation studies, for the development and pre-testing of advertising messages, package design evaluation, concept testing and new product testing. The major limitation of qualitative research is that its cost and its nature make it impossible to employ large samples and hence it can be dangerous applying it to large populations on the basis of the small sample involved.

Quantitative techniques

Quantitative research techniques include surveys, observation methods and experimentation of one type or another.

Surveys are a vast subject in themselves. There are three main types of survey depending on how the interviews are conducted: personal interviews are where the interviewer and the respondent come face to face for a question and answer session; telephone interviews, an increasingly used research technique, are conducted over the phone; and postal surveys use the mail services to send self-completion question-naires to respondents.

Each technique has its advantages and drawbacks. Personal interviews are the most expensive to conduct but offer the greatest flexibility. They are particularly useful where respondents are asked to react to attitudinal statements and more complex questions that may require some clarification by the interviewer.

Telephone interviews are particularly useful when data are required quickly. They do not entail the costs of physically sending interviewers into the field, they can be closely controlled, and the data collected can be entered directly on to computer for analysis. The majority of opinion polls are now conducted in this manner, facilitating 'next day' reporting in the sponsoring newspapers. The drawbacks of telephone interviews are that not everybody has a telephone and hence the sample achieved may be biased towards the more affluent in society (this problem is now less acute than a few years ago as more households now have telephones), and that the interview is less personal than a face-to-face encounter, requiring it to be kept relatively short. It is not possible to show prompts and other stimuli during a telephone conversation.

Postal surveys are the cheapest method of all. They are useful in locating geo-graphically dispersed samples and for situations where the questionnaire is long and detailed. Response rates, however, can be low and there is little control over who responds. The lack of personal contact requires a very clearly laid out questionnaire, well pre-tested to ensure clarity.

Observation techniques can be particularly useful where respondents are unlikely to be able or willing to give the types of information required. Crouch (1984) cites the example of research into what items a shopper has taken from a supermarket shelf, considered for purchase but not bought. Direct questioning after the shopping trip is unlikely to produce accurate data as the respondent simply will not remember. Observation of shopping behaviour in the store can provide these data.

Observation can be conducted by individuals, as in the case of the supermarket behaviour noted above or observation of traffic density on particular roads, or by instruments designed to monitor behaviour. The prime example of the latter is the 'PeopleMeter' recording device used in television viewing research. A black box is attached to the sets of a sample of viewers and records when the set was turned on and what channel was tuned to. Each individual in the household has a code key which is activated when he or she is in the room. Data are transmitted from the home to the research company via the telephone network overnight, enabling rapid analysis of viewing data.

In recent years PeopleMeters have been widely adopted throughout the developed and developing world as methods of monitoring TV viewing and audiences. Figure 6.2 shows the use of the technique world-wide as of May 1990.

The final type of quantitative research of interest here is experimentation. Experiments are carried out either in the field or in-house (laboratory). Field experiments take place in the real world and the subjects of the experiments typically do not know that they are part of an experiment. The prime example is test marketing,

COUNTRY	AGB	NIELSEN	OTHERS
Australia	●	●	
Belgium Flemish	●		●
French			●
Brazil			○
Canada		●	
Finland			●
France	●	●	●
Germany			●
Greece	●		
Hong Kong	○		
Ireland	●		
Italy	●		
Japan		○	○
Netherlands	●		
New Zealand	●		
Philippines	●		
Portugal	●		
Spain			●
Switzerland			●
Thailand	●		
Turkey	●		
UK	●		
US National		●	
Local		○	○
Total number of countries where PeopleMeter services operate	13	4	6
● PeopleMeter	○ Set Meter		

Source: *SRG News*, no. 63 (May 1990).

Figure 6.2 **TV meters world-wide**

where a new product will be marketed in a limited geographic region prior to a decision on whether to launch the brand nationally or internationally. In-house experiments are conducted in a more controlled but less realistic setting where the respondent knows he or she is taking part.

■   Broadbent (1983) describes the use of regional experiments in the development and testing of advertising copy for Cadbury's Flake. Cadbury's Flake competes in the confectionery market. The brand sales had grown steadily until 1977 when the total countline market went into decline. Flake sales, however, declined at twice the market rate. An attitudinal study was undertaken which showed that a high proportion of lapsed users found the product too messy or crumbly. As this represented the major reason for purchase by the heavy users of the brand it was not considered desirable to change the product design.

An alternative advertising message was developed emphasising 'every little piece of flake is sheer enjoyment' and making an art out of eating Flake. There were various techniques shown for getting the last crumbs — tipping back the chair, using a paper plate and sucking the last crumbs through a straw.

The new advertisements were tested in the Lancashire and Yorkshire television regions and sales were closely monitored compared to the rest of the country. Using syndicated sources and specially commissioned surveys it was estimated that in the 18 months of the test unit sales had increased by 16 per cent over and above what would have been expected. Both initial purchase and repeat purchase rates were shown to have increased. The campaign was judged to have turned the negative (mess) into a positive (delicious morsels of Flake) through the humour of the ads and was extended on a limited basis to other areas.   ■

There have been several recent innovations in test marketing. Full-scale testing, as described above, suffers from a number of problems. It is costly and time consuming, and it alerts the competition to changes in marketing strategy or new products about to be launched. As a result there has been an increase in other smaller-scale testing methods (see Saunders, 1985).

Mini test markets, such as the Taylor Nelson 'Model Test Market' and the RBL 'Minivan', offer the opportunity to introduce products into the real market on a limited and controlled distribution basis. They are good at estimating initial and repeat purchase rates but poor at evaluating the overall impact of the complete marketing mix.

Simulated supermarket tests make grocery products available in a simulated environment. They can be helpful in estimating trial rates, testing purchase intents created by exposure to test advertisements and testing individual elements of the marketing mix such as packaging, pricing and branding. Supermarket panels, recruited from among the shoppers of a particular chain, have their purchases recorded through laser scanning and related to purchase card numbers. These panels can be particularly useful in the limited market testing of new brands.

As with off-the-peg research, the variety of tailor-made research available is very wide indeed. There are a great many market research agencies available with varying expertise and skills. While it is still true to say that the bulk of expenditure on marketing research comes from the larger, fast-moving consumer goods companies, it is possible for smaller companies to take advantage of the research services and sources available (especially off-the-peg research).

Market research techniques are also increasingly being used to investigate non-commercial problems. Research was used heavily, for example, to investigate drug abuse by young people prior to the 1985 advertising campaign designed to tackle the problem. The Oxfam charity has used survey research to help it understand the motivations behind charity donations and to help identify 'prime donor segments'. During the run-up to the 1992 general election in the UK both large political parties spent heavily on market and opinion research to gauge the mood of voters. Opinion poll results (sponsored by the media and political parties) were published almost daily in the three weeks running up to the election.

In the context of competitive positioning, marketing research provides the raw data with which it is possible to segment the market creatively, and can help to identify current and potential product positionings.

6.3   The marketing research process

A typical segmentation and positioning research project might combine the use of several of the above techniques to investigate a particular market. Figure 6.3 shows the various stages.

6.3.1   Problem definition

The first step is to define clearly the problem to be tackled. Typically, a series of discussions between marketing research personnel (internal or external to the

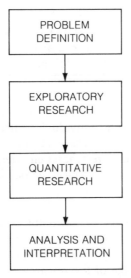

Figure 6.3 Stages in a comprehensive marketing research project

company) and marketing decision makers are necessary to ensure that the research project is tackling the correct issues.

6.3.2   Exploratory research

As part of problem definition, and a starting point in the research process itself, exploratory research will be used to identify information gaps and to specify the need for further research.

Initially, secondary sources could be utilised. Company records could be employed, alongside off-the-peg desk research, to quantify the market and draw its preliminary boundaries.

Qualitative research might then be used to explore with customers, and/or potential customers, why they use the particular product and how. At this stage group discussions may be relevant in many consumer markets. In industrial markets, while group discussions are successfully employed, a preferred route is often personal, depth interviews with key customers.

In a segmentation and positioning study the focus of this qualitative research will be to identify the prime motivators to purchase (i.e. the major benefits being sought) and any demotivators. The research should also seek to identify relevant competitors and explore their strengths and weaknesses in serving the market. Finally, hypotheses about how the market could be segmented should be developed that can be further researched during the later stages of the research project.

6.3.3   Quantitative research phase

While qualitative research will help in formulating hypotheses about how the market is segmented and what factors influence purchase, because of the small and normally non-representative samples involved it is unlikely to be adequate in itself for segmentation purposes. Typically, it will be followed by a quantitative study (a personal survey most often) utilising a sufficiently large and random sample to enable market segment sizes to be estimated and strength of opinions to be gauged.

Such a quantitative study might ask respondents to evaluate competing products on a series of attributes that have been identified as important during the qualitative research. Further, respondents could be asked to rate how important, to them personally, each attribute is and to express what characteristics their 'ideal' product would have. Background customer characteristics could also be collected to enable any market segments uncovered to be described in ways helpful to further marketing activity (see Chapter 8).

Experimentation might also be used in the quantitative phase of a segmentation and positioning study. Product samples might be placed with existing and potential customers to gauge reaction to new or improved products. Conjoint analysis experiments might be used to estimate reaction to hypothetical product combinations (see Chapter 9).

6.3.4   Analysis and interpretation

Following data collection, statistical techniques and models can be employed to turn the data generated into meaningful information to help with the segmentation. Factor analysis might be used to reduce a large number of attitudinal statements to their underlying dimensions, or underlying factors. Cluster analysis could be used to group respondents on the basis of several characteristics (attitudes, likes, dislikes or background demographics) into meaningful segments. Perceptual mapping techniques could be employed to draw models of customer perceptions on two, three or more relevant dimensions. These techniques are discussed in more detail in Chapter 10.

Finally, the results will be presented to and discussed with the senior marketing decision makers to aid their interpretation of the market in which they are operating.

The essence of a successful research project is to use the data gathering and analysis techniques which are relevant both to the product type being investigated and the stage in the research project where they are being employed. By utilising innovative techniques and looking at markets afresh, it is often possible to gain new insights into market structure and hence aid the sharpening of target market definition.

The next section in this chapter looks at how information is organised within the company.

6.4   Organising the customer information

6.4.1   Marketing information systems (MIS)

Information is organised within the company through the *marketing information system* (MIS). This system may be formally structured, physically consisting of several personnel and a variety of computer hardware and software, or it may be a very informal collection of reports and statistics piled on an executive's desk or even in his or her head!

Conceptually, however, the system can be represented as in Figure 6.4 (developed from Little, 1979). The information system has five basic components: a market research interface concerned with collecting and gathering raw data from the marketing environment; the raw data collected through the market research interface; statistical techniques that can be used to analyse, synthesise and collate the raw data, to turn it into information; market models that utilise both the raw data and statistical techniques to describe the market place, to simulate it or to predict it; and finally a managerial interface that allows the decision maker access to the information and models to aid his or her decision making.

Raw data
As discussed above, data comes into the system from a variety of sources, from internal and external, secondary and primary sources. The data are stored in various forms (e.g. on paper, in people's heads, on computer). Increasingly, data are being stored

on machine-readable media such as magnetic tape or hard and soft disc. The increased availability of computer hardware and software, especially with the advent of the microcomputer, has made it increasingly possible to store large amounts of data in a form that is readily accessible and easily analysed.

Statistical techniques

The processes available to synthesise and summarise the raw data are called *statistics*. A wide variety of statistics are available but often the most important are the simple ones which allow data to be summarised (such as averages, means, standard deviations, ranges, etc.) so that many small, often diverse observations can be condensed into a few important numbers. For a comprehensive review of statistical techniques available to analyse marketing data, see Green, Tull and Albaum (1988).

Market models

A model is a representation of the real world. Most managers have an implicit model in their own minds of the markets in which they operate. For example, they can give

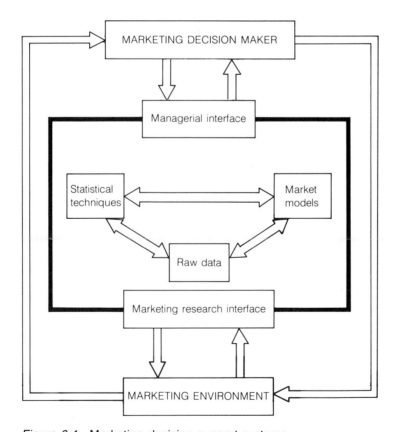

Figure 6.4 Marketing decision support systems

an expectation of the effect of changing price on sales of the product based on their experiences. This is essentially their internal model of the price/sales relationship. In examining data through the use of statistical techniques, the analyst may wish to test out the model he or she already has of the market. Alternatively, the objective may be to build a new model of the market to help managerial understanding of the forces that affect demand and overall company performance. In essence, models provide theories that 'seek to bring order to the chaos of collected facts' (Little, 1979).

Managerial interface

For the information system to be of value to the marketing decision maker requires that he or she has access to that system in such a way as to facilitate and encourage easy use. The interface between the manager and the MIS can consist of an individual (a marketing information officer), a report or set of reports produced on a regular or intermittent basis, or, increasingly commonly, a computer terminal or a micro-computer. With the relevant software to facilitate use of the MIS, direct 'hands on' access for the decision maker can encourage wider use of the system and experimentation with the various models developed.

6.4.2   Marketing decision support system (MDSS)

In the last decade there has been a change in emphasis in marketing from information systems (MIS) to marketing decision support systems (MDSS). The distinction may seem merely one of semantics, but it is, in fact, fundamental. While MIS placed the emphasis on provision of information, primarily in the form of facts and figures, MDSS changes the emphasis to aiding decision making through the provision of question and answer facilities. In other words, MDSS allows analysis rather than merely retrieval of information.

Decision support systems can have several types of output. These have been grouped into two types: data oriented and model oriented.

Data-oriented decision support systems focus on data retrieval and simple analysis using statistical techniques. This can include, for example, straightforward data retrieval of such items as stock levels. Systems of this type are effectively information systems rather than decision support systems as defined above.

Model-oriented decision support systems, on the other hand, focus on simulation and representation of aspects of the real world. Accounting models, for example, calculate the consequences of planned actions for the financial performance of the company. Representational models estimate the consequences of action of one type or another. An advertising model may estimate the effects of running a particular advertising campaign. Optimisation models provide guidelines for action by generating the optimal solutions consistent with a series of constraints. For example, given an advertising budget, a target audience and a required average viewing frequency, an optimisation model could be used to select the most effective combination of media and insertions.

Implementation of MDSS in marketing has, however, been slower than predicted. In 1977 Jobber (1977) concluded from a survey of 153 of the UK Times Top 500 companies that implementation had been slow (fewer than half the firms interviewed had a marketing information system let alone an MDSS). For those that did have a system of some type it was often of a very low level of sophistication. The majority were used primarily as data storage and retrieval systems with only a very small minority attempting model building or simulation.

The use of decision support systems in marketing is now developing more rapidly with the advent of computer hardware and software. They have been pioneered in the USA by researchers such as Little (1979) and in Europe by Naert and Leeflang (1978). Several characteristics of MDSS that differentiate them from their predecessors (the information systems of the 1970s) deserve emphasis:

- MDSS support decisions! They are not merely data retrieval systems but are actively designed to help managers make better decisions. In addition they support, rather than replace, managerial decision making.
- MDSS are essentially interactive. They allow the manager to ask questions, receive inputs and experiment with decisions to estimate the likely outcomes. As such they are more effective where a manager has the scope to use the system directly.
- MDSS should be flexible and easy to use. Ease of use is a major characteristic essential to gaining widespread use of an innovation such as MDSS in many organisations. Flexibility is desirable to allow the system to respond to a variety of information and decision support needs.

6.4.3 Expert systems for marketing decision support

More recent developments in computer hardware and software offer exciting opportunities for marketing management. Developments in expert systems and artificial intelligence, which enable the modelling of not only marketing phenomena but also the decision-making processes of 'experts' in the field, promise to revolutionise the whole field of decision support. The direction in which these developments will move is difficult to predict at present (see the special edition of the *International Journal of Research in Marketing*). What is certain, however, is that marketing decisions will become more data based (there is already a data explosion in marketing) and there will be an increased need to organise those data in meaningful ways to enable them to be used quickly and effectively. In particular, increased computing and modelling power will enable decisions to be tested out in simulated environments prior to implementation in the real world.

6.5 Conclusions

Understanding customers is central to developing a coherent positioning strategy.

This chapter has examined, first, the types of information about customers that can be useful in determining competitive position, and second, the marketing research methods available for collecting that information. The process typically undertaken to identify potential market segments and their needs was then discussed. Finally, developments in organising and presenting data were examined.

SEVEN

Competitor analysis

A horse never runs so fast as when he has other horses to catch up and outpace.

Ovid, *The Art of Love*, AD 8

Introduction

Sun Tzu (see Clavell, 1981), the great Chinese general from the fourth century BC, encapsulates the importance of competitor analysis:

If you know your enemy as you know yourself, you need not fear the result of a hundred battles. If you know yourself but not the enemy, for every victory you gain you will suffer a defeat. If you know neither the enemy nor yourself, you will succumb in every battle.

What was true of war in the fourth century BC is equally true of business today. Without a knowledge of competitors' strengths and their likely actions, it is impossible to formulate the central component of marketing strategy: finding a group of customers for whom one has a competitive advantage over the competition. It must also be true that, since competitive advantage is a relative concept, a company that has poor understanding of its competitors can have no real understanding of itself.

Japan's leading companies retain Sun Tzu's obsession with competitor analysis. Although successful eastern and western companies are alike in many ways (Doyle, Saunders and Wong, 1986), the commitment of Japanese companies to gathering information remains a distinguishing feature (Kotler, Fahay and Jatusripitak, 1985). In contrast, the situation in many western companies has led Porter (1980) to comment that 'despite the clear need for sophisticated competitor analysis in strategy formulation, such analysis is sometimes not done explicitly or comprehensively in practice'.

This chapter provides a framework for the essential activity of competitor analysis. It covers three areas:

- The competitive positions, strengths and intentions of rivals.
- The choice of 'good' competitors.
- The origin and sources of competitive information.

7.1 The dimensions of competitor analysis

In the medium term the focus of competitor analysis must be firms within the same strategic group as the company concerned. In the longer term, however, there is a danger in the analysis being so constrained. The industry as a whole must be scanned for indirect competitors which may have the resources or the need to overcome the entry barrier to the incumbent's strategic group. Although entry barriers may be high, if the incumbent's strategic group shows high profits or growth potential beyond the rest of the market, it is likely to attract new entrants. The European luxury car makers showed this myopia with their focus being concentrated upon each other rather than the Japanese mass manufacturers. For a long time the Japanese have been building up a reputation in terms of quality and technology which they are now exploiting, together with their huge resources, to compete against the Europeans in the American market. Notice how, after discounting the Japanese a few years ago, some of the companies are scampering for cover under the wing of an industrial giant.

A second source of threat could be potential entrants into an industry, or substitutes. Part of the failing of EMI in the body scanner market was its neglect of the entrants that EMI's hugely profitable success in the new market would be likely to attract. Rather than build defences or coalitions against the almost inevitable onslaught, the company chose to continue exploitation of the market as if it was the sole supplier. Perhaps EMI's greatest failings were to fall behind in product quality and not to develop a support network for its product.

In the longer term, substitutes are the major threat to an industry. These not only bring with them new processes and products with advantages that can totally undermine the incumbents' capabilities, as the scanner did for certain forms of X-ray machine, but they are also likely to bring with them new and hungry competitors which are willing to question conventional industry practices. Once IBM entered the PC market it was quite successful relative to its target competitors, such as Apple and Hewlett Packard, but had great difficulty in handling the new competition, such as Compaq and Amstrad, which IBM's standardised PC attracted.

Competitor analysis therefore involves evaluating a series of concentric circles of adversaries: innermost are the direct competitors within the strategic group, next are companies within the industry which are driven to overcome the entry barriers to the strategic group, and outermost potential entrants and substitutes (Figure 7.1).

Porter (1980) distinguishes four dimensions of competitor analysis: *future goals* and *assumptions* which drive the competitor, and *current strategy* and *capabilities* which describe what the competitor is doing and what it can do (Figure 7.2). The aim in gathering these is not just to describe the competitor, but to gauge the competitor's future intentions or, more importantly, what the competitor is likely to do in response to the evaluating firm's own actions.

Future goals can give guidance on three levels. They can indicate where the company is intending to develop and in which markets, either industrially or internationally, major initiatives can be expected. The areas of expansion could indicate markets which are to be particularly competitive, but may simultaneously signify companies not so committed. Where the intention is profitable co-existence, it is often better to compete in areas which are deemed of second interest to major companies rather than to compete directly. Such was the opportunity created when both General Motors and Ford declared that the small car markets in America and Europe were

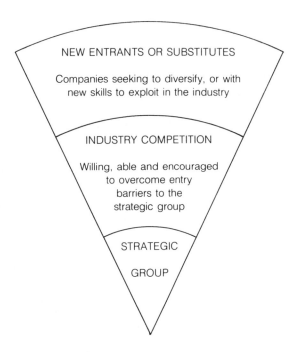

Figure 7.1   The targets of competitor analysis

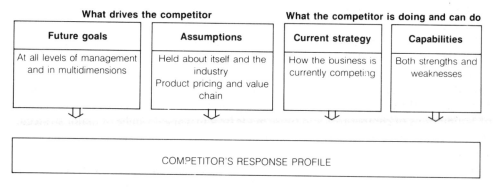

Source: Based on Porter (1980), p. 49.

Figure 7.2   The components of competitor analysis

intrinsically unprofitable and therefore of little interest to them. Goals may also give a guide to the intensity of competitor activity. When the likes of Procter and Gamble declare that they are only interested in being the number one or the strong number two in markets in which they operate, it is to be anticipated that they will compete very hard for new markets they enter. Finally, a company's goal can indicate the type of trade-off it is likely to make when faced with adversity. The obsession of many American overseas subsidiaries with the need to report back steady and slowly increasing profits has meant that they have often been willing to relinquish market share in order to achieve their short-term profit goals.

The goals can have implications across the broad portfolio of a company's activities. When competing against a diversified company, ambitious goals in one sector may indicate that commitment to another is diminishing. Equally, very large and diversified companies may often not be able to take advantage of their huge financial strengths because of their unwillingness to make strategic shifts in their resources. There is also a chance that financially driven companies like Britain's GEC may be unwilling to take the risks of new ventures, preferring instead to pick the bones of those who were damaged in taking the risk.

Assumptions that a firm has about itself and the market can be a source of opportunity or threat. Examples of flawed assumptions being made by companies and their dire consequences are many. In the 1960s Cunard assumed that, as the cost of transatlantic travel was so high, people would want a leisurely crossing rather than spending a large amount of money in flying the Atlantic in a few hours. The result of this faulty logic by Cunard, and other operators of passenger liners, was a massive increase in the tonnage of liners being constructed in their last few years of useful life. Similarly, Dunlop's assumption that it was pre-eminent in rubber technology in tyres meant that it neglected Michelin's development of steel-braced radials. The result was a catastrophic decline in Dunlop's own market share, accompanied by a decline in the total market size which occurred because of the longer life of Michelin's new development. Having assumed its pre-eminence in an established market, Dunlop's position was made intractable by its inability to develop new products.

Dunlop and Cunard were not untypical in their inability to see changing market conditions. As Foster (1986a) says, there is a tendency for incumbent companies to dismiss incipient new technologies as of little significance or maybe catering for some faddish segment of the market. Such was the case of the Swiss watch industry when first faced by the competition from Japanese digital alternatives. Thus, the evaluation of assumptions of competitors and those made by a firm itself can be of major strategic significance to a company. Having said this, there is a clear gap between the need and the ability of firms to question their own assumptions.

Analyses of how major firms often react to technological threats (Cooper and Schendel, 1976) show they are rarely able to change their historic orientation. O'Shaughnessy (1988) explains how incumbents often avoid the problems rather than take evasive action. There is, he says, a tendency for firms to: force the evidence to fit preconceptions; become deaf to any evidence at odds with their beliefs; predict the most feared competitive action as a defence in case there is any future post mortem after such action occurs; predict that competitive action will be that to which the manager's favourite strategy is an effective counter strategy as a way of getting support for that strategy.

7.1.1   Value chain analysis

By default, firms often make major assumptions about their role and position within the value chain. Porter (1985) identifies five primary activities which add value to the final output of a company (Figure 7.3).

- *Inbound logistics* involve managing the flow of products into the company. Recent attention to just-in-time manufacturing has shown how important this can be to the efficient operation of a company, and how by management of its suppliers and their quality, a company can add to the quality of its final products.
- *Operations* has long been seen as the central activity of businesses. These comprise the processes whereby the inbound items are changed in form, packaged and tested for suitability for sale. Traditionally, this has been viewed as the area where value is added to a company's products. At this stage, value can be added beyond the normal capital and manpower inputs by the maintenance of high quality, flexibility and design.

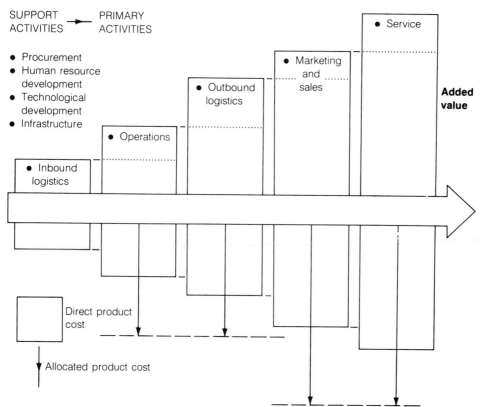

Figure 7.3 Value chain and direct product costing

- *Outbound logistics* carry the product from the point of manufacture to the buyer. They therefore include storage, distribution, etc. At this stage, value can be added through quick and timely delivery, low damage rates and the formulation of delivery mechanisms which fit the operations of the user. Within the fertiliser industry, for instance, ICI has added value to its products by offering blends which fit the specific needs of farmers at certain times of the year and delivery modularisation which fits the farmers' own systems. Taking it a stage further, deliveries can be taken to the field rather than to the farm, and even spreading can be be undertaken by the supplier.
- *Marketing and sales* activities inform buyers about products and services, and provide buyers with a reason to purchase. This can involve feedback which allows the user company to fit its operation's outbound logistics to user requirements, or helping customers understand the economic value of products that are available. Taking again the ICI example, part of the company's marketing activity involves showing how some of its products can be used to equalise the workload on a farm throughout the year and therefore use the overall labour force more efficiently.
- *Service* includes all the activities required to keep the product or service working effectively for the buyer, after it is sold and delivered. This can involve training, return of goods policies, consultation hot-line and other facilities. Since customer satisfaction is central to achieving repeat sales and word-of-mouth communication from satisfied customers, after-sales service is clearly a major part of added value.

In support of the primary activities of the value chain, Porter also identified support activities. These are procurement, human resource development, technological development and infrastructure. These, of course, feed into each stage of the primary activities of the value chain.

There are several ways in which analysis of the value chain can provide an insight into competitors.

- It can reveal cost advantages that competitors may have because of their efficient manufacture, inbound or outbound logistics. It may also reveal why, with better marketing sales and service, the company making intrinsically similar products may be achieving higher added value.
- Many conventionally oriented companies perceive operations as their primary source of added value and therefore leave opportunities for competitors to gain by taking a more extended view of the value they can add in the customer's eyes.
- Where the value added is costed effectively, it can help locate economical ways of adding value to the customer. There are often numerous ways of achieving this, such as the efficient management of single sourcing and just-in-time inbound logistics; total quality being incorporated in the operations and so reducing the service requirements and perhaps adding to the appeal of the marketing and sales activity by offering extended warranties; and well-targeted marketing and sales activities which assure that maximum perceived added value is

communicated to the customer while lower marketing and sales activity is occurring than if blanket sales activity was attempted.

A company's assumptions about how its costs are allocated across products and elements of the value chain can provide clear competitive guidelines. For instance, many companies add most of their overheads to manufacturing operations where inputs can usually be measured. This occurs despite products having vastly different inbound logistics, outbound logistics, marketing, sales and service expenditures. The result can be that the final prices of the products in the market place have little bearing upon the overall inputs and the value chain. Equally, where the overheads are allocated equally across products, direct product pricing can show where some products are being forced to carry an excessive burden of overheads, so allowing a competitor to enter the market and compete effectively on price.

When a company is competing in many different markets, it is very likely that its allocated product costs are completely out of line with some of the markets in which it is competing. This can act as an overall constraint upon its intention to support those products or give them little commitment to it. IBM encountered this problem in its PC marketing, where the margins are totally incapable of carrying the allocated overheads which were borrowed from their mainframe and mini business. This became particularly true in IBM's venture into the home computer market with the 'Peanut', which was launched with a totally inappropriate performance:price ratio.

7.1.2   Current strategy

Current strategy is the least subjective element of competitor analysis. It involves asking the basic question: 'What exactly is the competitor doing at the moment?' This requires making as full as possible a statement of what each competitor is trying to do and how it is trying to achieve it. It is an essentially complex activity where the components of marketing strategy outlined in Figure 2.1 can give some structure.

The process is one for defining product market strategies. As such it starts with *corporate strategy*. Where the competitor is part of a large diversified company this can be crucial because it may give some insight into the competitor company's commitment to the strategic group of companies being investigated. Next comes the *strategic purpose*, which can suggest the priority that the companies give to market share and profitability, and view the extent to which the strategic group is consistent with the company's strengths.

Core strategy looks at the main thrust of the competitor's quest for increased profitability. A defensive company may be looking for productivity improvements, in which case it may willingly relinquish market share. Alternatively, it may be aggressively trying to take market share from other competitors or looking at ways of carrying its strengths into related markets.

Although within a strategic group there may be companies with overlapping *competitive positions*, it is likely that at any one time competitors have a distinct focus, either accidentally or deliberately. Their goal could also be trying to serve the whole market, focusing on a few customer targets or trying to find niches for which they can provide an exclusive service. The mechanisms of promotional activity in selling also mean that it is usually necessary for a competitor within a strategic group to depend upon one means of positioning its product: for example, Volvo on safety, Saab on machismo, BMW on technology and Audi on being German. A feature of many markets is the extent to which the *competitor target* is usually the leading company. This can be the case even for small companies and hence provide opportunities for those companies who are willing to take a broader view.

Most successful companies attempt to build their strategies on a differential advantage they have over others in the market. This is an important consideration in two ways. It is clearly necessary to base the *differential advantage* on customer target, and it is important to avoid basing one's competitive strategy on trying to build strengths where one is always going to be weak relative to competitors. For instance, in the jewellery trade it is possible to compete through design or distribution but absolutely impossible to try to compete with the De Beers through securing one's own supply of rough diamonds.

Compared with other issues the *marketing mix* is quite basic. However, many attempts to enter new markets have failed because of the entrant misunderstanding the competitive levels of expenditure or being unwilling to spend at the going rate.

Consideration of *organisation* is fundamental because of the way that it can dictate strategy. For a long time Procter and Gamble's brand management structure was held up to be a marketing ideal. This was probably the case when the American market was dominant and lessons learnt there were relatively easily transferred downstream to less developed parts of the world. However, with America's relative economic decline compared to the rest of the world, Unilever's more flexible structure allowed it to transfer ideas across boundaries more easily and be more flexible to emerging local needs. Indeed, Procter and Gamble itself has now moved away from its product-managed structure.

7.1.3   Capability profiles

The assessment of a company's capabilities involves looking at its strengths and weaknesses to determine what it can do. It is the final diagnostic step in competitor analysis. Whereas a competitor's goals, assumptions and current strategy would influence the likelihood, time, nature and intensity of a competitor's reactions, its capabilities will determine its ability to initiate and sustain moves in response to environmental or competitive changes. A market audit (Chapter 5) will provide an array of the various issues that could be included at this stage. From these, competitors' relative strengths concerning *key factors for success* in the industry can be defined. MacDonald (1984) suggests keeping these to a minimum of seven or eight to assure concentration. Among these could be operational areas (such as research and engineering or financial strength) or generic skills (such as the company's ability to

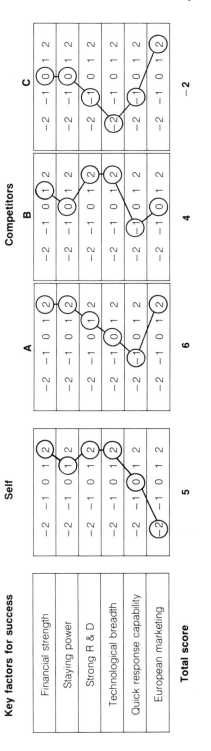

Figure 7.4 Competitors' capabilities

grow, quick response capability, ability to adapt to change, staying power or innovativeness).

Figure 7.4 shows a summary sheet which a company has used to assess its relative capability. Six dimensions have been determined as critical and the company has rated itself and three competitors on each key factor on a scale ranging from -2 (meaning very poor) to $+2$ (meaning very good). The result is profiles which suggest the companies are quite similar in their overall capabilities, and average scores which clearly identify the company on a par with competitors A and B overall. However, the total score should not be allowed to cloud the differences of the main protagonists in the market, since their relative strengths clearly show that they move in different directions given similar opportunities. For instance, Company A could build upon its European strength in marketing applied technology, whereas Company B may be forced to depend upon differentiation achieved through technological breadth and strength in R & D to maintain its market position. However, if the technology or market shifts in a direction which requires major expenditures, Company B may be weakened compared to Company A or 'Self'. An inspection of the competitive capabilities also suggests that, although Company C looks weak overall, it could be a good acquisition by 'Self'. Although weak in the financial and technological areas, it has a strong European marketing presence and therefore may be capable of providing rapid access to the European markets.

7.2 Competitors' response profiles

The aim of competitor analysis is to determine competitors' response profiles: that is, a guide to how competitors might behave when faced with various environmental and competitive changes. This covers such questions as:

- *Is the competitor satisfied with its current position?* One that is satisfied may allow indirect competitors to exploit new markets without being perturbed; alternatively, one that is trying to improve its current position may be quick in chasing market changes or be obsessed by improving its own short-term profits performance. A knowledge of a company's future goals will clearly play an important part in answering this question.
- *What likely moves or strategy shifts will the competitor make?* History can provide some guide as to the way that companies behave. Goals, assumptions and capabilities will also give some guide to how the company can effectively respond to market changes. After looking at these a company may be able to judge which of its own alternative strategies is likely to result in the most favourable reaction on the part of the competitors.
- *Where is the competitor vulnerable?* In commerce, as in war, success is best achieved by concentrating strength against weakness (Clausewitz, 1908). It takes no great insight to realise that it would be foolish for a company to take on a market leader in the areas where it is strongest, but successions of large companies

(including Xerox, GE and ICL) took on IBM at its own game and lost. Much better to compete against IBM in niche markets which its size means it cannot cover effectively, i.e. in rapidly changing markets where their bureaucracy means they cannot move swiftly, or in high-volume/low-margin markets where it has no understanding of distribution systems. The complacency of the leader in markets can provide major opportunities. The competitor's own feeling of invulnerability may be its own weakness, which could lead it to a Tyson-like downfall. In truth businesses, like armies, cannot defend on all flanks, from all positions, at all times. No company is ever all powerful in all places.

- *What will provoke the greatest and most effective retaliation by the competitor?* Whereas market leaders may accept some peripheral activity, because of perceived low margins, anti-trust laws or the scale involved, other actions are likely to provoke intense retaliation. This is what Rolls-Royce learnt to expect whenever it approached the American market for aero engines, what Freddie Laker found when he openly challenged the major carriers on the Atlantic route, and what the small Yorkshire-based company Dalepak found, when its chopped meat burgers starting making inroads into Unilever's market share. There is little interest in even the most powerful company unleashing the wrath of a strong competitor when there are less sensitive routes to success available.

Besides providing a general guideline, a competitor's response profile depends on obtaining a view of how a competitor is likely to respond, given various stimuli. Porter (1980) suggests examining the way a competitor may respond to the feasible strategic moves by a firm and feasible environmental changes. This involves assessing the vulnerability of a competitor to the event, the degree to which the event will provoke retaliation by the competitor and, finally, the effectiveness of the competitor's retaliation to the event.

The aim is to force a company to look beyond its own moves and towards those of its competitors — and, like a great player of chess, to think several moves ahead. A firm should think of its moves in a broad, strategic framework rather than the incremental manner in which strategies often emerge. By following a series of seemingly small incremental shifts in pricing and promotion, a firm may be perceived to be making a major play in the market place and incur the wrath of major players. It is clearly better for Black to consider the alternative moves carefully rather than make a series of moves, each one of which makes local sense, without regard to White's countermoves and the long-term consequences of incremental action.

7.3 Choosing good competitors

When a company chooses to enter a market, it also chooses its competitors. In the selection of new opportunities, therefore, it is important to realise that not all competitors are equally attractive. Just as markets can be attractive and a company's strengths can fit those markets, so competitors can be attractive or unattractive. Porter

	Balance	**Strength**	**Weakness**
Competitive maturity	• Understand the rules • Realistic assumptions • Support industry structure	• Credible/ viable • Know the industry costs	• Clear weaknesses • Limited strategic concept
Reconcilable goals	• Moderate strategic stake • Accept current profitability • Desire cash generation	• Comparable ROI targets	• Short time horizons • Risk-averse

Figure 7.5 Good competitors

(1985) lists the characteristics which make a good competitor. In Figure 7.5 these features are organised to show how certain features of competitors can make them attractive.

The competitively mature company understands the market it is operating in and enhances, rather than destabilises, the environment of the strategic group. The good competitor can help promote the industry's stability by understanding the rules governing the market and by holding realistic assumptions about the industry and its own relative position. In this way, it is unlikely to embark upon strategies which are unprofitable and result in zero-sum competition, such as precipitating price wars or unprofitable practices. Among the British clearing banks in the late 1980s both the Midland Bank and Lloyds introduced interest-bearing current accounts. This gave them a short-term competitive edge, but once the market leaders followed, the result was everyone losing money on this major part of their business. Once locked in, it was difficult for all the banks to extricate themselves from this self-defeating position.

A company making unrealistic assumptions about itself and the market can equally damage industrial stability. Within the European and American automobile market it is clear than an excess of capacity is being constructed. In the medium to long term this can be nothing but suicidal for the industry as a whole.

A good competitor can support industry structure if it invests in developing its own product and enhancing quality differentiation and market development, rather than embarking on confrontational price cutting or promotional strategies. In that way, barriers to entering the industry are enhanced because the market becomes relatively fragmented and the impact of one company or new entrant is diminished. The global pharmaceutical industry tends to have this structure, where legislation and the differentiation of drugs allow a large number of medium-sized companies to survive in many of the world's leading markets.

A further advantage of a competitively mature company is that it can provide a steady pressure towards the efficient operations of those with whom it is competing.

It can provide a respectability and standards in the way that IBM did in the PC market, and ensure that the market does not become too comfortable for the incumbents. The danger then, as many state monopoly industries have shown, is that once the protection is removed, or competition is allowed, they find themselves too weak, fat or rigid to change themselves. The application of the pressure becomes more even when the leading competitor has a thorough understanding of industry costs and therefore sets standards for cost-efficient services rather than imbalanced offerings.

Finally, the existence of the credible and viable large company within the strategic group can act as a deterrent to other entrants. A good competitor, therefore, can provide both a pressure to keep its competitors lean and an umbrella under which the industry can develop steadily.

A good competitor is a company which has a clear understanding of its own weaknesses and therefore leaves opportunities for others in the market. Within the British banking market after the Big Bang, there was clearly a shortage of good competitors when, once the market was deregulated, many clearing banks acquired diverse activities and offered excessive salaries in areas which they did not understand. The result was overcapacity, collapsing profits and a weakening of the British banking industry generally. A wiser competitor would have been more aware of its strengths and weaknesses and would have avoided ventures which would not only weaken its profitability but also damage the market. In this sense, a company with a limited strategic concept, or a clear idea of the business it is in, is a better competitor than one with wider or more vague statements about its intent. Richard Branson's Virgin Airlines is a far better competitor than was Freddie Laker's ill-fated operation, since Branson had a well-defined target market and limited growth objectives. In contrast, Laker made unrealistic assumptions about his own abilities and the overall effects of price cutting within the market. He was therefore a direct danger to the major operators, whereas Virgin Airlines is not.

A good competitor will have reconcilable goals which make it comfortable within the market in which it operates, less likely to make massive strategic shifts and tolerant of moderate intrusion. Where its strategic stake is moderate, a good competitor may not see market dominance or the maintenance of its own market position as a principal objective. If under pressure, it may be willing to retreat from the market, or when faced with greater opportunities, it may choose to grow elsewhere.

Moderation in desired profitability is also an advantageous characteristic of a competitor. If they are driven by the need to increase the returns obtained, the industry's ability is likely to be disturbed by major investments in new products, promotional activity or price cutting. A company that accepts its current profitability will be a seeker of stability rather than new opportunities.

The desire of a competitor to maintain its cash flow can have a further impact on promoting industry's stability. Most ventures which involve destabilising an industry depend upon investing in research and development, marketing and/or construction of new cost-cutting plant. A company with strict cash requirements is therefore less likely to embark upon such costly ventures.

The reconcilable goals of a good competitor can also provide a beneficial steady pressure upon the other companies within the industry. If a competitor has comparable return on investment targets from its stakeholders it will face similar competitive pressures to the rest of the industry. In contrast, a competitor which is state owned, and therefore does not face the same profitability requirements, or one which is funded from markets with different expectations from one's own, can be unhealthy. Within the European Community, the British Steel Corporation for a long time faced a regulated market against European competitors which were all subsidised heavily by their respective governments. Rather than competing with these, however, it chose to concentrate on speciality steels where the competitors were often in the private sector and therefore faced similarly realistic expectations. In a global context, many firms have found it very difficult competing with the Japanese, who have a lower cost of money from their home stock market, which is also less volatile and responsive to short-term changes than its western counterparts.

A feature of many western companies which has made them good competitors for the Japanese has been their short time horizon. This means that, when faced with adversity, the western companies which the Japanese face have often cut back investment to maintain short-term profitability, or taken a fast route to corporate success rather than investing for internal growth. With the UK market for dried milk products, Cadbury found Carnation a particularly attractive competitor because its American owners were seeking a quick return on their investment while Cadbury, who had a more long-term commitment to the market, was willing to invest to gain market share.

Risk aversion can also lead to a competitor being more attractive. Where there is a fear of making errors, there are likely to be followers within an industry, and this gives more agile companies a chance to gain an advantage when the technology or market changes.

Clearly, finding a market in which the competitors are good on all fronts is unlikely, just as it is impossible to find a market which is completely attractive and consistent with a company's own strengths. But by examining competitors and looking for markets where they tend to be good rather than wayward, a company is likely to face a more stable environment in which opportunities are there to be taken.

The diversity of competition makes it difficult to draw up generic classes of companies which are likely to be good competitors. Some groups can be identified as likely to be good or bad competitors, but in all these cases there are likely to be many exceptions to the rule. Porter identifies smaller divisions of diversified firms as one likely group of good competitors. These may not be viewed as essential to the long-term corporate strategy and often face tough profitability targets. In a global sense, this is particularly true of American multinationals which have shown a remarkable willingness to retreat home when faced with adversity. They are also often given particularly tough profitability objectives with little support or understanding in the overseas market. Part of this comes out of the belief that what is good enough for the home market is good enough for the overseas subsidiaries, and that all the major lessons can be learnt at home (Wright, Saunders and Doyle, 1990).

Another group of potentially good competitors can be old-established companies with a dynastic interest in the industry. This can be because the companies are strong and set high standards but are careful (as in the case of Sainsbury and Marks & Spencer in the UK), or because they are moderate in their expectations (as many British textile companies have been).

Among groups that are unlikely to be good are new entrants from other industries which break the mould of established competition in the markets. In microcomputers these would be Amstrad in the UK and Compaq in the USA. Others could be new entrants into a market which have made major investments and therefore have a large stake in terms of ego and money in making the venture a success. By not understanding the market they may destabilise competition and be willing to forgo profits for a long time. These can be very large companies at times, such as Unilever in the American market, which has a number three position in terms of household products and a desperation to grow in order to become viable; or Japanese automobile companies in Europe and America, which have been building industrial capacity which requires their taking a huge market share in both continents. To the incumbents these are bad competitors. Of course, the issue here is not good or bad from an ethical point of view. They are just bad competitors to compete with, although the new standards they bring to an industry and the services they provide to the consumer can do great good to the consumers and the economies concerned. Moreover, they *are* good at competing, just not good to be competing against.

7.4   Obtaining competitive information

The inability of commanders to obtain and use military intelligence is one of the major reasons for displays of military incompetence (Dixon, 1976). The same is true of competitive intelligence. Also, given the competitive nature of both war and commerce, it is not surprising that the means of gathering information on an enemy or the competition are similar in both method and ethics. And, in both cases, the illegality of methods has not been a barrier to their use. Here we examine the alternative means of gathering competitive information. In doing so, we follow a sequence of declining morality but seek to make no judgement about the ethics of many approaches mentioned.

At the most basic level a company can collect *published statistical information* on competitors and markets. Many companies will have such information on their records from market studies or from published sources on public companies. A problem with many of these sources is their disaggregation and the frequent inconsistency between various government statistics and those provided by a range of marketing research companies. Some of this is due to sampling problems, particularly in some government statistics, such as Business Monitors, where the respondents are little controlled. Although factual and quantitative, this sort of information is limited by its historic basis.

A company's own *propaganda* — in other words, its public relations activities — can add texture to background statistical information. The need to communicate to shareholders and intermediaries in markets means that frequent marketing or technological initiatives are broadcast widely. A danger here, clearly, is the public relations involvement of the competitors. Investigative journalism can lead to more open disclosures, but here again usually the press is dependent upon the goodwill of a company in providing information. Nevertheless, such sources can give a splendid feel for a company's senior executives. In that light the information can be akin to the information that great generals try to gather on each other.

An increasingly frequent source of information on a company is *leakages* from employees which get into the hands of press, either intentionally or unintentionally. Since these often have to be newsworthy items, such information is usually limited in context, but once again it can give texture to other information. Firms which are more aggressive seekers of information may take positive steps in precipitating the giving of information: for instance, by grilling competitors' people at trade shows or conferences, or following plant tours and being a particularly inquisitive member of a party. Although leakages may involve one of the competitor's employees being indiscreet, they do not involve the researching company in unethical activities. Many of the practices which follow hereon may be deemed by some as less worthy.

A company can gather information from *intermediaries* or by posing as an intermediary. Both customers and buyers can have regular contact with competitive companies, and can often be a source of valuable information, particularly to the salespeople or buyers from a researching company with whom they have regular contact. It is also possible to pose as a potential buyer, particularly over the phone, to obtain some factual information such as price, or to obtain performance literature.

Many industries have policies of not recruiting between major companies or, as in the United States, have regulations regarding the nature of an individual's work after he or she has moved from company to company. However, a company would be naive if it did not thoroughly debrief *competitors' former employees* when they join the company and, where there is a strong market leader, it is very common for that company's employees to be recruited by smaller companies. For a long time in the UK Procter and Gamble, and Unilever, for instance, have been a training ground for marketing people in many other industries. When they move they also carry with them a great deal of useful information on their previous employers' products, methods and strategies. Many large employers are very much aware of this and often request people who are leaving to clear their desks and leave immediately once their intent to move is known. Even if competitors' employees are not primarily recruited, the interviewing process itself can often provide useful information, particularly since the person being interviewed may be eager to impress the potential employer.

Surveillance is widely used within counter-espionage but is less common as a means of gathering competitive information. Some of the methods used can be quite innocuous, such as monitoring competitors' employee advertisements or studying aerial photographs. Others are very sensible business practices, such as reverse engineering — that is, tearing apart the competitors' products for analysis. Less acceptable, and certainly less hygienic, is the practice of buying a competitor's garbage to sift for useful memoranda or components. Bugging is a controversial means of surveillance which is becoming more common now that equipment is inexpensive, reliable and small enough to be hidden. Not only have Nixon's American presidential campaign organisers been found using this method, but also Dixons, the retailers, was suspected of doing so during their acquisition of Currys.

Dirty tricks have always been a danger of test marketing, but with the current availability of mini test markets (Saunders, Sharp and Witt, 1987), a new dimension has emerged. Their speed means that while a company is test marketing its products over a matter of months, a competitor can buy supplies, put them through a mini test market, find their market appeal and maybe experiment with alternative defensive strategies, before the test-marketed product is launched. Unilever's subsidiary Van den Berghs is reputed to have done just this when Kraft launched its Carousel margarine. Using mini test markets they were able to find out that, although the Kraft product had a high trial rate, few people adopted it in the long term and therefore it was of no great danger to Unilever's leading products.

A final means of gathering information is the use of *double agents*, either placed in a competitor's company purposely or recruited on to the pay roll while still working for the competitor. One can easily imagine how invaluable such people could be over the long term. We know that such individuals are common in military espionage, although few examples have come to light in business circles. One wonders how many leading companies would be willing to admit that they have been penetrated, even if a double agent were found within them.

7.5 Conclusions

Over the last few years competitive strategy has emerged as one of the major foundations of business strategy. Just as following markets is fundamental to business success, so is a complete understanding of competitors, their strengths, weaknesses and likely responses.

This chapter suggests that the focus of competitor analysis should be on strategic groups but should not neglect other firms in the industry which have the ability to overcome entry barriers or potential entrants to the industry. It provides some frameworks for analysing competitors and suggests the importance of thinking through their likely responses. It also suggests that when entering markets and instituting strategies firms should be looking for 'good' competitors which can stabilise markets, provide opportunities and apply a downward pressure upon performance.

Finally, means of gathering competitive information are presented. Although as important as marketing information, these data are rarely gathered systematically or comprehensively. There is also such a multiplicity of sources which have to be assessed that there is little chance of doing so on an *ad hoc* basis. There is therefore good reason for incorporating a competitive information system within any marketing information system that exists, and having people responsible for ensuring its maintenance. In competitive strategy, just as in war, it is impossible to exaggerate the importance of gathering information on the adversaries a company faces. As Sun

Tzu says: 'An army without spies is like a man without ears or eyes' and, because of this, 'to remain in ignorance of the adversary's condition simply because one grudges the outlay of a few hundred ounces of silver in honours and emoluments, is the height of inhumanity'.

Identifying current and future competitive positions

The third part of the book addresses in closer detail the issues and techniques behind segmentation and positioning research.

Chapter 8 discusses the *principles behind and foundations of segmentation studies* and approaches. Alternative bases for segmenting *consumer* and *industrial* markets are compared. The chapter concludes by discussing approaches to *identifying, validating and describing* market segments.

Chapter 9 examines the techniques of *segmentation research* in detail. Two fundamentally different approaches are discussed. Under the first, termed *a priori*, the bases for segmenting are decided in advance and typically follow product/brand usage patterns (e.g. heavy users) or customer demographic characteristics (e.g. age in consumer markets, SIC in industrial markets). The second approach, *post hoc or cluster based*, searches for segments on the basis of a set of criteria but without preconceived ideas as to what structure in the market will emerge. The chapter goes on to discuss methods of *collecting* segmentation data (relating back to the methods discussed in Chapter 6) and ways of *analysing* those data to identify and describe market segments, and finally addresses the issue of *validating* empirically the segmentation structure uncovered.

Chapter 10 examines *positioning research*. It starts by assessing methods of *identifying competitors*, *position analysis* and *alternative positioning processes*. Evolving positioning is then discussed in relation to *strategic options* open to the organisation.

EIGHT

Segmentation concepts and principles

... the benefits which people are seeking in consuming a given product are the basic reason for the existence of true segmentation.

Haley (1968)

Introduction

A major feature of modern markets is the extent to which many have become segmented. Where there are differences in customer needs or wants, or in their attitudes and predispositions towards the offerings on the market, there are opportunities to segment the market:

If you can divide a larger market into smaller segments with different preferences and subsequently adjust your product (or service) to the preferences in the different segments, then you reduce the overall distance between what you are offering to the market and what the market requires. By doing so the marketer improves his competitive position.

(Hansen, 1972)

Seen in the above light, segmentation is a logical extension of the marketing concept itself.

8.1 Underlying premises

Day *et al.* (1979) argue two underlying premises for effective segmentation of a market. First, customers seek the benefits that products provide rather than the physical products themselves. Under this view a particular product or service constitutes a particular combination of the benefits and their resultant costs. Products and services are seen as 'benefit bundles'.

Second, customers and potential customers view the available benefit bundle alternatives from the vantage point of usage contexts of which they have experience or the specific applications they are considering. It is the usage to which the product or service will be put that dictates the bundle of benefits required. Clearly, where there are different usage contexts requiring a different bundle of benefits, distinct ('use/benefit') market segments exist.

There are three basic propositions behind segmentation as an approach to marketing:

- Customers differ from one another in some respect which could be used to divide the total market. If they do not, if they are totally homogeneous, there is no need or basis on which to segment the market. In reality, all customers differ in some respect. The key to whether a particular difference is useful for segmentation purposes lies in the extent to which the differences are related to different behaviour patterns (e.g. different levels of demand for the product or service, or different use/benefit requirements) or susceptibility to different marketing mix combinations (e.g. different product/service offerings, different media, messages, prices or distribution channels).

- Segments can be identified by measurable characteristics to enable their potential value as a market target to be estimated (see Garda, 1981). Crucial to utilising a segmentation scheme to make better marketing decisions is the ability of the marketing strategist to evaluate segment attractiveness and the current or potential strengths the company has in serving a particular segment. Evaluation of segments and selection of market targets are discussed in Chapter 11.
- Selected segments can be isolated from the remainder of the market, enabling them to be targeted with a distinct market offering. Where segments are not distinct, they do not form a clear target for the company's marketing efforts.

For any segmentation scheme to be useful, it must possess the above three characteristics.

The major issues in segmentation studies centre around the bases on which the segmentation should be conducted and the number of segments relevant to a particular market. The selection of the basis for segmentation is crucial to gaining a clear picture of the nature of the market. The creative selection of different segmentation bases can often help to gain new insights into old market structures which, in turn, may offer new opportunities.

In addition to choosing the relevant bases for segmentation, to make the segments more accessible to marketing strategy, the segments are typically described further on common characteristics. Segments formed, for example, on the basis of brand preference may be further described in terms of customer demographic and attitudinal characteristics to enable relevant media to be selected for promotional purposes and a fuller picture of the chosen segments to be painted.

Below we examine the major bases used in consumer and industrial segmentation studies.

8.2   Bases for segmenting consumer markets

The variables used for segmenting consumer markets can be broadly grouped into three main classes:

- Background customer characteristics.
- Customer attitudes.
- Customer behaviour.

The first two sets of characteristics concern the individual's predisposition to action, whereas the final set concern actual behaviour in the market place.

8.2.1   Background customer characteristics

Often referred to as classificatory information, background characteristics do not change from one purchase situation to another. They are customer specific but not specifically related to his or her behaviour in the particular market of interest.

Background characteristics can be classified along two main dimensions (see Figure 8.1). The first is the origin of the measures. The measures may have been taken from other disciplines and hence are not marketing specific but believed to be related to marketing activity. Non-marketing-specific factors include demographic and socioeconomic characteristics developed in the fields of sociology and demography. Alternatively, they may have been developed specifically by marketing researchers and academics to solve marketing problems. Typically, they have been developed out of dissatisfaction with traditional (sociological) classifications. Dissatisfaction with social class, for example, as a predictor of marketing behaviour has led to the development of life style segmentation and to the ACORN (A Classification Of Residential Neighbourhoods) and related classification schemes.

The second dimension to these characteristics is the way in which they are measured. Factors such as age or sex can be measured objectively, whereas personality and life style (collectively termed 'psychographics') are inferred from often subjective responses to a range of diverse questions.

	OBJECTIVE MEASURES		SUBJECTIVE MEASURES
NON-MARKETING SPECIFIC	**Demographics** Sex, age, geography, subculture **Socioeconomics** Occupation Income Education	P S Y C H O G R A P H I C S	**Personality inventories**
MARKETING SPECIFIC	**Consumer life cycle** **ACORN** **Media usage**		**Life style**

Figure 8.1   Background customer characteristics

Demographic characteristics

Demographic measures such as age and sex of both purchasers and consumers have been one of the most popular methods for segmenting markets.

- *Sex.* A basic segmentation of the market for household consumables and for food purchases is to identify 'housewives' as a specific market segment. For marketing purposes, 'housewives' can include both females and males who have primary responsibility for grocery purchase and household chores. This segmentation of the total potential market of, say, all adults will result in a smaller (around half the size) identified target. Many segmentation schemes use sex (male, female and housewife) as a first step in the segmentation process but then further refine their targets within the chosen sex category — see, for example, Fry and Siller (1970), who examine different social classes within the housewife macrosegment.

- *Age.* Age has been used as a basic segmentation variable in many markets. The market for holidays is a classic example with holiday companies tailoring their products to specific age groups such as 'under-30s' or 'senior citizens'. In these segmentation schemes it is reasoned that there are significant differences in behaviour and product/service requirements between the demographic segments identified.

The main reasons for the popularity of age and sex as segmentation variables have been the ease of measurement of these characteristics (they can be objectively measured) and their usefulness for media selection purposes. Widely available syndicated media research studies present data on viewing and reading habits broken down by these characteristics. Matching media selected to segments described in these terms is, therefore, quite straightforward.

- *Geographic location.* Geographic segmentation may be a useful segmentation variable, particularly for small or medium-sized marketing operations that cannot hope to attack a widely dispersed market. Many companies, for example, choose to market their products only domestically, implicitly excluding world-wide markets from their targets. Within countries it may also be possible to select regional markets where the company's offerings and the market requirements are most closely matched. Haggis, for example, sells best in Scotland, while sales of jellied eels are most successful in the East End of London.

- *Subculture.* Each individual is a member of a variety of subcultures. These subcultures are groups within the overall society which have peculiarities of attitude or behaviour. For a subculture to be of importance for segmentation purposes, Frank *et al.* (1972) proposed two major requirements: (a) that membership of the subculture is relatively enduring and not transient; and (b) that membership of the subculture is of central importance in affecting the individual's attitudes and/or ultimate behaviour.

The major subcultures used for segmentation purposes are typically based on racial, ethnic, religious or geographic similarities. In addition, subcultures existing within specific age groupings may be treated as distinct market segments. Punks, for example, form a distinct segment in the market for popular records.

The major drawback of all the demographic characteristics discussed above as bases for segmenting markets is that they cannot be guaranteed to produce segments which are internally homogeneous but externally heterogeneous in ways of direct relevance to the marketer. Within the same demographic classes there can be individuals who exhibit very different behavioural patterns and who are motivated by quite different wants and needs. Similarly, there may be significant and exploitable similarities in behaviour and motivations between individuals in different demographic segments. As a consequence, a generally low level of correspondence between demographics and behaviour has been found in the academic marketing research literature. Despite these drawbacks, however, their relative ease of measurement makes demographic characteristics popular among marketing practitioners.

Socioeconomic characteristics

Socioeconomic factors, such as income, occupation, terminal education age and social class, have been popular with researchers for similar reasons to demographics: they are easy to measure and can be directly related back to media research for media selection purposes. More importantly, the underlying belief in segmenting markets by social class is that the different classes are expected to have different levels of affluence and to adopt different life styles. These life styles are, in turn, relevant to marketing-related activity, such as propensity to buy certain goods and services.

There are several social class stratification schemes in use by marketing researchers.

Table 8.1 *UK socioeconomic classification scheme*

Class name	Social status	Occupation of head of household
A	Upper middle	Higher managerial, administrative or professional
B	Middle	Intermediate managerial, administrative or professional
C1	Lower middle	Supervisors or clerical, junior managerial, administrative or professional
C2	Skilled working	Skilled manual workers
D	Working	Semi-skilled and unskilled manual workers
E	Those at lowest levels of subsistence	State pensioners or widows, casual or lower-grade workers

In the UK the Market Research Society uses the standard scheme presented in Table 8.1.

For many marketing purposes, the top two and bottom two classes are combined to give a four group standard classification by social class — AB, C1, C2, DE. In the USA several alternative social class schemes have been used for segmentation purposes (see Frank, Massey and Wind, 1972). The most widely adopted, however, is that proposed by Warner (see Table 8.2).

Social class has been used as a surrogate for identifying the style of life that individuals are likely to lead. The underlying proposition is that consumers higher up the social scale tend to spend a higher proportion of their disposable income on future satisfactions (such as insurances and investments), while those lower down the scale spend proportionately more on immediate satisfactions. Socioeconomic class can therefore be particularly useful in identifying segments in markets such as insurance, home purchase, investments, beer and newspapers.

As with the demographic characteristics discussed above, however, it is quite possible that members of the same social class have quite different purchase patterns and reasons for purchase. Consider, for a moment, your peers, people you work with or know socially. The chances are they will be classified in the same social class as

Table 8.2 *The Warner index of status characteristics*

Class name	Description	Consumption characteristics
Upper-upper	Elite social class with inherited social position	Expensive, irrelevant, but purchase decisions not meant to impress; conservative
Lower-upper	*Nouveau riche*; highly successful business and professional; position acquired through wealth	Conspicuous consumption to demonstrate wealth, luxury cars, large estates, etc.
Upper-middle	Successful business and professional	Purchases directed at projecting successful image
Lower-middle	White-collar workers, small businesspeople	Concerned with social approval; purchase decisions; conservative; home and family oriented
Upper-lower	Blue-collar workers, technicians, skilled workers	Satisfaction of family roles
Lower-lower	Unskilled labour, poorly educated, poorly off	Attraction to cheap, 'flashy', low-quality items; heavy exposure to TV

you. The chances also are that they will be attracted to different sorts of products, motivated by different factors and make quite different brand choices.

Concern has been expressed among both marketing practitioners and academics that social class is becoming increasingly less useful as a segmentation variable. Lack of satisfaction with social class in particular, and with other non-marketing-specific characteristics as segmentation variables, has led to the development of marketing-specific measures such as stage of customer life cycle, the ACORN classification system and the development of life style research.

Stage of consumer life cycle

Stage of the family life cycle, essentially a composite demographic variable incorporating factors such as age, marital status and family size, has been particularly useful in identifying the types of people most likely to be attracted to a product field (especially consumer durables) and when they will be attracted. The producers of baby products, for example, build mailing lists of households with new-born babies on the basis of free gifts given to mothers in maternity hospitals. These lists are dated and used to direct advertising messages for further baby, toddler and child products to the family at the appropriate time as the child grows.

Stage of family life cycle was first developed as a market segmentation tool by Wells and Gubar (1966) and has since been updated and modified by Murphy and Staples (1979) to take account of changing family patterns. The basic life cycle stages identified are presented in Table 8.3.

In some instances, segmentation by life cycle can help directly with product design, as is the case with package holidays. In addition to using age as a segmentation variable, holiday firms target very specifically on different stages of the life cycle, from the Club Med emphasis on young singles, to Butlins family holidays and coach operators' holidays for senior citizens.

■ In the UK the Research Services Ltd marketing research company have developed a segmentation scheme based on a combination of consumer life cycle, occupation and income. The scheme, termed SAGACITY, defines four main life cycle stages (dependent, pre-family, family and late), two income levels (better off and worse off) and two occupational groupings (white collar and blue collar — ABC1 and C2DE). On the basis of these three variables, 12 distinct SAGACITY groupings are identified with different aspirations and behaviour patterns (see Crouch, 1984). ■

ACORN and related classificatory systems

As a direct challenge to the socioeconomic classification system, the ACORN (A Classification Of Residential Neighbourhoods) system was developed by the CACI Market Analysis Group. The system is based on population census data and classifies residential neighbourhoods into 36 types within 11 main groups (see Table 8.4). The groupings were derived through a clustering of responses to census data required by law on a ten-yearly basis. The groupings reflect neighbourhoods with similar characteristics.

Early uses of ACORN were by local authorities to isolate areas of inner-city deprivation (the idea came from a sociologist working for local authorities), but it

Table 8.3 *Stages of the family life cycle*

Stage	Financial circumstances and purchasing characteristics
Bachelor stage Young, single, not living at parental home	Few financial burdens, recreation oriented; holidays, entertainments outside home
Newly wed Young couples, no children	Better off financially, two incomes; purchase home, some consumer durables
Full nest I Youngest child under 6	Home purchasing peak; increasing financial pressures, may have only one income earner; purchase of household 'necessities'
Full nest II Youngest child over 6	Financial position improving; some working spouses
Full nest III Older married couples with dependent children	Financial position better still; update household products and furnishings
Empty nest I Older married couples, no children at home	Home ownership peak; renewed interest in travel and leisure activities; buy luxuries
Empty nest II Older couples, no children at home, retired	Drastic cut in income; medical services bought
Solitary survivor Still in labour force	Income good but likely to sell home
Solitary survivor Retired	Special needs for medical care, affection and security

Table 8.4 *ACORN: a classification of residential neighbourhoods*

ACORN group	Description
A	Agricultural areas
B	Modern family housing, higher incomes
C	Older housing of intermediate status
D	Poor-quality older terraced housing
E	Better-off council estates
F	Less well-off council estates
G	Poorest council estates
H	Multiracial areas
I	High-status, non-family areas
J	Affluent suburban housing
K	Better-off retirement areas

was soon seen to have direct marketing relevance, particularly because the data base enabled post codes to be ascribed to each ACORN type. Hence its use particularly in direct mail marketing.

Personality characteristics

Personality characteristics are more difficult to measure than demographics or socio-economics. They are generally inferred from large sets of questions, often involving detailed computational (multivariate) analysis techniques.

Several personality inventories have been used by segmentation researchers. Most notable are the Gordon Personal Profile (see Sparks and Tucker, 1971), the Edwards Personal Preference Schedule (see Alpert, 1972), the Cattell 16-Personality Factor Inventory (see, for example, Oxx, 1972) and the Jackson Personality Inventory (see Kinnear, Taylor and Ahmed, 1974). All were developed by psychologists for reasons far divorced from market segmentation studies and have, understandably, achieved only varied levels of success when applied to segmentation problems.

Perhaps the main value of personality measures lies in creating the background atmosphere for advertisements and, in some instances, package design and branding. Research to date, however, conducted primarily in the USA, has identified few clear relationships between personality and behaviour. In most instances, personality measures are most likely to be of use for describing segments once they have been defined on some other basis. As with the other characteristics discussed above, it is quite possible, indeed probable, that behaviour and reasons behind it will vary within segments defined on the basis of personality characteristics alone.

Life style characteristics

In an attempt to make personality measures developed in the field of psychology more relevant to marketing decisions, life style research was pioneered by advertising agencies in the USA and the UK in the early 1970s. This research attempts to isolate market segments on the basis of the style of life adopted by their members. At one stage these approaches were seen as alternatives to the social class categories discussed above.

Life style segmentation is concerned with three main elements: activities (such as leisure-time activities, sports, hobbies, entertainments, home activities, work activities, professional work, shopping behaviour, housework and repairs, travel and miscellaneous activities, daily travel, holidays, education, charitable work); interaction with others (such as self-perception, personality and self-ideal, role perceptions as mother, wife, husband, father, son, daughter, etc., communication, social interaction, communications with others, opinion leadership); and opinions (on topics such as politics, social and moral issues, economic and business—industry issues, technological and environmental issues).

A typical study would develop a series of statements (in some instances over 200 have been used!) and respondents would be asked to agree or disagree with them on a five- or seven-point agree/disagree scale. Using factor analysis and cluster analysis, groups of respondents are identified with similar activities, interests and opinions.

■ Segnit and Broadbent (1973), for example, found six male and seven female life style segments on the basis of responses to 230 statements. These have been used to segment markets by both publishers of newspapers (such as the *Financial Times* and *Radio Times*) and manufacturers (Beecham used the technique successfully to segment the shampoo market in the mid-1970s).

Martini advertising is directed at individuals on the basis of what life style they would like to have. It appeals to 'aspirational life style' segments.

Richards and Sturman (1977) report the use of life style as a basis for segmenting the market for brassières, identifying five segments: conservatives; fashion conscious; brand conscious; outgoing; and home/price oriented. ■

The most significant advantages of life style research are again for guiding the creative content of advertising. Because of the major tasks involved in gathering the data, however, it is unlikely that life style research will supplant demographics as a major segmentation variable.

Summary of background customer characteristics

The background customer characteristics discussed above all examine the individual in isolation from the specific market of interest. While in some markets they may be able to discriminate between probable users and non-users of the product class, they can rarely explain brand choice behaviour. Members of the same segments based on background characteristics may behave differently in the market place for a variety of reasons. Similarly, members of different segments may be seeking essentially the same things from competing brands and could be usefully grouped together. While traditionally useful for the purposes of media selection and advertising atmosphere design, these characteristics are often too general in nature to be of specific value to marketers. They are essentially descriptive: they describe who the consumer is, but they do not uncover the basic reasons why the consumer behaves as he or she does.

8.2.2   Attitudinal characteristics

Attitudinal characteristics attempt to draw a causal link between customer characteristics and marketing behaviour. Attitudes to the product class under investigation and attitudes towards brands on the market have both been used as fruitful bases for market segmentation.

Benefit segmentation

Benefit segmentation (Haley, 1968 and 1984) examines the benefits customers are seeking in consuming the product. Segmenting on the basis of benefits sought has been applied to a wide variety of markets such as banking, fast-moving consumer products and consumer durables. The building society investment market, for example, can be initially segmented on the basis of the benefits being sought by the customers. Typical benefits sought include high rates of interest (for the serious investor), convenient access (for the occasional investor) and security (for the 'rainy day' investor).

Benefit segmentation takes the basis of segmentation right back to the underlying reasons why customers are attracted to various product offerings. As such it is perhaps the closest means yet to identifying segments on bases directly relevant to marketing decisions. Developments in techniques such as conjoint analysis make them particularly suitable for identifying benefit segments (Hooley, 1982).

Perceptions and preferences

A second approach to the study of attitudes is through the study of perceptions and preferences. Much of the work in the multidimensional scaling area (Hooley, 1980) is primarily concerned with identifying segments of respondents who view the products on offer in a similar way (perceptual space segmentation) and require from the market similar features or benefits (preference segmentation). This approach to market segmentation is discussed further in Chapter 9.

Summary of attitudinal bases for segmentation

Segmentation on the basis of attitudes, both to the product class and the various brands on offer, can create a more useful basis for marketing strategy development than merely background characteristics. It gets closer to the underlying reasons for behaviour and uses them as the basis for segmenting the market. The major drawback of such techniques is that they require often costly primary research and sophisticated data analysis techniques.

8.2.3   Behavioural characteristics

The most direct method of segmenting markets is on the basis of the behaviour of the consumers in those markets. Behavioural segmentation covers purchases, consumption, communication and response to elements of the marketing mix.

Purchasing behaviour

Study of purchasing behaviour has centred around time of purchase (early or late in the product's overall life cycle) and patterns of purchase (identification of brand-loyal customers).

- *Innovators*. Because of their importance when new products are launched, innovators (those who purchase a product when it is still new) have received much attention from marketers. Clearly, during the launch of new products isolation of innovators as the initial target segment could significantly improve the product's or service's chances of acceptance on the market.

  Innovative behaviour, however, is not necessarily generalisable to many different product fields. Attempts to seek out generalised innovators have been less successful than looking separately for innovators in a specific field. Generalisations seem most relevant when the fields of study are of similar interest.

● *Brand loyalty.* Variously defined, brand loyalty has also been used as a basis for segmentation. While innovators are concerned with initial purchase, loyalty patterns are concerned with repeat purchase. As such they are more applicable to repeat purchase goods than to consumer durables, though they have been used in durables markets (see the example below). As with innovative behaviour research, it has not been possible to identify consumers who exhibit loyal behaviour over a wide variety of products. Loyalty, like innovativeness, is specific to a particular product field.

■ Volkswagen, the German automobile manufacturer, has used loyalty as a major method for segmenting its customer markets. It divides its customers into the following categories: first-time buyers; replacement buyers — (a) model-loyal replacers, (b) company-loyal replacers and (c) switch replacers. These segments are used to analyse performance and market trends, and for forecasting purposes. ■

Consumption behaviour

Purchasers of products and services are not necessarily the consumers, or users, of those products or services. Examination of usage patterns and volumes consumed (as in the heavy user approach) can pinpoint where to focus marketing activity. There are dangers, however, in focusing merely on the heavy users. They are, for example, already using the product in quantity and therefore may not offer much scope for market expansion. Similarly, they will be either current company customers or customers of competitors.

In the latter case, brand loyalty patterns may be set and competition could be fierce. Companies may be better advised to research further the light or non-users of the product to find out why they do not consume more of the product. In the growth stage of the product life cycle the heavy user segment may well be attractive; but when the market reaches maturity it may make more sense to try to extend the market by mopping up extra potential demand in markets that are not adequately served by existing products.

Product and brand usage has a major advantage over many other situation-specific segmentation variables in that it can be elicited, in the case of many consumer products, from secondary sources. The 'heavy users' of beer, for example, can be identified through the Target Group Index (TGI) (see Chapter 6) and their demographic and media habits profiled. For this main reason consumption is one of the most popular bases for segmenting consumer markets in the UK.

Communication behaviour

A further behavioural variable used in consumer segmentation studies has been the degree of communication with others about the product of interest.

Opinion leaders can be particularly influential in the early stages of the product life cycle. Record companies, for example, recognise the influence that disc jockeys have on the record-buying public and attempt to influence them with free records and other inducements to play their records. In many fields, however, identifying opinion leaders is not so easy. As with innovators, opinion leaders tend to lead opinion only in their own interest areas. A further problem with satisfying opinion leaders is that they tend to have fairly strong opinions themselves and can often be a very heterogeneous group (the 'pop' disc jockeys providing a good example).

In addition to information-giving behaviour (as displayed by opinion leaders), markets could be segmented on the basis of information-seeking behaviour. The information seekers may be a particularly attractive segment for companies basing their strategy on promotional material with a heavy information content.

Response to elements of the marketing mix

The use of elasticities of response to changes in marketing mix variables as a basis for segmentation is particularly attractive as it can lead to more actionable findings, indicating where marketing funds could best be allocated. Identifying, for example, the deal-prone consumer or the advertising-responsive segment has immediate appeal. There are, however, methodological problems in research to identify factors such as responsiveness to changes in price.

Summary of bases for segmentation

Many variables have been tested as bases for consumer segmentation, ranging from behaviour, to attitudes to background characteristics. The most used characteristics are product and brand usage and demographics/socioeconomics, primarily because of the ease of obtaining this sort of data from secondary sources. Ultimately, however, for a segmentation scheme to be useful to marketing management it should seek not only to describe differences in consumers but also to explain them. In this respect attitudinal segmentation can offer better prospects.

8.3   Bases for segmenting industrial markets

As with consumer markets, a variety of factors have been suggested for segmenting industrial markets. Indeed, industrial segmentation variables can be considered under the same headings.

8.3.1   Background company characteristics

Demographic characteristics of companies can be a useful starting point for industrial segmentation. Factors such as the Standard Industry Classification (SIC) and the geographic location can be particularly useful first-stage segmentation variables. In addition, factors such as number of employees or turnover can give an indication of the potential value of various customer segments. For example, companies selling ingredients for paint manufacture in the UK could initially segment the market by SIC to identify paint manufacturers, then by size of company as indicated by number of employees (there are only seven companies employing more than 750 employees and together they account for over 60 per cent of the paint market).

8.3.2   Attitudinal characteristics

It is possible also to segment industrial markets on the basis of the benefits being sought by the purchasers. An added complication in industrial markets, however, is the decision-making unit or DMU (see Chapter 6). For many industrial purchases, decisions are made or influenced by a group of individuals rather than a single purchaser. Different members of the DMU will often have different perceptions of what the benefits are, both to their organisation and to themselves.

In the purchase of hoists, for example, the important benefit to a user may be lightness and ease of use, whereas the purchasing manager may be looking for a cheaper product to make his or her purchasing budget go further. Architects specifying installations for new plant may perceive greater benefit in aesthetically designed hoists, and maintenance personnel may look for easy maintenance as a prime benefit.

Benefit segmentation, however, is at the centre of conventional wisdom on industrial selling, which emphasises selling benefits rather than features in any product or service. In communicating with the different members of the DMU, different benefits may be emphasised for each.

8.3.3   Behavioural characteristics

Even more so than in consumer markets, the 80/20 rule (80 per cent of sales typically being accounted for by only 20 per cent of customers) dominates many industrial markets. Identifying the major purchasers for products and services through volume purchased can be particularly useful. Also of interest may be the final use to which the product or service is put. Where, for example, the final consumer can be identified, working backwards can suggest a sensible segmentation strategy.

■   The paint market, for example, can be segmented at various levels. At the first level it can be divided into 'decorative paints', mainly used on buildings, and 'industrial paints', used in manufactured products. In 1982 general industrial paints by volume represented 24 per cent of the market, the automobile industry 14 per cent, professional decorative 42 per cent, and DIY decorative 22 per cent. Demand for vehicle paints relates to automobile sales (derived demand) and relates closely to demand in this market. In the general industrial paints sector there are various specialist segments such as marine coatings. Here ultimate product use dictates the type of paint and its properties, and is the basic method for segmentation (Chisnall, 1985).   ■

8.3.4   Summary of bases for segmenting industrial markets

The segmentation bases available for industrial marketing follow industrial buying behaviour, as those in consumer marketing follow consumer behaviour. Because of the presence, however, of particularly large individual customers in many industrial markets, usage-based segmentation is often employed. For smaller companies, geographic segmentation may be attractive, limiting their markets to those that are more easily served. Ultimately, however, in industrial and consumer markets the basic rationale for segmentation is that groups of buyers exist with different needs or wants (benefits sought), and it is segmentation on the basis of needs and wants that offers the closest approximation to implementing the marketing concept.

8.4 Identifying and describing market segments

It will be clear from the above that the first task the manager must face is to decide on what basis to segment the market. If product usage or background characteristics are selected, in many markets the segmentation can be accomplished from secondary sources (e.g. from TGI or AGB/TCA in consumer markets, or from SIC or Kompass in industrial markets). Where segmentation is being based on attitudes, however, there will often be insufficient data available from secondary sources. In these cases primary research will be necessary.

A typical primary research segmentation study could include initial qualitative research to identify major benefits to users and purchasers of the product or service under consideration. This would be followed by quantitative research to estimate the size of the potential segments and further to describe them in terms of other background characteristics. This methodological approach is described by Haley (1968).

8.4.1   First-order and second-order segmentation

There is a popular misconception among many marketing managers as to what constitutes a market segment.

In consumer marketing in particular, many managers will often describe the segmentation of their market and their selected market targets in terms of customer background characteristics. Thus, for example, a marketer of quality wines might describe the segmentation of the market in terms of social class, the prime target being the ABC1 social classes. From the above, however, it can be seen that this way of segmenting the market only makes sense if all ABC1s purchase quality wine for the same reasons. Where use/benefits of wine purchase differ substantially within a given social class, there is the opportunity to segment the market in a more fundamental way.

In reality, as the quote by Haley at the start of this chapter makes clear, the most fundamental way of segmenting markets is the marketing-oriented approach of grouping together customers who are looking for the same benefits in using the product or service. All other bases for segmenting markets are really an approximation to this. The wine marketer assumes that all ABC1s have similar benefit needs from the wines they purchase. Hence use/benefit segmentation can be referred to as *first-order segmentation*. Any attempt to segment a market should commence by looking for different use/benefit segments.

Within identified use/benefit segments, however, there could be large numbers of customers with very different backgrounds, media habits, levels of consumption and so on. Particularly where there are many offerings attempting to serve the same use/benefit segment, concentration on sub-segments within the segment can make sense. Sub-segments, for example, who share common media habits can form more specific targets for the company's offerings. Further segmentation within use/benefit segments can be termed *second-order segmentation*. Second-order segmentation is used to improve the ability of the company to tailor the marketing mix within a first-order segment.

In the wine example, the marketing manager may have identified a first-order segmentation in terms of the uses to which the wine was being put (e.g. as a meal accompaniment, as a home drink, as a social drink, as a cooking ingredient). The quality level of the wine might suggest use in the first segment as a meal accompaniment. Further research would then reveal within this segment further benefit requirements (e.g. price bands individual customers are prepared to consider, character of the wine preferred, etc).

Having further refined the target through matching the company's offerings to specific customer group requirements, the marketer may still find a wide variety of potential customers for the wines. Within the identified first-order segment, sub-segments based on demographic characteristics could be identified (e.g. AB social class, aged 35–55, male purchaser), enabling a clearer refinement of the marketing strategy.

8.5   The benefits of segmenting markets

There are a number of benefits that can be derived from segmenting a market:

- Segmentation is a particularly useful approach to marketing for the smaller company. It allows target markets to be matched to company competencies and makes it more possible for the smaller company to create a defensible niche in the market.
- It helps to identify gaps in the market: that is, unserved or underserved segments. These can provide areas for new product development or extension of the existing product or service range.
- In mature or declining markets it may be possible to identify specific segments that are still in growth. Concentrating on growth segments when the overall market is declining is a major strategy in the later stages of the product life cycle.
- Segmentation enables the marketer to more closely match a product or service to the needs of the target market. In this way a stronger competitive position can be built.
- The dangers of not segmenting the market when competitors do should also be emphasised. The competitive advantages noted above can be lost to competitors if the company fails to take advantage of them. A company practising a mass marketing strategy in a clearly segmented market against competitors operating a focused strategy can find itself falling between many stools.

8.6 Conclusions

In the increasingly fragmented markets of the 1990s and beyond, marketers are turning more and more to segmentation methods to identify prime market targets. A major decision facing most companies is what basis to segment on. There are a great many potential bases for segmentation in consumer and industrial, product and service and non-profit marketing.

Arguably the closest to extending the marketing concept, however, is the use/benefit segmentation approach suggested by Haley (1968) and developed by Day *et al.* (1979). While it does require considerable primary investigation, understanding the benefits customers derive in buying and/or consuming products and services is central to designing an integrated marketing strategy. The next chapter on segmentation research shows how these and other bases for segmentation can be developed.

NINE

Segmentation research

> ... researchers are anxious to find a magic formula that will profitably segment the market in all cases and under all circumstances. As with the medieval alchemist looking for the philosopher's stone, this search is bound to end in vain.
>
> Baumwoll (1974)

Introduction

Segmentation increases the effectiveness of marketing by accepting that people are neither all the same nor completely unalike. Instead of this, segmentation recognises the heterogeneity of markets but points to the efficient marketing practice of grouping potential customers into segments who tend to be homogeneous in their response to elements of the marketing mix. This allows scarce resources to be concentrated through a marketing mix designed to appeal to target market segments. Segmentation, therefore, has two elements: the theory of splitting markets into heterogeneous groups; and resource allocation to those groups using the marketing mix. This chapter focuses on how to identify the heterogeneous groups of customers who can be defined as segments. Chapter 11 and subsequent chapters then concentrate on the selection target segments and ways of approaching them.

Although it is a central part of most marketing programmes, there are circumstances in which segmentation may not be appropriate. A company following a segmented approach has either to choose a single market segment at which to aim, and therefore have a marketing mix which is inappropriate for other customers, or develop a series of marketing mixes appropriate for customer segments with different needs. Within British retailing the two approaches have clearly been used by Next, which expanded its retailing chains to cater for more and more needs of young professionals, and the Burton Group, which has used the differently positioned Top Shops, Evans, Harvey Nichols stores etc. to appeal to a variety of segments.

Both of these approaches have limitations. A single-focus company has limitations to its size because the market segment itself is limited. Therefore, like Next, it may be forced to attempt to sell an ever-increasing range of products to the same group of customers. This, of course, would be less of a problem to a small to medium-sized company following the dictum, 'Think small, stay small'. A company taking the multiple segment approach may face a diseconomy in managing, supplying and promoting in a different way to each of the segments it has chosen.

In some cases an economic alternative is to use an undifferentiated mix designed to appeal to as many segments as possible. The company does not fine tune its offering to any one segment but hopes to attract a sufficient number of customers from all segments with one mix. The company can, therefore, benefit from economies of scale in a simple operation, but may be damaged by the 'sameness' of the mix not appealing to the customers in each segment completely, or by better targeted competitors.

The appropriateness of segmenting or not segmenting depends on economies of scale, the cost of developing separate marketing mixes, and the homogeneity of needs of different markets — issues that are pursued more deeply in Chapter 11. Such are the similarities in demand for petroleum and retail grocery that the products being supplied by competitors converge as they all seek to develop a mix with broad market appeal. Certainly segments do exist, but they are not of significant magnitude or difference to justify separate appeals. The aerospace industry and automobile industry

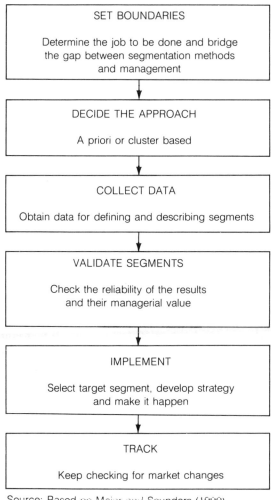

Source: Based on Maier and Saunders (1990).

Figure 9.1 A model for segmentation research

have markets which are diverse but in which development and manufacturing costs are such that it is not feasible to develop products to fit exactly all market needs. The successful companies therefore focus on a relatively small product range with variations which appeal to individual customer preferences.

However, even in markets whose main body does not demand segmentation there are often small-scale opportunities where companies can survive by pursuing a focus strategy: for instance, Marks & Spencer in food and Rolls-Royce in supplying the luxury car market. So, even in markets where the major players may be using a mass strategy, segmentation offers an opportunity for some smaller participants. For companies with small market share in particular, the rule is segment, segment, segment!

Whereas Chapter 8 concentrated on the role of segmentation and positioning, this chapter follows the process of identifying usable market segments. In doing this it follows a model developed by Maier and Saunders (1990) which takes segmentation research from entry to tracking. Within this framework the wide range of bases and algorithms for segmentation are explained (see Figure 9.1).

9.1   Setting the boundaries

Segmentation needs both market and technical expertise. This often necessitates a dialogue between a manager commissioning a segmentation study and an agency or individual conducting the necessary research. The value of the final segmentation results will depend on the effort the individuals concerned have taken in bridging the gap between the technical requirements of segmentation methods and the practical knowledge of marketing and sales management.

It is customary to see this bridge-building role as a responsibility of the modeller or marketing scientist, but since the marketing manager is going to depend on the results and is going to be responsible for implementing them, he or she has a vested interest in ensuring that a mutual understanding is achieved. Whereas the expert or modeller faces rejection if the technical gap is not bridged, the marketing manager may face failure in the market place if the relationship fails. When employing an agency, the marketing manager will certainly need to know how to cross-examine the agency to ensure its methods are appropriate and its assumptions valid.

The marketing scientist's entry into the segmentation process is similar to opening a sale. If good initial relationships are not formed, the chance of further progress is slight (Zunin, 1972). The marketing scientist has to establish his or her credibility by demonstrating personal expertise while fitting into the client's culture. As in selling, the prior gathering of information about the industry, the company and the personnel is beneficial. A grasp of terminology popular in the company is particularly useful. This preparation accelerates the formation of the mutual understanding thought necessary for successful model implementation (Duncan, 1974).

The role of the salesperson and the marketing scientist should be different because, although a salesperson usually has a limited set of products to sell, the marketing scientist should theoretically be able to choose without bias from a wide portfolio of appropriate techniques. Unfortunately, this perspective is an ideal, for many marketing scientists and agencies have a predisposition towards techniques with which they are familiar. So, in commissioning segmentation research, the marketing manager has to have sufficient knowledge to resist being supplied from a limited portfolio of solutions. On the other hand, in practice, it is not undesirable for the marketing scientists to favour methods they can champion and use effectively (Urban, 1974). The recommended communication pattern for implementation (Little, 1970 and 1975), therefore, falls somewhere between persuasion and mutual understanding (Churchman and Schainblatt, 1965).

The major lessons for entry are that the first contact is critical and that successful segmentation depends upon the marketing manager and the marketing scientist being sympathetic to each other's needs; not necessarily knowing each other's business perfectly, but certainly having the ability to ask the right questions.

At this stage it is unrealistic to fix marketing and financial objectives for the study, but it is necessary to agree the focus: that is, the product market to be investigated and the benefits sought. Multiproduct companies may choose to start with one application and proceed to others if the trial is successful. There may also be market structures — such as the division between industrial and consumer markets — which suggest a two-stage approach: the first stage breaking the market down into easily definable groups, and the second being involved with the segmentation analysis proper. In their segmentation analysis of the general practitioner (GP) market, Maier and Saunders (1990) used such a process by first dividing doctors into general practitioners and hospital doctors, this distinction being necessary because of the different jobs of the two groups. The second stage then focused upon the determining product usage segments within the GP market.

Agreeing on a focus reduces the chance of initial misunderstandings leading to dissatisfaction with the final results. It may also identify staff who could be consulted because of their required involvement at a later stage: for example, R & D staff, if the aim is to identify new product opportunities; or sales people, if the objective is sales allocation. At this stage participants are both learning and setting objectives. It may, therefore, be appropriate to start with an orientation seminar for managers on the state of the art of segmentation and model building (Little, 1975). This could be designed to conclude with a discussion and agreement of the focus of the segmentation project.

9.2 Deciding the approach

Strategies are fundamentally affected by the way a market is segmented, yet the segmentation methods available are so numerous that an exhaustive evaluation is impractical. However, a consensus has emerged which suggests that some criteria work better than others in certain applications. Table 9.1 is based on Wind's (1978)

Table 9.1 *Preferred bases for segmentation*

Bases	Applications					
	Understanding the market	Positioning	New product concept	Pricing decision	Advertising decision	Distribution decision
Benefits	✔	✔	✔		✔	✔
Purchase and usage	✔	✔				
Needs	✔					
Brand loyalty	✔					
Product preference		✔				
Reaction to new concepts			✔			
Price sensitivity				✔		
Deal proneness				✔		
Price sensitivity by usage				✔		
Media usage					✔	
Psychographic					✔	
Store patronage						✔
Hybrid	✔	✔			✔	

Source: Based on Y. Wind (1972) 'Issues and advances in segmentation research', *Journal of Marketing Research*, vol. 15, no. 1, p. 320, published by the American Marketing Association.

breakdown of preferred methods, but published information does not allow the table to be entirely comprehensive.

9.2.1   A priori methods

A priori, or off-the-peg methods appear to be the easiest way of segmenting markets. In their original form the process involved searching among demographic or socio-graphic characteristics (Figures 8.1 to 8.4), and identifying which of these form significant splits within the market place. Usually the search for appropriate criteria would be guided by some expectation of how the market could be divided.

There are some clear cases where a priori methods have proved a powerful tool for segmenting markets. The successful toy company Lego, for example, has carefully developed its assembly toys to fit the development of children from birth to mid-teens. Duplo, its pre-school product, starts with rattles and manipulative toys which are not immediately intended for assembly but do have fixture mechanisms which allow the child to progress into Duplo proper (chunky and brightly coloured bricks and shapes which can be assembled into all manner of toys). Duplo overlaps with Lego, a system of building bricks upon which the Lego empire was formed. Almost identical to Duplo parts in every other way, the Lego units are half the size and therefore suitable for a child's enhanced manipulative ability, and they allow more detail in construction. They are also cleverly designed to link with the Duplo units and therefore allow relatively easy progression from one to the other.

Another demographic segmentation criterion, from the life cycle, has been successfully applied in the package holiday market: in particular, Club 18–30 aimed at the single person or young marrieds, and Saga aimed at pensioners.

Despite their ease of use and intuitive appeal, attempts to validate an a priori basis for segmentation have met with little success. One of the earliest reported attempts to validate this approach was by Evans (1959), who sought to use demographic variables to distinguish between Ford and Chevrolet owners in the United States. He concluded that 'demographic variables is not a sufficiently powerful predictor to be of much practical use . . . [they] point more to the similarity of Ford and Chevrolet owners than to any means of discriminating between them. Analysis of several other objective factors also leads to the same conclusion.'

In other markets the conclusions have been similar. An Advertising Research Foundation study (Hildegaard and Krueger, 1968) into grocery products compared toilet tissue purchase behaviour with 15 socioeconomic characteristics to find that the predictive efficiency of the characteristics was virtually nil. Earlier Koponen (1960) had used J. Walter Thompson panel data on beer, coffee and tea to find similar results. An even bigger study by Frank, Massey and Boyd (1968) used panel data to compare 57 product categories ranging from foods to household products with demographic characteristics. Some relationships were found but no more than could have been expected to occur by chance if the data were random. Unfortunately, study after study throws doubt upon the direct usefulness of demographic characteristics as a predictor for product purchase.

These findings do not dispute the certainty that some products with clearly defined target consumers depend heavily on demographic characteristics: for instance, nappies purchased by families with babies, incontinence pads by older people and sanitary towels by women. However, evidence does seem to show that demographic characteristics alone are incapable of distinguishing between the subtle differences in markets which are not explained by the physiological differences between human beings.

9.2.2   Cluster-based a priori methods

Recently the traditional demographic and socioeconomic means of off-the-peg segmentation has been supplemented by more sophisticated methods being promoted by advertising and market research agencies. These encompass the subjective methods and the marketing-specific objective measures in Figure 8.1. Of these new techniques personality inventories were the first to be developed. As a consequence they are also those most widely investigated. Unfortunately, tests show them to be as unreliable as the less sophisticated demographic and socioeconomic methods.

In the analysis of the automobile market (Westfall, 1962) and food (Kamen, 1964) no evidence of consistency among personality groups was found. Although these measures do not seem to be universally strong, however, they do appear to have some slight discriminating power for high-involvement products such as deodorants and cigarettes. For instance, Koponen (1960) found some minimal difference between smokers and non-smokers on such variables as sex, aggression, achievement, dominance and compliance. However, the percentage of variance accounted for by both personality variables and demographic variables combined was less than 12 per cent.

Tucker and Painter (1961) studied numerous products to find significant but weak relationships between product preference and responsibility, emotional stability, sociability and ascendancy. But among all the products studied, personality variables only differentiated between the users of deodorants and cigarettes. Compared with demographic and socioeconomic off-the-peg methods, personality inventories appeared to have a slight but insubstantial advantage. They do appear to be able to discriminate to a small extent between some high-involvement products, but even in these cases they leave the majority of variance unexplained. Like demographic and socioeconomic methods, they appear to have a power to discriminate in markets where their measurement has a clear role, such as in smoking which reflects a drug dependency and in deodorants which suggest anxiety. However, the subtlety of personality measurement renders it less useful as an off-the-peg measure in most cases because the personality differences are less strong and obvious than the physiological differences which demographics can measure: introversion and dependency are well-defined personality traits but they are nowhere near as easily measured or as linked to behaviour as gender or age.

The introduction of CACI's ACORN geodemographic data base represented one of the biggest steps forward in segmentation and targeting techniques. Its basis was segments derived from published census information which provides a classification of neighbourhood based on housing types. Although the measure is crude, the great strength of the service depends on CACI's own research linking the neighbourhood groups to demographics and buyer behaviour, together with the ability to target households. The system, therefore, provides a direct link between off-the-peg segmentation and individuals, unlike earlier methods which only provided indirect means of contacting the demographic or personality segments identified.

Like the other a priori techniques, the limitations of CACI's approach are the variability within neighbourhoods and the similarity between their buying behaviour for many product classes. English (1989) provides an example of this where five enumeration districts (individual neighbourhood groups of 150 households) are ranked according to geodemographic techniques. Of the five, two were identified as being prime mailing prospects. However, when individual characteristics were investigated, the five groups were found to contain 31, 14, 10, 10 and 7 prospects respectively: the enumeration districts had been ranked according to the correct number of prospects, but neighbourhood classifications alone appeared to be a poor method of targeting. With only 31 prime target customers being in the most favoured enumeration district, 119 out of 150 households would have been mistargeted.

To be fair, like other means of off-the-peg segmentation discussed, geodemographics are powerful when related to products linked directly to characteristics of the neighbourhood districts: for instance, the demand for double glazing or gardening equipment. Even in the case provided, targeting upon the best enumeration districts increases the probability of hitting a target customer from less than 10 per cent to over 20 per cent, but misses are still more common than hits.

Life style segmentation provides an opportunity to overlay geodemographic data with life style characteristics. In this descriptive form they have existed for some time and have been associated with the original success of Storehouse's Habitat chain or the success of the Conservative Party in the 1986 general election. Life style characteristics have sometimes been used in conjunction with demographics, forming the second part of a two-stage segmentation. Third Age Research has done this after first identifying the over-65s as a target market and then breaking them up into life style segments of apathetic, comfortable, explorer, fearful, organiser, poor me, social lion, and status quo. To anyone who has contact with more than one older person, it is clear that these labels provide a much more powerful way of putting a face on the over-65s customer than does his or her age alone.

Recent developments have linked life style segments to customer data bases. In the UK there are currently four of these, all of which are established, successful and growing (Coad, 1989):

- *The Lifestyle Selector.* This is a UK data base started in 1985 by the American National Demographics and Lifestyle Company. The Lifestyle Selector collects data from questionnaires packed with consumer durables or from retailers and holds over 4.5 million returned, self-completed questionnaires.
- *Behaviour Bank.* This is the UK service provided by the American Computerised Marketing Technologies company. This collects its data from syndicated questionnaires distributed directly to consumers via magazines and newspapers, and holds over 3.5 million returned questionnaires.
- *Omnidata.* This is a result of a joint venture between the Dutch Post Office and the Dutch *Reader's Digest*. The company mails its questionnaires to all Dutch telephone subscribers and tries to induce them to respond by arguing that by doing so they would receive less junk mail. Twenty-three per cent of consumers have responded, and Omnidata has 730,000 households on file from a total of 5 million in Holland.
- *Postaid.* This is a Swedish organisation run by PAR, a company providing marketing research and a subsidiary of the Swedish Post Office. It was started in the early 1980s and, as with the Dutch system, was based on the idea that

people should be given the chance to determine the kind of mail they want to receive. The result is a data base containing a million of Sweden's 3.7 million households.

All the research carried out so far has been on generalised life style typologies and their comparative use in discriminating consumer attitudes and behaviour (Wilmott, 1989). The results are mixed, but the most recent study (O'Brien and Ford, 1988) suggests that such generalised typologies are less efficient as discriminators than traditional variables like social class or age. While the relative merit of demographic variables and life style tends to vary from situation to situation, overall, in the comparisons that have been conducted, life style comes out worst. It must therefore be concluded that, like their less sophisticated demographic brethren, life style segments are no panacea for marketing. Although, when added to data bases, they provide a powerful means of shifting from the target markets to individual customers, their low coverage renders them of limited value. Certainly life style segments provide a more graphic portrayal of customers than do demographics, but as yet their sophistication does not seem to pay dividends. As with single demographic variables, it is too much to hope that a single classification will work beyond markets for which it is particularly well suited.

To return to Lego, which has been so successful in using age as a way of discriminating between sectors in the market for construction toys, the company has found it necessary to develop a wide range of products covering the different needs of children: Lego Basic for 3- to 12-year-olds, which specialises in using the original Lego components as they were initially contrived; Fabuland aimed at 4- to 8-year-old girls and revolving around a fantasy theme based on animal characters; Legoland for 5- to 12-year-olds, which has the sub-themes of space, medieval life, pirates and modern suburbia; and Legotechnic for 7- to 16-year-olds, which has a focus on engineering mechanisms. Although the company used demographics as the first basis of segmentation, to go further depended upon identifying customer characteristics specific to the product in question.

9.2.3   The automatic interaction detection approach

The poor discriminating power of single off-the-peg variables can be theoretically overcome using *automatic interaction detection* (AID) to sort through large numbers of alternative bases to produce a hierarchy of means by which markets can be successively split. For instance, in examining the market for clothes, AID might first of all split the market by gender, then, examining males only, by age. Continuing AID would then examine one of these sub-groups, say males over 65, and discover that income provides a little more discriminating power. Unfortunately, AID has its drawbacks. The successive splitting of the market quickly produces very small cell sizes unless very large samples are available. Also, in application, it has been found to be unreliable and misleading (Doyle and Fenwick, 1975).

9.2.4   Post hoc methods using cluster analysis

Life style and geodemographic data bases depend upon some form of cluster analysis to group customers who are alike. In these cases, general attitude, behaviour, demographic and socioeconomic data are used to form groups deemed to be of general utility. For those companies willing to dedicate more resources to segmentation, it is possible to use the same approaches using dimensions pertaining to the particular market in question. In that way clusters of customers are formed into groups which have a direct relevance to the product or service being marketed.

Cluster-based segmentation depends on grouping potential customers on the basis of several dimensions simultaneously: for example, product usage, usage situation, brand preference and readership. This is quite different from AID, which partitions customers sequentially, first on one a priori criterion then on another. A major problem with customer segmentation from a practitioner's point of view is the seemingly incredible number of ways in which the process can be conducted. The most common is called *hierarchical clustering*, which starts with all the customers being treated individually and then forms segments comparing customers first of all to other customers who are most alike and then joining alike groups of customers together. However, even within hierarchical clustering there is a multiplicity of ways in which customers can be measured for alikeness and in which groups of customers can be treated.

Matters have also been made to look more complicated than they really are by writers referring to the same techniques in different ways and never quite understanding the jumble which has thereby been created. Fortunately, Punj and Stewart (1983) have brought order to this confusion and provided a thorough review of the results when various methods were compared.

The comparative studies consistently show two methods to be superior: Ward's (1963) method, which is one of the minimum variance approaches listed in Table 9.2; and the K-mean approach of interactive partitioning. In fact, an analyst does not have to choose between these two, because they can be used in combination, where Ward's method is used to form the initial number of clusters, say seven, and the K-mean approach used to refine that seven-cluster solution by moving observations around. If desired, after finding the best seven-cluster solution, Ward's method can then be re-engaged to find a six-cluster solution which is again optimised using K-mean.

This may seem a computationally cumbersome approach, but fortunately packages are available to allow the process to be used: these are CLUSTAN (Wishart, 1969) and Anderberg (1973). Of these, CLUSTAN is the only really viable alternative, since Anderberg, not untypically, has no user manual and can only handle binary data. So, at a stroke, by realising that Ward's method in conjunction with K-means is the best approach for forming cluster-based segments, the analyst has removed the necessity to sort among numerous cluster alternatives and is able to choose between the clustering programs which are available.

Table 9.2 *Clustering methods*

Favoured name	Method	Aliases
Hierarchical methods		
Single linkage	An observation is joined to another if it has the lowest level of similarity with at least one member of that cluster	Minimum method, linkage analysis, nearest neighbour cluster analysis, connectiveness method
Complete linkage	An observation is joined to a cluster if it has a certain level of similarity with all current members of that cluster	Maximum method, rank order typal analysis, furthest neighbour cluster analysis, diameter method
Average linkage	Four similar measures which differ in the way they measure the location of the centre of cluster from which its cluster membership is measured	Simple average linkage analysis, weighted average, centroid method, median method
Minimum variance	Methods which seek to form clusters which have minimum within-cluster variance once a new observation has joined it	Minimum variance method, Ward's method, error sum of squares method, H GROUP
Interactive partitioning		
K-means	Starts with observation partitioned into a pre-determined number of groups and then reassigns observation to cluster whose centroid is nearest	Non-hierarchical methods
Hill-climbing methods	Cases are not reassigned to a cluster with the nearest centroid but moved between clusters dependent upon the basis of a statistical criterion	

Source: Based on G. Punj and D.W. Stewart (1983) 'Cluster analysis in marketing research: review and suggestions for applications', *Journal of Marketing Research*, vol. 20, no. 2, Table 2, published by the American Marketing Association.

9.3   Collecting segmentation data

The data required for segmentation studies can be broken down into two parts: those which are used in conjunction with cluster analysis to form the segment; and those which are used to help describe the segments once they are formed. Cluster analysis will allow any basis to be used, but experience has shown that the most powerful criteria are those which relate to the attitude and behaviour regarding the product class concerned. These could include usage rate, benefits sought, shopping behaviour, media usage, etc. Examples are Lancaster and Saunders' (1978) analysis of the sixth-former market for higher education, which used the benefits sought as a segmentation criterion, Maier and Saunders' (1990) analysis of the general practitioner market, which formed segments on the basis of drugs prescribed, and the study by Jobber *et al.* (1989), which uses the results from conjoint analysis to segment computer systems users. Once these product, class, behaviour variables have been used to form a segment, the other demographic and psychographic information can be used to describe the clusters formed. One test of the validity of the results is the extent to which the clusters formed within product, class, behaviour do have significantly different psychographic and demographic characteristics.

The method of data collection depends on the usage situation. Where the aim is to define target markets for which products are to be designed or campaigns are to be directed via the mass media, then the data collection is usually by personal interviews using semantic scales which gauge whether a respondent agrees or disagrees with the statement. These results then provide a proxy to the continuous data which is the usual basis for cluster analysis. Where the segmentation in a study is to be used in conjunction with a data base which can rely on direct mailing, the data sources are much more limited. For example, all of the life style data bases mentioned earlier use simple checklists so that consumers have classified themselves according to their interests. In the data base segmentation study conducted by Maier and Saunders, the basis was product usage reports by general practitioners.

It is clearly a limitation of all data base methods that their data collection is constrained by the quality of data that can be obtained from a guarantee card or self-administered questionnaire. There inevitably tends to be an inverse correlation between the coverage in segmentation data bases and the quality of the data upon which they are formed. The life style segmentation bases are relatively rich yet cover only a relatively small percentage of the population. In contrast, CACI's ACORN data base covers the majority of households but is based upon very limited census returns. To add richness to their results CACI therefore conduct their own surveys at regular intervals to provide a more graphic portrayal of the customers within their enumeration districts.

9.4 Validation of segments

One of the beauties and problems of cluster analysis is its ability to generate seemingly meaningful groups out of meaningless data. This, and the confusion of algorithms, has frequently led to the approach being treated with scepticism. These uncertainties make validation an important part of segmentation research.

One favoured method of validation was mentioned above. Where product class behaviour or attitude was used to form the clusters, the extent to which those clusters also vary on demographic or psychographic variables is a measure of the cluster's validity. If the cluster is found to describe people with different beliefs and attitudes and behaviour, it would be expected that they could also have different demographic or psychographic profiles. Equally, from an operational point of view, if the market segments are demographically and psychographically identical, it is going to be very difficult to implement any plan based upon them.

Where sample data have been used to suggest segments and there is a hope to extrapolate those results to the major population, there is a need to test the reliability of the solution: to ask, 'Do the results hold for the whole population?' The most common way to test for this is cross-validation. It involves splitting the data that have been collected into two, using one set to form the first set of clusters and then using the second set to validate the results. A simple approach is to conduct the same cluster analysis on both samples and to compare them to see the similarity of the clusters in terms of their size and characteristics.

Since comparing two cluster analysis solutions tends to be rather subjective, several authors have recommended using discriminate analysis for cross-validation. This approach once again involves taking two samples and performing separate cluster analysis on each. One sample is then used to build a discriminate model, into which cases from the other samples are substituted. The reliability is then measured by comparing the allocation using discriminate analysis with the allocation by cluster analysis.

It is necessary to supplement this statistical validation with operational validation, which checks if the segments have managerial value. At a first level, this means the segments having face validity and appearing to provide marketing opportunities. If further endorsement is needed, an experiment can be run to test if the segments respond differently or not. For example, Maier and Saunders used a direct mailing campaign to a sample of GPs to show that their segments captured major differences in the doctors' responses to certain self-motioned activity.

9.5 Implementation

Implementation is best viewed not as a stage in segmentation research, but as the aim of the whole research process. Previously neglected (Urban, 1974), implementation has become one of the central issues in market modelling. However, it is often not considered by segmentation researchers. Schultz and Henry (1981) showed the consequence of this neglect with the distinction between a successful model, implementation and successful implementation. A successful model adequately represents the modelled phenomena, and implementation changes decision making, but a successful implementation improves decision making. In many cases it is worth going beyond the concept of implementation to implantation. By this we mean the results of the exercise, being not just used once, but adopted and used repeatedly once the marketing scientist has withdrawn from the initial exercise. This again suggests that implementation not only begins at the start of the segmentation research process, but continues long after the results have been first used by the marketing manager.

Successful implementation, therefore, depends on more than just the correct transfer of a model into action. The whole model-building process needs to be executed with implementation in mind. In particular, the segmentation research must be involved with the potential user in order to gain its commitment and ensure that the results fit its needs and expectations. An unimplemented segmentation exercise is truly academic in its more cynical sense.

Segment selection and strategy development are two critical stages which follow the technical activity of segmentation research. These are managerial tasks which are central to marketing strategy and upon which successful implementation depends. Chapter 11 focuses upon these and links them to the broader issues of strategic positioning.

9.6 Tracking

A segmentation exercise provides a snapshot of a market as it was some months before the results were implemented. Inevitable time delays mean that, from the start, the results are out of date, and as time goes on and consumers change it will inevitably become an increasingly poor fit to reality. Modelling myopia (Lilien and Kotler, 1983) occurs when successful implementation leads to the conviction that market-specific 'laws' have been found that make further analysis unnecessary. The converse is true: success means that modelling should continue. Customers and competition change. Successful implementation itself may also change the market and competitors' behaviour. In addition, application is likely to show bugs which may hamper the system's continued use, or wrinkles which may show how its usefulness can be extended.

The essence of tracking is twofold. It involves maintaining contact with users to ensure that bugs do not become a barrier to effective implementation and that the segments are interpreted correctly. It also means tracking the segment for stability. Implementation provides a natural experiment whereby the true characteristics of segments can be understood. Indications are that there is a great degree of variability in the way that individuals respond to sales promotion campaigns, etc. Through tracking the impact of various campaigns on segmentation, it may be possible to refine and detail the sort of promotional activity which is appropriate for them. If the segments do not prove to be stable, showing either gradual changes or a radical shift, that itself can create a major opportunity. It may indicate that a new segment is emerging or that segment needs are adjusting, and so enable an active company to gain a competitive edge by being the first to respond.

9.7 Conclusions

Considerable research has shown that the naive user of segmentation can be easily confused and disappointed. The traditional off-the-shelf methods have proved to be a poor guide to segmenting markets other than those which have a direct and immediate link to the markets concerned: that is, gender-based or race-based products. Although more expensive, and providing a much more graphic view of the market place, the more modern off-the-shelf psychographic methods appear to provide little advantage. Like demographic bases for segmentation, they do work in certain circumstances but only when the products from the segmentation criteria are very closely related.

The need to find segmentation bases which are closely associated with the product market in question means that successful implementation often involves a company developing product-specific bases. Here there is a potential barrier because of the perceived complexity of cluster analysis and the confusion that researchers have created by their own misunderstandings. Although once a major block to implementation, sufficient case law on using cluster analysis in marketing has been accumulated to allow some of the confusion to be removed. Comparative studies come down firmly in favour of Ward's method in conjunction with iterative partitioning. Few of the computer packages available can do this, so a selection of clustering algorithms and the computer package used to run it becomes routine.

There is much scepticism about the results from cluster analysis. This is justifiable, given the confusion of the algorithms used, the tendency of cluster analysis to produce results even if the data are meaningless, and the lack of validation of those results. Being aware of these dangers, it is vital that validation — both statistical and operational — has a central role within segmentation research. In particular, tests should be done to see if the segments formed can be replicated using other data, and to check that the segments are managerially meaningful and respond differently to elements of the marketing mix.

Segmentation researchers have indeed failed to find a single criterion which will fit all markets, despite the claims of those selling life style segmentation. However, rather than finding a single criterion, researchers have found consistently reliable methods of using product market data to segment customers into groups which are of managerial significance. In the search for a universal segmentation criterion no philosopher's stone has been found, but researchers have instead discovered how to make philosopher's stones.

TEN

Positioning research

You don't buy coal, you buy heat;
You don't buy circus tickets, you buy thrills;
You don't buy a paper, you buy news;
You don't buy spectacles, you buy vision;
You don't sell products, you create positions.

Introduction

In marketing, segmentation and positioning are as inseparable as bubble and squeak. While segmentation identifies homogeneous groups of potential customers, positioning research shows how those customers perceive the competing products or services. Both segmentation and positioning research are therefore ways of enhancing a picture of how customers in a market can be grouped, and how those customers group the products or services on offer.

Businesses started by selling products, and advertisers taught them how to give the products personality. Positioning shifts the emphasis of marketing from the product to 'the battle for your mind' (Ries and Trout, 1981). In their seminal work, Ries and Trout explained how 'Positioning starts with the product. A piece of merchandise, a service, a company, an institution, or even a person . . .'. But positioning is not what you do to a product; positioning is what you do to the mind of the prospect. In other words, you position the product in the mind of the prospect.

Positioning now has a central role within modern marketing, providing a bridge between the company and its target customers, describing to customers how the company differs from the current or potential competitors. Positioning therefore becomes the actual designing of the company's image so that the target customers understand and appreciate what the company stands for in relation to its competitors (Kotler, 1991).

Within the definition of positioning lie the roots of positioning research. It is about groups of customers and groups of competitors, and is therefore a multidimensional problem. It is also about perceptions, beliefs and attitudes about competitors, products and the wants and needs of customers. It is therefore concerned with psychology and understanding how people perceive markets. Positioning research brings this multidimensionality and psychology together by using a series of techniques designed to extract consumer perceptions.

Central to this process are a series of computer programs which are suitable for various data-gathering techniques. These, and the various positioning alternatives, are the focus of this chapter. It starts with the need to identify competitors correctly and then uses an example to show how a perceptual map can be developed. Alternative competitive positions are then discussed.

10.1   Identifying the competitors

There are two reasons why the identification of direct competitors is an important first step in positioning research. The first concerns data gathering, where it is essential to limit the number of brands considered in order to make data gathering less onerous for respondents. This is a particularly important issue in positioning research because, as will be shown, many of the techniques which have to be used depend on paired comparisons and so increase in length with the square of the number of brands involved. This potential explosion in the amount of data with a number of brands considered also suggests that limiting the number of brands can result in significant data-processing efficiencies.

The second reason for excluding indirect competitors is the impact they can have upon the products of greatest concern. For example, a company analysing the market for hover mowers might be interested in how customers perceive competitors' brands (i.e. Flymo, Qualcast, and Black and Decker) and the products they sell. When buying such a product a customer is likely to have a reasonable idea about the likely size and cost of the item he or she wishes to buy, and therefore gives most attention to products within that price performance envelope. Among the competitors the customer is likely to see various dimensions of importance, such as value for money, reliability, safety and convenience, and it is the relationships between the direct competitors with which positioning is particularly involved. If the direct competitors have not been correctly identified, the researcher may include within the survey manufacturers of sit-upon mowers (i.e. Lawnflight, Laser and Toro). This would not only add to the burden of respondents whose perceptions are being sought, but could also change the perceptions since, when compared with sit-upon mowers, conventional handmowers may all look similarly inexpensive, time consuming and compact.

The mower market is relatively simple compared with some others. Consider the problem faced by a company wishing to launch a low-alcohol lager. Should the competitors be low-alcohol lagers or should they include low-alcohol beers as well? Or maybe the study should be extended to include other low-alcohol drinks such as shandy, cider or wine. In Britain, the rapid increase in the consumption of soft drinks which has been associated with the concern for the health and safety of alcohol consumption may suggest that soft drinks also should be considered as an alternative to low-alcohol lagers, but should diet and caffeine-free versions also be considered? Perhaps it is just a matter of taste, and it is more appropriate to compare low-alcohol drinks with drinks with normal alcohol content. Production orientation is a danger when trying to reduce the number of product alternatives. A brewer may well consider low-alcohol lagers or other lagers as the direct competitors, but certain customer groups may easily associate low-alcohol drinks with cokes or other beverages. It is clearly necessary to take a customer-oriented view of the direct competitors.

One way of defining direct competitors is to look at panel data to see what customers have done in the past. By tracking the past purchases of customers, it may be possible to identify product alternatives when switching takes place. The danger in this approach is the dissociation of the purchasers from the user's situation and the user. For instance, a buying pattern which shows the purchase of low-alcohol lagers, lemonade, beer and coke could represent products to be consumed by different people at different times, rather than switching between alternatives. Another approach is to determine which brands buyers consider. For consumer durables, customers might be asked what other brands they considered in their buying process. For low-involvement products, it may be inappropriate to ask buyers about a particular purchase decision, so instead they could be asked what brands they would consider if their favourite one was not available.

Day *et al.* (1979) propose a more exhaustive process introduced in Chapter 2 as a cost-effective way of mapping product markets. Start by asking 20 or so respondents the use context of a product, say a low-alcohol lager. For each use context so identified, such as the lunchtime snack, with an evening meal, or at a country pub, respondents are then asked to identify all the appropriate beverages. For each beverage so identified, the respondent has to identify appropriate use context. Once again the process is continued until an exhaustive list of contexts and beverages is produced. A second group of respondents would then be asked to make a judgement as to how appropriate each beverage would be for each usage situation, the beverages then being clustered on the basis of the similarity of their usage situation. For instance, if both low-alcohol lager and coke were regarded as appropriate for a company lunchtime snack but inappropriate for an evening meal, they would be considered as direct competitors.

Rather than using consumers, it can be tempting to use a panel of experts or retailers to guide the selection of direct competitors. This could be quicker than using customers but is likely to lead to a technological definition of preference. As Saunders and Watt (1979) have shown, there can be a vast difference between what is perceived by experts and what is perceived by customers. Since the focus of positioning is to gauge customers' preference, it is therefore difficult to justify using anyone other than customers to define competitors.

10.2 Position analysis

To explain position analysis we will follow a case involving the positioning of leisure facilities accessible from the East Midlands of the United Kingdom. For the sake of simplicity only the major attractions and segments are considered in this case.

Interviews with respondents revealed six leisure centres which, although very different in their provision, were all seen as major attractions. These were as follows:

- The American Adventure theme park: a completely modern facility, with a Wild West emphasis but also including other American themes such as GI and space exploration.

- Alton Towers: recently acquired by Madame Tussaud's, this is a large leisure facility based around a derelict country house. It has inherited several natural features, such as the house itself, the gardens and lakes, but particularly focuses upon dramatic, white-knuckle rides.
- Belton House: one of many country houses owned by the National Trust. Like most of these, it has splendid gardens and furnished accommodation, which visitors may see. Untypical of National Trust properties, the house also has a large adventure playground in a wood beside the house, this being a venture started by the family who owned the house prior to its passing on to the National Trust.
- Chatsworth House: one of the largest stately homes in Britain and still the residence of the owning family. Its extensive grounds and the house itself make it a popular place for families to visit.
- Warwick Castle: one of the best kept and most visited medieval castles in Britain. Like many estates it has been lived in from medieval times, and in this case the owners have built a country house into the fabric of the building. Owned by Madame Tussaud's, the castle's attractions have been extended beyond the building and its gardens, to include contemporary waxworks within the furnished accommodation, medieval knights cavorting, torture chambers, etc.
- Woburn Abbey and Safari Park: like Chatsworth, still the residence of the family owning the estate. However, the family in this case have developed two distinct attractions, the house and the safari park, the latter also having a fairground, etc.

Although these attractions differ widely in their appeals, ownership and background, the respondents' interviews clearly indicated that they were direct competitors, and were alternatives they would choose between when deciding on an outing.

10.2.1   Determine the competitive dimensions

The positioning research process (Figure 10.1) shows the determination of competitive dimensions, competitors' positions and the customers' positions as parallel phases. This is because there are certain techniques which can be used to extract all these simultaneously. In this case the phases are taken in sequence. Details of the other approaches that are available are given later.

10.2.2   Determine the competitors' positions

It is an odd feature of many of the techniques used in positioning research that the competitors' positions can be determined before it is understood how the customer is differentiating between them. Such an approach was used to represent the leisure park market in the East Midlands. The approach is called *similarities-based multidimensional scaling*. Respondents were given a shuffled stack of cards which contained all possible combinations of the six leisure parks. There were fifteen pairs

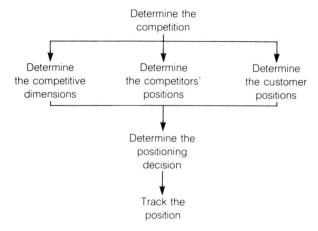

Figure 10.1 The positioning research process

in all, ranging from American Adventure linked to Alton Towers, to Warwick Castle linked with Woburn Safari Park. The respondents were then asked to rank the pairs in accordance with their similarity, the pair most alike being on the top and the pair most unalike being on the bottom. Since this can be a rather cumbersome process, it is sometimes advisable first of all to ask respondents to stack the cards into three piles representing those pairs that are very similar, those pairs that are very unalike and a middling group. The respondent then has to rank the pairs within each group.

Figure 10.2 presents the ranking from one such process. It shows that the respondent thought Belton House and Woburn Safari Park were the most similar. As the next most similar, the pair of Belton House and Chatsworth House was chosen, and so on, until the least similar pair of the American Adventure and Chatsworth House. An indication that the respondent is using different criteria to judge each pair is shown by the judgement that Belton is similar to Woburn and Chatsworth, but Woburn and Chatsworth are not alike. Such are the permutations and combinations of pairs

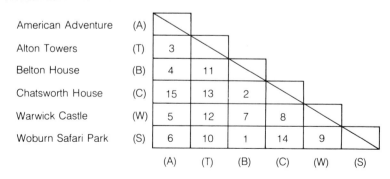

Figure 10.2 Individual similarity matrix of leisure facilities

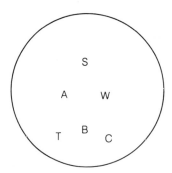

A = American Adventure
T = Alton Towers
B = Belton House
C = Chatsworth House
W = Warwick Castle
S = Woburn Safari Park

Figure 10.3 Perceptual map of product positions

each respondent can choose that it is almost inevitable that each individual's similarity matrix is different.

The objective from this point is to develop a plot of the stimuli (leisure parks) which shows those that respondents said were similar close together, and those that respondents said were dissimilar far apart. Although this is a difficult task to conduct manually, computers are particularly adept at finding such solutions and researchers within multidimensional scaling have produced many computer packages which can be used (Green, Carmone and Smith, 1989). A multidimensional package called KYST can be used to produce perceptual maps from the similarities matrix provided and many other data formats (Kruskal, Young and Seery, 1973). The map produced (Figure 10.3) shows some of the detail from a similarity matrix (Figure 10.2). Chatsworth House, Alton Towers and Woburn Safari Park are some distance apart, while American Adventure, Alton Towers and Belton House are somewhat closer together.

There are two reasons why the fit is not perfect:

● The perceptual map presented in Figure 10.3 is in two dimensions whereas the customers' perception of the market is rather more complex than that.
● The perceptual map is an aggregate of a number of customers' views whereas the similarity matrix in Figure 10.2 represents the views of one customer.

KYST can produce a perceptual map of a single customer, but it is more common to produce a map which aggregates either all customers or gives a segment's view.

10.2.3   Determine the competitive domain

Two methods of determining competitive dimensions are not recommended. The first is using experts' judgements which, like their judgements of competitors, are likely to be different from those of customers. The second is trying to eyeball the perceptual map to try and work out what the dimensions represent. Such maps are often ambiguous and there is a particular danger of researchers superimposing their own views of what is going on. A better, but still imperfect, technique is to ask customers directly how they differentiate the market. The problem here is that customers may give a relatively simplistic answer which may not represent all the dimensions they may use to differentiate product offerings.

More useful is a research-based approach where respondents are asked first to choose two or more similar products and say why they consider them to be alike, then to choose some products they consider to be quite dissimilar and say why they see them as unalike. An approach like this was used to determine the dimensions of the perceptual space for the leisure facilities.

The respondents were first asked why they chose the first pair (Woburn Safari Park and Belton House) as most alike. They were then asked what made Belton House and Chatsworth House alike, and so on, until the respondents had difficulty saying that pairs were alike at all. The opposite tack was then taken, where the respondents were asked to explain why they considered pairs to be unalike: first of all, the most dissimilar pair of Chatsworth House and American Adventure, then Chatsworth House and Woburn Safari Park, etc. The result was a long list of attributes which was reduced to ten after some similar ones were combined and less frequently used ones were deleted. The ones remaining were

- Big rides
- Educational
- Fun and games
- Sophisticated
- Noisy
- For teenagers
- Strong theme
- For all the family
- Synthetic/artificial
- Good food.

Kelly grids are a popular market research technique which could also have been used to identify the dimensions underlying the perceptual map:

- Respondents are presented with three stimuli (in our case recreation centres) and asked to state one way in which two of them are alike and yet different from the third.
- The criteria upon which the two were said to be alike (say, noisy) is labelled

'the emergent pole' and associated dissimilarity (say, quiet) is labelled 'the implicit pole'.
- The remaining stimuli (leisure centres) are then sorted equally between the two poles.
- Another three stimuli are selected and the process is repeated until the respondent can think of no new reasons why the triad are alike or dissimilar.

To find how the dimensions fit the perceptual map in Figure 10.3, respondents were asked to rank each of the leisure facilities on the basis of the attributes identified. Once again, the result is a series of matrices which are difficult to analyse manually and, once again, computers come to our aid: in this case, a package called PREFMAP (Chang and Carol, 1972) which takes the perceptual map of product positions in Figure 10.3 and fits the dimensions as they best describe the respondents' perceptions. To identify the meaning of these vectors, each one can be traced back through the centre of the perceptual map.

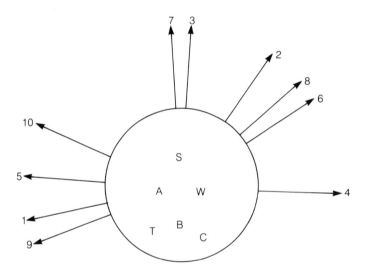

Leisure centres (stimuli)
A = American Adventure
T = Alton Towers
B = Belton House
C = Chatsworth House
W = Warwick Castle
S = Woburn Safari Park

Dimensions (vectors)
1 = Big rides
2 = Educational
3 = Fun and games
4 = Sophisticated
5 = Noisy/rowdy
6 = Pre-teen
7 = Theme
8 = For all the family
9 = Artificial/synthetic
10 = Good food

Figure 10.4 Perceptual map of product positions and dimensions

The score of each of the leisure centres (stimuli) on the dimension (vector) is measured by its relative position as the vector is traced back. For instance, the respondents see Chatsworth House as being the most sophisticated, followed by Warwick Castle, Belton House, Woburn Safari Park, American Adventure and Alton Towers. In almost complete opposition to sophistication is vector 5, representing noisy and rowdy, on which Alton Towers and American Adventure scored the highest. Projecting back vector 7, which represents a strong theme, shows the highest scoring leisure centre to be Woburn Safari Park, followed by the American Adventure and Warwick Castle with an almost equal rating, and finally Belton House, Alton Towers and Chatsworth House.

Once again, it is likely that the respondents' individual or aggregated scores are not perfectly represented by the map that has been generated. This is inevitable, considering that the picture is now trying to represent even more information in the same two dimensions. The magnitude of this problem can be reduced by resorting to portraying the picture using three or more dimensions, but usually the situation becomes less understandable rather than more understandable as the map goes beyond our normal experience. It may also be that segments of the market have distinctly different views and therefore it is more appropriate to produce maps which represent their different perceptions rather than aggregating the market as has been done so far.

10.2.4   Customer positions

A two-stage process was used to add customer positions to the perceptual map of leisure centres. First, respondents were asked to rate the leisure centres in terms of their preference. Cluster analysis was then used to form segments with similar preferences (Chapter 9). This indicated the presence of three main clusters. Analysis of their demographic characteristics revealed these to be mature couples or young sophisticates, who found Chatsworth House and Belton House as most attractive; young families, who preferred American Adventure and Woburn Safari Park; and wild young things, who were most attracted by Alton Towers and Woburn Safari Park.

Once again, PREFMAP was used to locate these segments in relation to product position. However, in this case the segments were to be expressed as ideals points within the body of the map rather than as vectors in the way that the dimensions were examined. Figure 10.5 gives the final map. This shows clearly the strategy of American Adventure, the latest of the leisure centres to enter the market. Aimed at the family market, it has big rides, good food and plenty of opportunity for fun and games, particularly for the very young children. Although lacking sophistication and being perceived as artificial, it is well positioned for young families. Less successful appears to be Belton House, where the National Trust has found itself running a country estate, with which it is very familiar, and an adventure playground, with which it is unfamiliar. Although the house and gardens may provide the sophistication and tranquillity desired by the mature couples, the existence of the adventure playground would make it too rowdy for them. Equally, the direction of so many

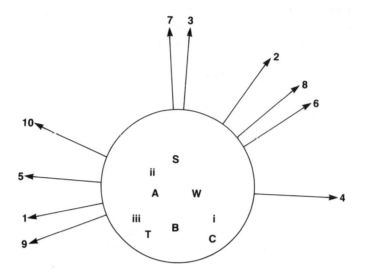

Leisure centres (stimuli)
A = American Adventure
T = Alton Towers
B = Belton House
C = Chatsworth House
W = Warwick Castle
S = Woburn Safari Park

Segments (points)
i   = Mature couples
ii = Young families
iii = Wild young things

Dimensions (vectors)
1 = Big rides
2 = Educational
3 = Fun and games
4 = Sophisticated
5 = Noisy/rowdy
6 = Pre-teen
7 = Theme
8 = For all the family
9 = Artificial/synthetic
10 = Good food

Figure 10.5 Perceptual map of product positions, dimensions and strengths

resources into maintaining the house and gardens to National Trust standards provides facilities which are unlikely to be attractive to the wild young things (which the National Trust probably thinks is good) or young families.

The map also shows the dangers of product positioning without consideration of market segments. The positions of the leisure centres suggest that there may be an opportunity to develop one which excels in the provision of an educational experience for the pre-teens, or for all the family. Vacant that position may be, but it is dangerously away from the needs of the three major segments which have been identified in this case. Maybe the mums and dads would have liked such a leisure centre, but the kids would be happier with a less pretentious, synthetic place providing fun and games.

10.3 Alternative positioning processes

In developing positioning maps, researchers are spoilt by the number of alternative approaches that can be used (see Hooley, 1979). For instance, PREFMAP allows the stage where segments were formed from individuals to be missed out and so produces a map representing the ideal point of each individual. Rather than the picture seen in Figure 10.5, which presents the ideal points of each segment, the map would then show the product positions, the market dimensions and the position of each individual relative to the product. From there it may be possible to eyeball the positions of individual respondents to identify a group which is worthy of being targeted.

Another package, MDPREF (Chang and Carroll, 1987) can be used to combine the identification of the perceptual map of product positions and underlying dimensions. This would have required respondents to rate leisure parks along each of the dimensions, such as 'for all the family' or 'sophisticated', and then involved aggregating the results to arrive directly at a map similar to Figure 10.4.

Anyone who starts to use this diversity of approaches will find that the map produced depends upon the approach used. This is because of the differences in the data-gathering techniques and the methods used to optimise the results. In that way, the use of multidimensional scaling to produce perceptual maps is similar to cluster analysis where the results depend on the clustering algorithm used (see Chapter 9). But, just as in cluster analysis, this should not be seen as a defect but as the realisation that there are numerous ways of looking at a market. Life would be more convenient if there were just one map which represented a market, but any attempt to compress the richness of a market into so simple a perspective is likely to result in opportunities being lost, or never seen.

Only a few years ago, access to the packages was difficult, and the programs themselves were poorly documented and hard to use. Now the situation has changed completely. They, along with other reasonably user-friendly data analysis packages, are available in PC form (Smith, 1988) and are routinely used by leading market research companies.

10.4 Positioning alternatives

In trying to position their products, companies face a battle for attention and distinctiveness within an 'overcommunicated society' (Ries and Trout, 1986). Even though there may be numerous products on the market, consumers are rarely able to name more than a few. This was the problem faced by Audi, when it realised that people mentioned Mercedes, BMW and Volkswagen as German cars, with all the connotations of quality and reliability that entails, but often omitted Audi. The result was the *Vorsprung Durch Technik* campaign, which concentrated upon the Germanness of the product and, through rallying and the Quatro, upon their technical excellence. Ever the number four, in 1990 Audi had to change tack once again to maintain a foothold on the product ladder by successfully associating itself with green issues.

In their exposition of the existence of a product ladder, Ries and Trout noted that in markets the second firm usually enjoys half the business of the first firm, and the third firm enjoys half the business of the second, etc. This flows through into profitability and return investments where, in the long term, profitability follows the market share ranking of the companies. Leading companies can also achieve major economies in advertising and promotion (Saunders, 1990). Part of the reason for this is the tendency for people to remember the number one. When asked who was the first person successfully to fly alone across the Atlantic, most people would correctly answer Charles Lindbergh, but how many people can name the second person? It is similar with the first and second people to set foot on the moon, or climb Mount Everest.

The importance of leadership is fine for market leaders such as Mercedes in luxury cars, Hilton in hotels, Coca-Cola in soft drinks and Nescafé in coffee, but it leaves lesser brands with an unresolved problem. Positioning points to a way of these brands establishing a strong place in the minds of the consumer despite the incessant call for attention from competing products. This involves consistency of message and the association of a brand with ideas that are already strongly held within the consumer's mind.

A matrix of alternative generic positions and positioning strategies is available (Figure 10.6). Generic positions provide the broad alternatives: consolidation, latent position, deposition and membership position. The consolidation position might be

GENERIC POSITION

STRATEGY	Consolidation	Latent position	Deposition	Membership
Attributes	Volvo	Radion		Lloyds Bank
Price/quality	Sainsbury		Intercity	
Competition			Intercity	Swiftair Express
Application		Polaroid		
User	Swissair			
Product class				Toyota

Figure 10.6   Positioning alternatives

used by market leaders, such as Boeing in civil aircraft, or British Aerospace in the corporate jet markets, which uses typical consolidation copy in the adverts for the market-leading 125 executive jet: 'market leader . . . 750 sales . . . and accelerating'. For this highly technical purchase, the emphasis is on the aircraft having more than 50 per cent of the sales in its market sector, rather than on the performance of the aircraft. The consolidation position can also be appropriate for non-leaders with a strong image. Volvo, like the Volkswagen before it, concentrated on the ruggedness and safety of its saloon cars, while others concentrated on performance, exclusivity and styling. The consumer believes the products to be unstylish, safe, conservative and rugged. From the advertising, this position is reinforced by using appeals based on fear and the safety of the family or children: 'Are they as safe around the town as they are around the house?'

While making headway against established competition can be difficult, where there is an unfulfilled need or want, a company can use latent positioning to establish a reputation. Such was the appeal of Sensodyne toothpaste, the first product to focus on the comfort of people with sensitive teeth; or Lever's highly successful Radion automatic soap powder, which focused upon removing 'dirt and odours'! The Radion campaign took unsubtlety to the extreme — a brutal name with possible association with strength and radioactivity, a brash, day-glo orange, green, yellow and blue pack, and the parody of an advert which displays the wife's distaste of the smell of her husband's armpit. Although Lever Brothers received no advertising awards, they did achieve 9 per cent market share in the UK market in the first year. Helped by their radical positioning, this massive gain within an established market was achieved without particularly cannibalising any of Unilever's other brands.

Depositioning is directly competitive, although the competitors may not always be mentioned. For instance, in the Barclaycard campaign Alan Whicker comments on the universal usability of Visa, which is 'more than can be said for certain other charge cards I could mention'. Although American Express is not mentioned, it is certainly imputed by referring to charge cards and the exotic locations involved in the ads. Besides promoting the advantage of Barclaycard, this also tends to undermine the prestige position occupied by American Express. A similar campaign is used by British Rail's Intercity service, which makes a direct comparison between the comfort and convenience of travelling by rail, and the crowding and inconvenience of air travel: 'When you travel on business, it's the same old story.'

Membership positioning is attractive for lower-order companies within a product market. This Lloyds Bank does by identifying itself as one of the Big Four and projecting the range of facilities and services it provides for the consumer and the business user.

Within each of the generic positions, the positioning strategy determines the means by which each of the product's positions are communicated. Aaker (1982) identified six of these.

■ Positioning by attribute, as used by Volvo, Radion and Lloyds Bank, where their distinctiveness or similarity to other products is stated.

,s price/quality as a basis for its dominant position in the market place: 'Good food
, Sainsbury's.'

ɔn is the main emphasis of British Rail's Intercity campaign, although the generic strategy
.osition the competitor. An alternative competitor-based position is used by the Royal Mail's
, service, which, although less expensive, seeks to be seen as a courier service: 'By air,
.nd, by Swiftair, by hand.'

,plication is used by Polaroid to position its EMI System range as a piece of communication
,quipment rather than a fun camera: 'Now when you describe it, everyone will get the picture . . .
What will Polaroid do for you today?'

User portraits are used to position Swissair within the overcrowded and protected European airline
industry: for instance, 'Swissair customer portrait 69, photographed by Nikolaus Schmid-Burgk,
Elizabeth Princess of Shchsen-Weimar and Eisenach, managing directrice of an eminent jewellery
company, Munich . . . She chooses Swissair because it's a gem of an airline.' In contrast, Lufthansa,
which has a similar profile in the market place, focuses on its attributes of safety and reliability:
'We have people who check the people who check the people who check the aircraft.'

Product class association is now being used strongly by the Japanese motor manufacturers, as
they attempt to move upmarket. The advertising of Toyota and Nissan particularly associates them
with Porsche and, more creatively, Mazda associates its sports cars with the golden age of MG,
Austin Healey and Triumph. ■

A feature of many successful products is their ability to hold their position over
many years and so give themselves a strong identity. Even though the product may
have many different attributes, as does Coffeemate, the emphasis has remained upon
it making 'good coffee taste great'. This is despite the alternative claim that it contains
fewer calories and is more economical to use than ordinary milk. To help it retain
this consistency throughout generations of competitors, common brand managers
and advertising campaigns, Unilever developed the concept of the positioning bridge,
which provides a clear focus and eases internal communications about the brand's
identity. This is a deceptively simple tool, which seeks to anchor the product to its
core identity. It involves using two words — one functional, one emotional or
psychological — that give the essence of a brand's position in the market place: for
instance, for the fabric conditioner Comfort, loving softness; for the washing powder
Persil, caring whiteness; and for the washing-up liquid Fairy, gentle relationships.

Like marketing in general, the essence of positioning is simplicity and tenacity:
distilling the miscellaneous features of a product, its competitors and the market place
into a simple message that is easy to understand, and then focusing the promotional
effort of a company on retaining that idea. Simple to say; hard to do; easy to forget.

10.5 Evolving positioning

Despite the good sense of taking great pains to hold a brand's position, there are
changes in the market place and over a product's life cycle which necessitate strategies

being altered. During introduction, the positioning objective is to establish the product's foothold in the market; to create awareness of the product and what it provides (Figure 10.7). The path to be followed depends upon the needs being fulfilled by the product, whether functional, symbolic, or experiential (Park, Jaworski and MacInnis, 1986).

At the introduction stage, a functional product may focus upon the application of the product and its problem-solving capabilities. Where the needs being fulfilled are symbolic, it is more likely that the positioning will depend upon relating to the user or product class association; and when the needs are experiential, concentrated upon the attributes of the user once again. At this stage, the positioning message is likely to be relatively unsophisticated, although the brand could be distinct: for example, Mars Bars, Imperial Leather soap or the original pine furniture-based Habitat chain.

As competition increases and the product becomes well known, an elaboration of the positioning process becomes appropriate. The products associate themselves more clearly, such as Mars Bars, which associate themselves with an active life style rather than indulgence, and Imperial Leather, which associates itself with beauty and sophistication. In this elaboration, products can move towards either specialisation or generalisation. Specialisation has been appropriate for tactiles, such as superglues, where the single product is now fragmented into a market with numerous products for specific applications. A case of generalisation has been WD 40, a lubricant initially sold as a 'magic' liquid spray which helped cars start in awkward conditions. Despite the product having many more capabilities, it was focused totally on that single application. Stimulated by the increased reliability of cars and competition, WD 40

	Introduction	Elaboration	Fortification
Positioning objective	Establish image	Enhance value of the image	Brand concept association
Functional	Functional problem-solving capabilities	Problem-solving/ specialisation	Image bundling: new products with functional concepts
Symbolic needs	Reference group/ ego enhancement association	Market shielding	Image bundling: new products with symbolic concepts
Experiential	Cognitive/ sensory stimulation concepts	Brand assessory/ brand network	Image bundling: new products with experiential

Source: Based on Park, Jaworski and MacInnis (1986), Figure 1, p. 137.

Figure 10.7 Positioning life cycle stages

has changed its distribution and promotion to position itself as an aerosol-based, general-purpose lubricant. In a similar way, the simple style of Habitat became more complex in the 1970s and 1980s, as it began to accommodate ranges aimed at different target market segments. The basic appeal still remained design-oriented, economic goods, but hi-tech and classical lines were added to the original fresh, pine image. The objective at this elaboration stage of the positioning will be to enhance the perceived value of the product. The developments show greater concern for identifying the customer and the advantages communicated.

Late in the life of a product, positioning may take up a fortification role. Here image bundling may occur where the strengths of the original brand are used to umbrella new products. Whereas in the elaboration stage, the position of Mars Bars was very clearly identified and the Mars Group launched products to cater for new segments without using the Mars brand name itself (e.g. Snickers), in the fortification stage the Mars Bar image has clearly been bundled with Mars ice-cream and drinks brands: a move also used by the company with its Snickers product in an attempt to defend an initial gain in the ice confectionery market. In a similar way, Cussons, the manufacturers of Imperial Leather, have chosen to trade upon the Imperial Leather brand name when launching hair and body shower gel, shampoos, etc.

The demise of the Next chain in the UK in the late 1980s clearly shows the danger of excessive use of a brand in the fortification of markets. Unless carefully controlled, the otherwise clearly defined position can be diluted by proliferation with associated products, which dilute the original clarity upon which market success depends. There are also indications (Saunders, 1990) that the use of brands in this way can be dangerous, since it deludes managers into thinking that the use of an umbrella brand name reduces the necessary expenditure for a new product to be launched. So common is this error that umbrella brands have a significantly lower success rate than brands launched without the benefit of an associated parent brand.

10.6 Conclusions

Positioning is now centre stage of the marketing planning process and, like segmentation, it has a simplicity which almost defies contradiction. As soon as marketing orientation changes the focus of a company from the product to the customer, the customer's mind must become central to marketing. Doubtless, intuition and creativity can lead to marketing strategies based upon radically new positions in the same way that new products can emerge from the mind of a genius. But geniuses are few, so one has to depend upon method rather than near madness to delve into the mind of the buyer. Fortunately, following the exposition of positioning by Ries and Trout, there has been a rapid development in the adoption of mathematical methods and associated data collection techniques, which have allowed perceptual markets to be expressed graphically.

As with marketing generally, the analytical techniques that are available will never replace the individual's insights which are central to creative marketing decisions, but they can provide a fresh view of markets which would not otherwise be seen. They can provide ways of visualising the customer's mind explicitly and provide a systematic way of determining and tracking positioning strategy. The perceived complexity of positioning research may be a barrier to its adoption by marketing managers of the qualitative tradition. But if they neglect the opportunities that positioning research provides, they are in danger of taking an unnecessarily simplistic view of the market: like trying to understand a polychromatic world using a monochromatic picture.

PART FOUR

Competitive positioning strategies

The final part of the book looks at implementation of competitive positioning strategies.

Chapter 11 discusses ways of *selecting market targets* from those uncovered through segmentation and positioning research. Two key dimensions are suggested for making the selection of target markets. First is the *relative attractiveness* of each potential segment. This will be dependent on many factors including size, growth prospects, margins attainable and competitive intensity. The second key dimension is the *strength of the organisation* in serving that potential target market. This is determined by the core competencies of the organisation, its current and potential marketing assets and the resources it is prepared to put into the market, all relative to competitors.

Chapter 12 focuses on methods for *building defensible market positions* once the target market has been decided. Routes to achieving *cost leadership* and *differentiation* are examined and the critical factors for maintaining position addressed.

Chapter 13 concludes the substantive part of the book by examining *strategies for building position, holding position, harvesting, niching and divesting*. Finally, the issues of the *managerial skills and competencies* necessary for each strategy are discussed.

Chapter 14 concludes the book by reviewing the key issues addressed and suggesting future developments in the field of *competitive positioning*.

ELEVEN

Selecting market targets

Attacking a fortified area is an art of last resort.

Sun Tzu, *c.*500 BC

Introduction

One of the most fundamental decisions a company faces is its choice of market or markets to serve. Unfortunately, many firms enter markets with little thought to their suitability for the firm. They are entered simply because there may appear to be an attractive market for the firm's products.

Chapter 8 was concerned with the different ways in which markets could be segmented. Alternative bases for segmentation were examined and the benefits of adopting a segmentation approach discussed. Chapter 9 then looked at the research techniques available to help segment markets. In this chapter market targeting is discussed in more detail. In particular, the process of identifying the market segments where the company's capabilities can be used to the best advantage is considered, together with the selection of the appropriate marketing strategy.

In deciding on the segment or segments to target, three basic questions need to be asked:

- How is the market segmented?
- How attractive are the alternative segments?
- Where do our current or potential strengths lie?

11.1 Defining how the market is segmented

As discussed in Chapter 8, there are many ways in which markets could be segmented. Often a useful starting point is to ask how management view the market, on the basis of their experiences in the market place. Management definition of market segments may typically be on the basis of products/services offered or markets served.

11.1.1 Products or services offered

Describing segments on the basis of products or services offered can lead to broad-based segmentation of the market.

189

■ John Deere, for example, competing against the much larger Caterpillar company in the US crawler tractor (bulldozer) market, initially segmented the market into 'large' and 'small' bulldozers. On the basis of its marketing assets (defined in terms of better service support through local dealer networks and lower system price) Deere decided to concentrate its efforts in the small bulldozer market, thus avoiding head-on competition with Caterpillar, which was stronger in the large bulldozer market. ■

Many market research companies, operating in the service sector, define their market segments in terms of the services they offer: for example, the market for retail audits, the market for telephone surveys, the market for qualitative group discussions and the market for professional (industrial) interviewing.

Underlying this product- or service-based approach to identifying markets is a belief that segments defined in this way will exhibit the differences in behaviour essential to an effective segmentation scheme. The strategy adopted by Deere made sense, for example, only because the requirements of purchasers and users from large and small bulldozers were different. Where the requirements of customers are essentially the same, but are satisfied by different products or services, this segmentation approach can lead to a myopic view of the market.

11.1.2   Market or markets served

Many companies now adopt a customer-based or markets-served approach to segmenting their markets. Segments are defined in terms of the customers themselves rather than the particular products they buy. In consumer markets management may talk in terms of demographic and socioeconomic segments, while in industrial markets definitions may be based on SIC or order quantity. A particularly useful approach in many markets is to segment on the basis of the benefits the customer is seeking in consuming the product or service, and/or the uses to which the product or service is put.

■ Van den Berghs (a subsidiary of Unilever) has been particularly successful in segmenting the market for 'yellow fats' on the basis of the benefits sought by consumers (see Broadbent, 1981).

The market, which comprises butter, margarine and low fat spreads, stood at £600m at retail selling price (RSP) in 1979. It was a static market with no overall growth. Within the market, however, there were some important changes taking place. There had been a marked trend away from butter to margarine, primarily because of the increasing price differential (butter and margarine were roughly equivalent prices in the mid-1970s but since then butter prices had increased more rapidly, widening the gap). Coupled with this came increased price sensitivity as the UK economy entered the recession of the late 1970s/early 1980s.

Van den Berghs was quick to spot a market opportunity as it segmented the market. There were at least five benefit segments identified:

Segment 1 consisted of customers who wanted a 'real butter taste' and were not prepared to forgo that taste at almost any price. This segment chose butter, the top-selling brands being Anchor, Lurpak and Country Life.

Segment 2 were customers who wanted the taste, feel and texture of butter but were concerned about its price. They were typically not prepared to sacrifice on taste and not convinced that existing margarines could satisfy them. These customers would typically choose the cheapest butter available, such as supermarket own label.

Segment 3 were ex-butter users who were prepared to accept existing margarines as a substitute and even found that they offered additional benefits over butter, such as softness and ease of spreading. Also attractive to this segment were tub packaging and larger packs. They were more price sensitive than Segment 2. The leading brand in this segment was Stork.

Segment 4 were a growing minority segment concerned with diet and weight control. In particular they were concerned with calories and with fat content. Outline was a leading brand. More recently, St Ivel Gold has been particularly successful in appealing to this segment.

Segment 5 were concerned with health in general and particularly the effects of cholesterol. Of special appeal to this segment were spreads low in cholesterol and high in polyunsaturated fats. The market leader in this segment was Flora.

Van den Berghs had achieved around 60 per cent of the total market in 1980 through recognising the segmentation described above and positioning its brands such that they attracted specific individual segments. Segment 1 was deliberately not targeted specifically. Krona, a block margarine with (in blind tests) a very similar taste to butter, was launched at a premium price and high margins to attract Segment 2 customers as they traded down from butter. Segment 3 was secured by Van den Berghs' leading brand Stork, while Segments 4 and 5 were served by Outline and Flora respectively. ■

Central to the success of Van den Berghs and other creative marketers has been an unwillingness merely to accept the segmentation of the market adopted by others. In many fast-moving consumer products markets, and in grocery marketing in particular, there has been a tendency to segment too much on the basis of background customer characteristics or volume usage. By looking beyond these factors to the underlying motivations and reasons to buy, companies can often create an edge over their competitors.

Once the segments have been identified, the alternatives need to be evaluated on the basis of market attractiveness and company strength or potential strength in that particular market segment. This evaluation is carried out across a number of factors.

11.2 Determining alternative market attractiveness

A number of factors should be considered in evaluating market, or specific segment, attractiveness. Abell and Hammond (1979) categorise the factors under four main headings:

- Market factors.
- Economic and technological factors.
- Competitive factors.
- Environmental factors.

Other writers, notably Robinson, Hitchins and Wade (1978), Patel and Younger (1978) and Day (1986), have amplified and extended these factors.

11.2.1   Market factors

Size of the segment

Clearly, one of the factors that makes a potential target attractive is its size. Volume markets offer greater potential for sales expansion (a major strategic goal of many companies). They also offer potential for achieving economies of scale in production and marketing, and hence a route to more efficient operations.

Segment growth rate

In addition to seeking scale of operation, many companies are actively pursuing growth objectives. Typically, it is believed that company growth is more easily achieved in growing markets.

Stage of industry evolution

Chapter 4 (Figure 4.2) looked at the characteristics of markets at different stages of evolution. Depending on the company's objectives (cash generation or growth), different stages may be more attractive. For initial targeting, markets in the early stages of evolution are generally more attractive as they offer more future potential and are less likely to be crowded by current competitors (see competitive intensity below). Typically, however, growth requires marketing investment (promotion, distribution, etc.) to fuel it, so that the short-term returns may be modest. Where more immediate cash and profit contribution is sought, a mature market may be a more attractive proposition requiring a lower level of investment.

Predictability

Chapter 4 also stressed the predictability of markets as a factor influencing their attractiveness to marketers. Clearly, the more predictable the market, the less prone it is to discontinuity and turbulence, the easier it is to predict accurately the potential value of the segment. The more certain, too, is the longer-term viability of the target.

Price elasticity and sensitivity

Unless the company has a major cost advantage over its main rivals, markets which are less price sensitive, where the price elasticity of demand is low, are more attractive than those which are more sensitive. In the more price-sensitive markets there are greater chances of price wars (especially in the mature stage of industry evolution) and the shake-out of the less efficient suppliers.

Bargaining power of customers

Those markets where buyers (ultimate customers or distribution chain intermediaries) have the strongest negotiating hand are often less attractive than those where the supplier can dominate and dictate to the market.

■ In the UK grocery market, the buying power of the major supermarket chains is considerable. Together the top ten chains supply around 80 per cent of the nation's food shopping needs. Food manufacturers and processors compete vigorously for shelf space to make their products available to their ultimate consumers. Indeed, some supermarket chains are now moving towards charging food manufacturers for the shelf space they occupy.

Similarly, in the market for military apparel, a concentration of buying power (by the government) dictates to potential entrants on what basis they will compete. ■

Seasonality and cyclicality of demand

The extent to which demand fluctuates by season or cycle also affects the attractiveness of a potential segment. For a company already serving a highly seasonal market, a new opportunity in a counter-seasonal market might be particularly attractive, enabling the company to utilise capacity year round.

■ The Thomson publishing group found the package tour market highly attractive for primarily cash flow reasons. The company needed to bulk-purchase paper for printing during the winter months and found this a severe drain on cash resources. Package holidays, typically booked and paid for during the winter months, provided a good opportunity to raise much-needed cash at the crucial time. Thomson Holidays, founded originally as a cash flow generator, has gone on to become a highly successful package tour operator. ■

11.2.2   Economic and technological factors

Barriers to entry

Markets where there are substantial barriers to entry (e.g. protected technology or high switching costs for customers) are attractive markets for incumbents but unattractive markets for aspirants. While few markets have absolute barriers to entry in the long term, for many companies the costs of overcoming those barriers may make the venture prohibitively expensive and uneconomic.

Barriers to exit

Conversely, markets with high exit barriers, where companies can become locked into untenable or uneconomic positions, are intrinsically unattractive. Some new target opportunities, for example, may have substantial investment hurdles (barriers to entry) that, once undertaken, lock the company into continuing to use the facilities created. In other markets, powerful customers may demand a full range of products/services as the cost of maintaining their business in more lucrative sectors.

When moving into high-risk new target markets, a major consideration should be exit strategy in the event that the position becomes untenable.

Bargaining power of suppliers

The supply of raw materials and other factor inputs to enable the creation of suitable products and services must also be considered. Markets where the suppliers have monopoly or near monopoly power are less attractive than those served by many competing suppliers (see Porter, 1980).

Level of technology utilisation

Use and level of technology affect the attractiveness of the target differently for different competitors. The more technologically advanced will be attracted to markets which utilise their expertise more fully and where that can be used as a barrier to other company entry. For the less technologically advanced, with skills and strengths in other areas such as people, markets with a lower use of technology may be more appropriate.

Investment required

Size of investment required, financial and other commitment, will also affect the attractiveness of the market and could dictate that many market targets are practically unattainable for some companies. Investment requirements can form a barrier to entry that protects incumbents while deterring entrants.

Margins available

Finally, margins will vary from market to market, partly as a result of price sensitivity and partly as a result of competitive rivalry. In grocery retailing, margins are notoriously low (around 2–4 per cent), whereas in other markets they can be nearer 50 per cent or even higher.

11.2.3   Competitive factors

The third set of factors in assessing the attractiveness of potential market targets relate to the competition to be faced in those markets.

Competitive intensity

Competitive intensity concerns the number of serious competitors in the market. Markets may be dominated by one (monopoly), two (duopoly), a few (oligopoly) or none ('perfect competition') of the players in that market. Entry into markets dominated by one or a few key players requires some form of competitive edge over them that can be used to secure a beachhead. In some circumstances it may be that the existing players in the market have failed to move with changes in their markets and hence have created opportunities for more innovative rivals.

Under conditions of perfect or near perfect competition, price competitiveness is particularly rife. The many small players in the market offer competitively similar products so that differentiation is rarely achieved (the stalemate environment of Figure 4.5), and if it is, then it is usually on the basis of price rather than performance or quality. To compete here requires either a cost advantage (created through superior technology, sourcing or scale of operations) or the ability to create a valued uniqueness in the market.

In segments where there are few or weak competitors, there may again be better opportunities to exploit.

■   In the early 1980s Barratt Developments made a major impact on the house-building market. Its segmentation of the market identified the need for specialist housing at various consumer life cycle phases. The first venture was Studio Solos, designed for young single people. In the first year of sales Barratt sold over 2,000 (2 per cent of total new home sales). In the USA the same strategy was adopted to spearhead the company's international expansion (70 per cent of Barratt's US sales coming from Solos).

At the same time, in the UK the company successfully developed retirement housing for pensioners, one- and two-bedroom apartments in blocks featuring communal facilities and wardens. In both retirement homes and Solos, Barratt was among the first aggressively to pursue the markets it had identified. Indeed, the company would argue that it was among the first to recognise that the housing market was segmented beyond the traditional product-based segmentation of terraces, semis and detached. ∎

Quality of competition

Chapter 7 discussed what constitutes 'good' competitors — those that can stabilise their markets, do not have overambitious goals and are committed to the market. Good competitors are also characterised by their desire to serve the market better, and hence will keep the company on its toes competitively rather than allow it to lag behind changes in the environment. Markets which are dominated by less predictable, volatile competitors are intrinsically more difficult to operate in and control, and hence are less attractive as potential targets.

Threat of substitution

In all markets there is a threat that new solutions to the customer's original problems will be found that will make the company's offerings obsolete. The often quoted example is substitution of the pocket calculator for the slide rule, though other less dramatic examples abound. With the increasing rate of technological change experienced in the 1980s and 1990s, it is probable that more products will become substituted at an accelerating rate. Two strategies make sense. First, for the less technologically innovative, seek market targets where substitution is less likely, but beware being lulled into believing that substitution will never occur!

Second, identify those targets where your own company can achieve the next level of substitution. Under this strategy, companies actively seek market targets which are using an inferior level of technology and are hence vulnerable to attack by a substitute product. Hewlett Packard's success with laser printers followed by ink jet printers in the PC peripherals market (attacking dot matrix printers) is a classic example.

Degree of differentiation

Markets where there is little differentiation between product offerings present significant opportunities to companies that can achieve differentiation. Where differentiation is not possible, a stalemate will often exist and competition will degenerate into price conflicts which are generally to be avoided.

11.2.4 Environmental factors

Exposure to economic fluctuations

Some markets are more vulnerable to economic fluctuations than others. Commodity markets in particular are often subject to wider economic change, meaning there is less direct control of the market by the players in it.

■ The New Zealand wool export industry was badly affected in mid-1990 by an Australian decision, in the face of declining world demand and increasing domestic stockpiles, to lower the floor price on wool by 20 per cent. Australia is such a dominant player in the commodity world market that New Zealand exporters were forced to follow suit. ■

Exposure to political and legal factors

As with exposure to economic uncertainty, markets which are vulnerable to political or legal factors are generally less attractive than those which are not. The exception, of course, is where these factors can be used positively as a means of entering the markets against entrenched but less aware competitors: for example, when protection is removed from formerly government-owned monopolies.

Degree of regulation

The extent of regulation of the markets under consideration will affect the degree of freedom of action the company has in its operations. Typically, a less regulated market offers more opportunities for the innovative operator than one which is closely controlled.

Again there is an exception, however. Regulated markets might afford more protection once the company has entered. This might be protection from international competition (e.g. protection of European car manufacturers from Japanese car imports by quotas), which effectively creates a barrier to (or a ceiling on) entry. The warning should be sounded, however, that experience around the world has generally shown that protection breeds inefficiencies and when that protection is removed, as is the current trend in world trade, the industries thrown into the cold realities of international competition face major difficulties in adjusting.

Social acceptability and physical environment impact

Increasingly, with concern for the environment and the advent of green politics, companies are looking at the broader social implications of the market targets they choose to go after. Especially when the company is widely diversified, the impact of entering one market on the other activities of the company must be considered.

In the 1970s Barclays Bank was forced to reconsider its activities in South Africa because of the impact on its business in the UK and elsewhere. Many other companies ceased to trade in South Africa for similar reasons. With the South African government's move towards a more pluralist society, the abolition of apartheid and the resumption of sporting links with South Africa, many companies are now seeking to re-establish trading links.

With increasing concern for the natural world, its fauna and flora, some cosmetics companies are now looking to non-animal ingredients as bases for their products, and manufacturers of aerosols are increasingly using non-ozone-depleting propellants in place of CFCs. The Body Shop, a cosmetics and toiletries manufacturer and retailer, has built its highly successful position in the market on a clear commitment to the use of non-animal ingredients.

Summary

The quality of a market is dependent on a number of factors. Other factors being equal, segments which are big and growing offer the best prospects for the future. Other factors rarely are equal, however, and size and growth are not the only criteria that should be taken into consideration. Of prime importance is the scope for building a valuable and defensible position for the company in that segment. This will also require a clear identification of the company's strengths with regard to the proposed segment.

11.3   Determining current and potential strengths

Abell and Hammond (1979) discuss the assessment of a firm's strength, or ability to serve a particular market, under three main headings:

- The firm's current market position.
- The firm's economic and technological position.
- The firm's capability profile.

11.3.1   Current market position

Relative market share

In markets which the company already targets, market share serves two main functions. First, it acts a barometer of how well the company is currently serving the target. A higher share will indicate better performance in serving the needs of the customers. Second, market share can, of itself, confer an advantage in further penetrating the market. High-share brands, for example, typically have high levels of customer awareness and wide distribution. Share of market is a prime marketing asset that can be used to develop the company's position further (see Chapter 5).

Rate of change of market share

Absolute market share in itself can confer a strength on the company. So too can rapidly increasing share. Growing share demonstrates an ability to serve the market better than those competitors currently losing share. A company with a low but increasing share of the market can demonstrate to distributors the need for increased shelf space and availability.

Exploitable marketing assets

Central to this book has been the identification and exploitation of the company's marketing assets. In target markets where marketing assets have potential for further exploitation (e.g. a favourable image, brand name or distribution network), the company has potential strength on which to build.

Identifying marketing assets was discussed at length in Chapter 5. Of interest here is how those marketing assets affect the strength of the company in serving particular market segments. What may, for example, be a strength with one target segment may be a weakness with another.

- ■ The image of John Player No. 6 as an ordinary, everyday cigarette was seen to be an advantage in the mass, filter-tipped cigarette market. When used in the king-size sector of the market, however, where prestige and sophistication are more important, that image was a clear disadvantage. The company therefore developed other brands to cater to that market (such as the Lambert and Butler brand). ■

Unique and valued products and services

In potential markets where the company has superior products and services, and these are different in a way valued by the customers, there is potential for creating a stronger competitive position.

Similarly, a competitive advantage based on low price relative to the competition is likely to be attractive to price-sensitive segments. It may actually deter segments more motivated by quality.

11.3.2 Economic and technological position

Relative cost position

The company's cost structure relative to competitors was listed as a potential marketing asset in Chapter 5. Low relative production and marketing costs — through technological leadership, exploitation of linkages, or experience and scale effects — give a financial edge to the company in the particular market (see Hall, 1980).

Capacity utilisation

For most companies, the level of capacity utilisation is a critical factor in its cost structure. Indeed, the PIMS study has shown that capacity utilisation is most crucial to small and medium-sized companies (see Buzzell and Gale, 1987). Few companies can hope to achieve 100 per cent utilisation (there will inevitably be downtime in manufacturing and slack periods for service companies), and indeed running at 'full' capacity may produce strains on both systems and structures. What is clearly important in any operation is to identify the optimum level of utilisation and seek to achieve that.

Technological position

Having an exploitable edge in technology again creates a greater strength for the company in serving a market. That may or may not be leading-edge technology. In some markets a lower-technology solution to customer requirements may be more suitable than state-of-the-art applications. Again the key is matching the technology to the customer's problems or requirements.

11.3.3   Capability profile

The third set of factors affecting competitive strength centre around the resources that can be brought to bear in the market.

Management strength and depth

A major asset, and hence potential strength, of any company is its human resources, and particularly its management strength and depth. The skills and competencies of the staff working in an organisation are the strengths with which it can exploit opportunities in the market place. Particularly in service organisations (such as consultancy companies or health services), the strength of the supplier often comes down to the individual skills of the managers who deal directly with the customers.

Marketing strength

Marketing strength stems from experience and synergy with other product areas. Companies operating primarily in consumer markets often believe they have superior marketing skills to those operating in slower-moving industrial markets. They then see these markets as areas where they can use the fast-moving consumer goods (FMCG) skills they have learned elsewhere to good effect. Experience of transferring skills from one business sector to another, however, has not been universally successful.

Forward and backward integration

The extent of control of the supply of raw materials (backward integration) and distribution channels (forward integration) can also affect the strength or potential strength of a company in serving a specific target. Where integration is high, especially in markets where supplier and buyer power is high (see above), the firm could be in a much stronger position than its rivals.

11.3.4   Summary

The important point to consider when assessing company or business strength is that strength is relative both to competitors also serving the segment and to the requirements of the segment.

One technique that can be useful in assessing current strengths in serving particular markets is the product–customer matrix (see Figure 11.1). This matrix presents a summary of the current products (or services) offered by the company tabulated against segments served. For industrial marketers with several particularly large customers, the customers may well be best considered individually. The technique summarises the sales value of each product to each customer or segment (outer circle) and the actual sterling contribution as a proportion of that sales value (inner circle). The final row and column summarise product sales value and contribution across customers, and customer sales value and contribution across products, rescaled for ease of presentation.

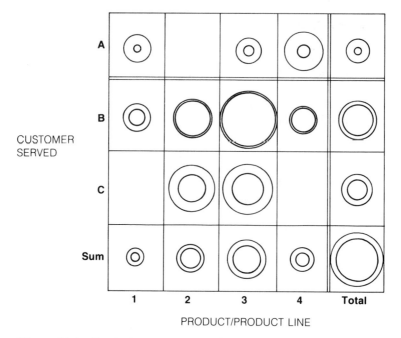

A

B

CUSTOMER
SERVED

C

Sum

| | 1 | 2 | 3 | 4 | Total |

PRODUCT/PRODUCT LINE

Figure 11.1   Product–customer matrix

It can be seen in the example of Figure 11.1 that the bulk of sales come from products 2 and 3. The company's main strengths seem to be in serving segments B and C. Segment A is not currently a major contributor for the company, even though turnover is approaching that of segment C. Similarly, products 1 and 4 are not major current earners and, unless they are developments for the future or service lines to enable the company to serve the profitable segment B, they should be considered for deletion from the product portfolio.

11.4   Putting it all together

Several authors have suggested the use of portfolio matrices as a useful way of summarising the alternative business investment opportunities open to a multiproduct company. Such matrices have also been used to assess the balance of the portfolio of businesses the company operates (see Chapter 3). The same techniques can be usefully adapted to help with the selection of market targets.

Techniques such as the directional policy matrix developed by the UK Chemical Division of Royal Dutch Shell (Robinson, Hitchins and Wade, 1978) or the GE matrix (Wind and Mahajan, 1981), while generally considered as methods for modelling existing portfolios, are actually, in many instances, better suited to deciding which markets to target in the first place. An adapted model is presented in Figure 11.2.

MARKET SEGMENT ATTRACTIVENESS

		Unattractive	Average	Attractive
CURRENT AND POTENTIAL COMPANY STRENGTHS IN SERVING THE SEGMENT	**Weak**	Strongly avoid	Avoid	Possibilities
	Average	Avoid	Possibilities	Secondary targets
	Strong	Possibilities	Secondary targets	Prime targets

Figure 11.2   Target market selection

Under this approach the factors deemed relevant in a particular market are identified (typically from the factors listed above) and are each assigned weights depending on their perceived importance. The subjective choice and weighting of the factors to be used in the analysis ensures that the model is customised to the needs of the specific company. The process of selecting and weighting the factors can, in itself, prove a valuable experience in familiarising managers with the realities of the company's markets. Where appropriate, factors can be more objectively assessed through the use of marketing research or economic analysis.

Once the factors have been determined and weighted, each potential market segment is evaluated on a scale from 'excellent = 5' to 'poor = 1' and a summary score on the two main dimensions of 'market segment attractiveness' and 'company business strength in serving that segment' is computed using the weightings. Sensitivity analyses can then be conducted to gauge the impact of different assumptions on the weight to attach to individual factors and the assessments of targets on each scale.

The resulting model, such as that shown in Figure 11.3 for a hypothetical company, enables the alternatives to be assessed and discussed objectively. Ideally, companies are looking for market targets in the bottom right-hand corner of Figure 11.3. These opportunities rarely exist and the trade-off then becomes between going into segments where the company is strong, or can become so, but which are less attractive (e.g. target opportunity 1), or alternatively tackling more attractive markets where the company is only average in strength (target 2).

To develop defensible positions in the market place, the former (sticking to areas of current or potential strength) often makes the most sense. Indeed, many would argue (see Ohmae, 1982) that most companies are better advised to consolidate in apparently less attractive markets where they have considerable exploitable strengths than to 'chase the rainbows' of seemingly attractive markets where they are only average or weak players.

Where business strength is weak, investment should be avoided in average or unattractive markets (target 7); in very attractive market segments, some strengths could be built or bought in through merger/acquisition (e.g. target 3). Similarly,

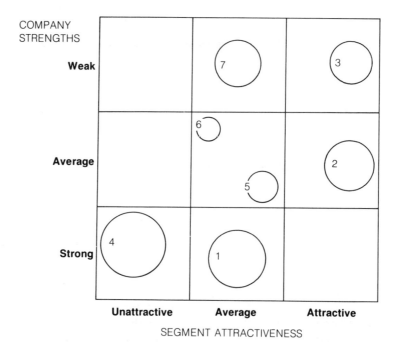

Figure 11.3 Evaluating market targets for a hypothetical company

investment in unattractive segments should be avoided unless particular company strengths can lead to a profitable exploitation of the market (target 4). Market segments of medium attractiveness where the company has medium strength should be invested in selectively (targets 5 and 6).

A further factor in selecting target markets for the overall business is how those individual targets add up: that is, the overall portfolio of businesses or markets the company is operating in (see Chapter 3). Companies are typically seeking to build a balanced portfolio of activities — balanced in terms of cash use and generation, risk and return, and focus on the future as well as on the present.

■   A prime example of a company using the above approach to selecting new market targets on a world scale is Fletcher Challenge Ltd. With assets in 1990 valued at over £6 billion, turnover of £4.11 billion and pretax profit of £345 million, it is New Zealand's largest and most successful company.

Fletcher Challenge (FC) examines opportunities for acquisition or further investment on the basis of two sets of factors — industry attractiveness and potential business strength in serving that market.

Industry, or target, attractiveness is determined by the following key factors: FC looks for markets with a steady demand growth (growing markets are easier to exit if difficulties arise); which are low in customer concentration (are not dominated by a handful of large customers); where there are substantial barriers to entry (in scale of operations, level of technology employed and control of the inputs and supporting industries); where participants are few and competitors are 'good' (up to two or three major players, in the market for the long haul); where prices are stable (absence of price wars or wild fluctuations); and where there is a steep cost (experience) curve where Fletcher Challenge's scale of operations will yield lower costs.

Company strength in serving the targets is examined in the following main areas: Fletcher looks for markets where it is, or believes it can become, the market leader; where it can utilise its technological expertise to the full; where it can achieve a cost leadership position; where it can manage intergroup (competitor) understandings; and where it can keep control of the market (especially in pricing).

The acquisitions and expansion strategies of Fletcher Challenge from the mid-1980s have consistently met the above criteria. ■

11.5 Alternative targeting strategies

As noted by Kotler (1991), there are three broad approaches a company can take to its market, having identified and evaluated the various segments that make up the total. The company can pursue undifferentiated marketing, essentially producing a single product designed to appeal across the board to all segments; differentiated marketing, offering a different product to each of the different segments; or concentrated marketing, focusing attention on one, or a few, segments.

11.5.1 Undifferentiated marketing

An undifferentiated marketing approach entails treating the market as one whole, rather than as segmented, and supplying one standard product or service to satisfy all customers. It is the approach carried out in the cost leadership strategy of Porter (1980). This approach was particularly prevalent in the mass marketing era in the days before the emergence (or recognition!) of strongly identified market segments. More recently, however, as the existence of market segments has become more widely accepted, the wisdom of such an approach in all markets except where preferences are strongly concentrated has been called into doubt.

11.5.2 Differentiated marketing

Differentiated marketing is adopted by companies seeking to offer a distinct product or service to each chosen segment of the market. Thus a shampoo manufacturer will offer different types of shampoo depending on the condition of the hair of the customer. The major danger of differentiated marketing is that it can lead to high costs, both of manufacturing and of marketing a wide product line. Depending on the company's resources, however, differentiated marketing can help in achieving overall market domination (this is the strategy pursued in the yellow fats market by Van den Berghs, see above).

11.5.3   Focused marketing

For the organisation with limited resources, however, attacking all or even most of the potential segments in a market may not be a viable proposition. In this instance, concentrated or focused marketing may make more sense. Under this strategy the organisation focuses attention on one or a few market segments and leaves the wider market to its competitors. In this way it builds a strong position in a few selected markets, rather than attempting to compete across the board (either with undifferentiated or with differentiated products).

The success of this approach depends on clear, in-depth knowledge of the customers served. The major danger of the strategy, however, is that over time the segment focused on may become less attractive and limiting on the organisation.

■   Lucozade is a glucose, carbonated drink first made in the 1930s. In the late 1970s the brand, which was focused on the sick child and offered as a highly concentrated source of energy that was quickly assimilated into the bloodstream, appeared to be in terminal decline. This was partly due to the fact that the population was growing healthier and the use of the product was declining. The concentration on the sick child market had created a strong position for Beecham Foods, marketers of Lucozade, in an increasingly unattractive market.

Without destroying the strength enjoyed by the brand in its original segment, the company set about broadening the customer base for the product (see Broadbent, 1981). New potential uses were identified and the product was essentially targeted at a broader segment — any member of the family wanting highly concentrated energy quickly absorbed. Initial redefinition of the target segment saw the product advertised to mothers as a quick pick-me-up, and subsequently to fully fit young adults (using the sportsman Daley Thompson in the advertisements). Lucozade was effectively retargeted as an enjoyable source of energy in health as well as sickness.   ■

The most effective strategy to adopt with regard to target market selection will vary from market to market. Certain characteristics of both the market and the company, however, will serve to suggest the type of strategy that makes most sense in a given situation.

11.6   Choosing between strategies

Figure 11.4 (from Cravens, 1982) shows the major factors that should be taken into consideration when deciding on the type of strategy to pursue. A mass marketing strategy (or undifferentiated marketing) makes more sense when customer needs and wants are similar (i.e. when preferences are concentrated). It also makes more sense in small and simple markets where the scope for segmentation is less. A mass marketing strategy is more likely to be pursued by companies already dominant in the market, with high market shares and substantial resources, experiencing weak or low levels of competition and where economies of scale are greatest.

Conversely, a niche strategy (or concentrated, focused marketing) makes more sense where preferences are clustered (i.e. clear segmentation of the market exists), the

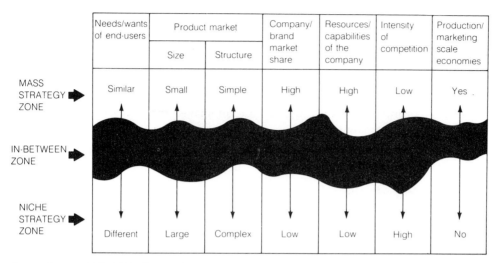

	Needs/wants of end-users	Product market		Company/ brand market share	Resources/ capabilities of the company	Intensity of competition	Production/ marketing scale economies
		Size	Structure				
MASS STRATEGY ZONE	Similar	Small	Simple	High	High	Low	Yes
IN-BETWEEN ZONE							
NICHE STRATEGY ZONE	Different	Large	Complex	Low	Low	High	No

Source: Cravens, D.W. (1982), *Strategic Marketing*. Homewood, Ill.: R.D. Irwin, p. 189.

Figure 11.4   Factors affecting the choice of a target market strategy

market is large and complex, the company has a small share of the overall market, with a relatively low level of resources, in the face of heavy competition, and where economies of scale of operations are not significant.

In any one market it is unlikely that all the factors will point in the same direction. Weighing up the factors and making decisions is the role of the marketing strategist. Increasingly, however, some degree of targeting of marketing effort is becoming essential.

11.7 Conclusions

The selection of which potential market segment or segments to serve is the crucial step in developing a comprehensive marketing strategy. Until the targets have been clearly identified, their requirements and motivations fully explored, it is not possible to take fully rational decisions concerning the remainder of the marketing mix.

Building and maintaining defensible positions

Competitive Strategy is the search for a favourable competitive
position in an industry. Competitive Strategy aims to establish a
profitable and sustainable position against the forces that determine
industry competition.

Porter (1985)

Introduction

Chapter 11 discussed the choice of target market suited to the strengths and capabilities
of the firm. This chapter focuses on methods for creating a competitive advantage
in that chosen target market. While few advantages are likely to last for ever, some
bases of advantage are more readily protected than others. A key task for the strategist
is to identify those bases which offer the most potential for defensible positioning.

As noted in Chapter 2, Porter (1980) has identified two main routes to creating
a competitive advantage. These he termed *cost leadership* and *differentiation*. In
examining how each can be achieved, Porter (1985) takes a systems approach, likening
the operations of a company to a *value chain* from the input of raw materials and
other resources through to the final delivery to, and after-sales servicing of, the
customer. The value chain was discussed in the context of competitor analysis in
Chapter 7 and was presented in Figure 7.3.

Each of the activities within the value chain, the primary activities and the support
functions, can be used to add value to the ultimate product or service. That added
value, however, is typically in the form of lower cost or valued uniqueness.

The main factors affecting each route are discussed below.

12.1 Creating cost leadership

Porter (1985) has identified several major factors that affect costs. These he terms
cost drivers. They are shown in Figure 12.1 and each is reviewed briefly below.

12.1.1 Economies of scale

Economies of scale are perhaps the single most effective cost driver in many industries.
Scale economies stem from doing things more efficiently or differently in volume.

In addition, sheer size can help in creating purchasing leverage to secure cheaper and/or better quality (less waste) raw materials and securing them in times of limited availability.

There are, however, limits to scale economies. Size can bring with it added complexity, which itself can lead to diseconomies. For most operations, there is an optimum size above or below which inefficiencies occur.

12.1.2   Experience and learning effects

Further cost reductions may be achieved through learning and experience effects. Learning refers to increases in efficiency that are possible at a given level of scale through having performed the necessary tasks many times before.

In the 1960s the Boston Consulting Group extended the recognised production learning curve beyond manufacturing and looked at increased efficiency that was possible in all aspects of the business (e.g. in marketing, advertising and selling) through experience. BCG estimated empirically that, in many industries, costs reduced by approximately 15–20 per cent each time cumulative production (a measure of experience) doubled. This finding suggests that companies with larger market share will, by definition, have a cost advantage through experience, assuming all companies are operating on the same experience curve.

Experience can be brought into the company by hiring experienced staff, and enhanced through training. Conversely, competitors may poach experience by attracting away skilled staff.

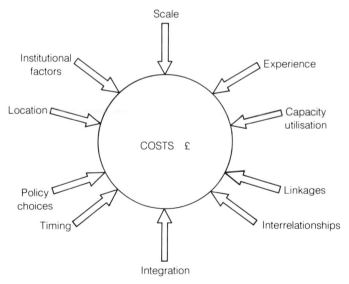

Source: Based on Porter (1985).

Figure 12.1   Cost drivers

The experience curve as an explanation of costs has come under increasing scrutiny recently. Gluck (1986) argues that when the world changed from a high-growth, 'big is beautiful', mentality to a low-growth, 'big is bust' realisation, the experience curve fell into disfavour. He concludes that in today's business environments competitive advantages that rely too heavily on economies of scale in manufacturing or distribution are often no longer sustainable. In addition, a shift in the level or type of technology employed may result in an inexperienced newcomer reducing costs below those of a more experienced incumbent, essentially moving on to a lower experience curve. Finally, the concept was derived in manufacturing industries and it is not at all clear how applicable it is to the service sector.

12.1.3   Capacity utilisation

Capacity utilisation has been shown to have a major impact on unit costs. The PIMS study (see Buzzell and Gale, 1987) has demonstrated a clear positive association between utilisation and return on investment (ROI). Significantly, the relationship is stronger for smaller companies than for larger ones. Major discontinuities or changes in utilisation can add significantly to costs, hence the need to plan production and inventory to minimise seasonal fluctuations. Many companies also avoid segments of the market where demand fluctuates wildly for this very reason (see Chapter 11 on factors influencing market attractiveness).

12.1.4   Linkages

A further set of cost drivers are linkages. These concern the other activities of the firm in producing and marketing the product that have an effect on the costs. Quality control and inspection procedures, for example, can have a significant impact on servicing costs and costs attributable to faulty product returns. Indeed, in many markets it has been demonstrated that superior quality, rather than leading to higher costs of production, can actually reduce costs (Peters, 1988).

External linkages with suppliers of factor inputs or distributors of the firm's final products can also result in lower costs. Recent developments in just-in-time manufacturing and delivery (JIT) can have a significant impact on stockholding costs and work in progress. Beyond the cost equation, however, the establishment of closer working links has far wider marketing implications. For JIT to work effectively requires a very close working relationship between buyer and supplier. This often means an interchange of information, a meshing of forecasting and scheduling, and the building of a long-term relationship. This in turn helps to create high switching costs (the costs of seeking supply elsewhere) and hence barriers to competitive entry.

12.1.5   Interrelationships

Interrelationships with other SBUs in the overall corporate portfolio can help to share experience and gain economies of scale in functional activities, such as marketing research, research and development, quality control, ordering and purchasing.

12.1.6   Degree of integration

Decisions on integration, e.g. contracting out delivery and/or service, also affect costs. Similarly, the decision to make or buy components can have major cost implications. The extent of forward or backward integration extant or possible in a particular market was discussed in Chapter 11 as one of the factors considered in assessing target market attractiveness to the company.

12.1.7   Timing

Timing, though not always controllable, can lead to cost advantages. Often the first mover in an industry can gain cost advantages by securing prime locations, cheap or good-quality raw materials, and/or technological leadership. Second movers can often benefit from exploiting newer technology to leap-frog first mover positions.

   As with other factors discussed above, however, the value of timing goes far beyond its impact on costs. Abell (1978) has argued that a crucial element of any marketing strategy is timing, that at certain times 'strategic windows' are open (i.e. there are opportunities in the market that can be exploited) while at other times they are shut. Successful strategies are timely strategies. A prime example would be the impact of the more economical Japanese cars in the US market after the 1973 oil crisis and subsequent price rise, while American-made cars were still in the 'gas guzzler' era.

12.1.8   Policy choices

Policy choices, the prime areas for differentiating discussed below, have implications for costs. Decisions on the product line, the product itself, quality levels, service, features, credit facilities, etc. all affect costs. They also affect the actual and perceived uniqueness of the product to the consumer and hence a genuine dilemma can arise if the thrust of the generic strategy is not clear. The general rules are to reduce costs on factors which will not significantly affect valued uniqueness, avoid frills if they do not serve to differentiate significantly, and invest in technology to achieve low-cost process automation and low-cost product design (fewer parts can make for easier and cheaper assembly).

12.1.9   Location and institutional factors

The final cost drivers identified by Porter (1985) are location (geographic location to take advantage of lower distribution, assembly, raw materials or energy costs) and institutional factors such as government regulations (e.g. larger lorries on the roads can reduce distribution costs but at other environmental and social costs). The sensitivity of governments to lobbyists and pressure groups will dictate the ability of the company to exercise institutional cost drivers.

12.1.10   Summary of cost drivers

There are many ways in which a company can seek to reduce costs. In attempting to become a cost leader in an industry, a firm should be aware, first, that there can only be one cost leader, and second, that there are potentially many ways in which this position can be attacked (i.e. through using other cost drivers). Cost advantages can be among the most difficult to sustain and defend in the face of heavy and determined competition.

That said, however, it should be a constant objective of management to reduce costs that do not significantly add to ultimate customer satisfaction.

12.2   Achieving differentiation

Most of the factors listed above as cost drivers could also be used as 'uniqueness drivers' if the firm is seeking to differentiate itself from its competitors. Of most immediate concern here, however, are the policy choices open to the company. These are summarised in Figure 12.2.

12.2.1   Product differentiation

Product differentiation seeks to increase the value of the product or service on offer to the customer. Levitt (1986) has suggested that products and services can be seen on at least four main levels. These are the core product, the expected product, the augmented product and the potential product. Figure 12.3 shows these levels diagrammatically. Differentiation is possible in all these respects.

At the centre of Levitt's model is the core or generic product. This is the central product or service offered. It is the petrol, steel, banking facility, mortgage, information, etc. Beyond the generic product, however, is what customers expect in addition, the expected product. When buying petrol, for example, customers expect easy access to the forecourt, the possibility of buying by credit card, the availability of screen wash facilities, air for tyres, radiator top-up and so on. Since most petrol forecourts meet these expectations they do not serve to differentiate one supplier from another.

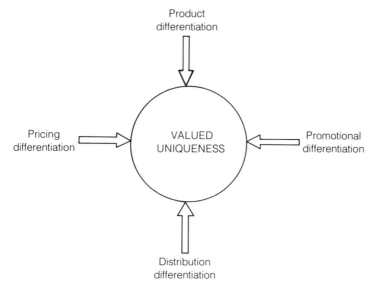

Figure 12.2 Uniqueness drivers

At the next level, Levitt identifies the augmented product. This constitutes all the extra features and services that go above and beyond what the customer expects, that convey added value and hence serve to differentiate the offer from that of competitors. The petrol station where, in the self-serve 1990s, one attendant fills the car with petrol while another cleans the windscreen, headlamps and mirrors is going beyond what is expected. Over time, however, these means of distinguishing can become copied, routine and ultimately merely part of what is expected.

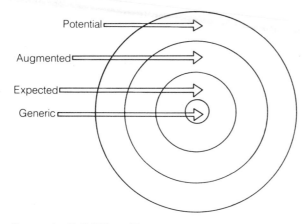

Source: Levitt (1986), p. 79.

Figure 12.3 Levels of product

Finally, Levitt describes the potential product as all those further additional features and benefits that could be offered. At the petrol station these may include a free car wash with every fill up, gifts unrelated to petrol and a car valeting service. While the model shows the potential product bounded, in reality it is bounded only by the imagination and ingenuity of the supplier.

Peters (1988) believes that, while in the past suppliers have concentrated on attempts to differentiate their offerings on the basis of the generic and expected product, convergence is now occurring at this level in many markets. As quality control, assurance and management methods become more widely understood and practised, delivering a performing, reliable, durable, conforming offer (a 'quality' product in the classic sense of the word) will no longer be adequate. In the future he predicts greater emphasis on the augmented and potential product as ways of adding value, creating customer delight and hence creating competitive advantage.

Differentiating the core and expected product

Differentiation of the core product or benefit offers a different way of satisfying the same basic want or need. It is typically created by a step change in technology, the application of innovation. Calculators, for example, offered a different method of solving the basic 'calculating' need than the slide rules that they replaced. Similarly, the deep freeze offers a different way of storing food to the earlier coldstores, pantries and cellars.

Augmenting the product

Differentiation of the augmented product can be achieved by offering more to customers on existing features (e.g. offering a lifetime guarantee on audio tape, as Scotch provide, rather than a one- or two-year guarantee), or by offering new features of value to customers. There are two main types of product feature that can create customer benefit. These are performance features and appearance features.

Analysis of product features must relate those features to the benefits they offer to customers. For example, the introduction of the golf-ball typewriter did not change the core benefit (the ability to create a typewritten page of text or numbers). It did, however, allow different typefaces and different spacings to be used, thus extending the value to the customer who wanted these extra benefits. In estimating the value to the consumers of additional product features and their resulting benefits, conjoint measurement (see Green and Wind, 1975) can be particularly useful. This technique has been successfully applied to product features by companies operating in the audio market and to service features by building societies in high-interest accounts.

In the lawnmower market, Flymo introduced the rotary-blade hover mower as a means of differentiating from the traditional rotating cylinder blade. In some markets, especially where lawns were awkwardly shaped or steeply sloping, the ease of use of the hover mower made it a very attractive, differentiated product. In other markets, however, the market leader, Qualcast, was able to retaliate by showing the advantage of the conventional mower in having a hopper in which to catch the grass cuttings.

Under the Flymo system, the cuttings were left on the cut lawn. More recent developments have seen the introduction of rotary hover mowers with hoppers.

A prime factor in differentiating the product or service from that of competitors is quality. Quality concerns the fitness for purpose of a product or service. For manufactured products, that can include the durability, appearance or grade of the product, while in services it often comes down to the tangible elements of the service, the reliability and responsiveness of the service provider, the assurance provided of the value of the service and the empathy or caring attention received (see Parasuraman, Zeithaml and Berry, 1988). Quality can reflect heavily both on raw materials used and the degree of quality control exercised during manufacture and delivery.

Of central importance is the consumer's perception of quality, which may not be the same as the manufacturer's perception. Cardozo (1979) gives an example of where the two do not coincide:

> ■ The marketing research department of a manufacturer of household paper goods asked for consumer evaluation of a new paper tissue. The reaction was favourable, but the product was not thought to be soft enough. The R & D department then set about softening the tissue by weakening the fibres and reducing their density. In subsequent usage tests, the product fell apart and was useless for its designed purpose. Further tests showed that to make the product 'feel' softer required an actual increase in the strength and density of the fibres. ■

Quality has been demonstrated by the PIMS project to be a major determinant of commercial success. Indeed, Buzzell and Gale (1987) concluded that relative perceived quality (customers' judgements of the quality of the supplier's offer relative to its competitors) was the single most important factor in affecting the long-run performance of a business. Quality was shown both to have a greater impact on ROI level and to be more effective at gaining market share than lower pricing.

Closely related to perceptions of quality are perceptions of style, particularly for products with a high emotional appeal, such as cosmetics. In fashion-conscious markets such as clothes, design can be a very powerful way of differentiating. Jain (1990) notes that Du Pont successfully rejuvenated its market for ladies' stockings by offering different coloured tints and hence repositioned the stockings as fashion accessories — a different tint for each different outfit.

Packaging too can be used to differentiate the product. Packaging has five main functions, each of which can be used as a basis for differentiation:

- Packaging stores the product, and hence can be used to extend shelf life, or facilitate physical storage (e.g. tetra-packs for fruit juice and other beverages).
- Packaging protects the product during transit and prior to consumption to ensure consistent quality (e.g. the use of film packs for potato crisps to ensure freshness).
- Packaging facilitates use of the product (e.g. applicator packs for floor cleaners, wine boxes, domestic liquid soap dispensers).
- Packaging helps create an image for the product through its visual impact, quality of design, illustration of uses, etc.
- Packaging helps promote the product through eye-catching, unusual colours and

shapes etc. Examples of the latter are the sale of wine in carafes rather than bottles (Paul Masson California Wines) and the sale of ladies' tights in egg-shaped packages (L'eggs).

A particularly effective way of differentiating at the tangible product level is to create a unique brand with a favourable image and reputation. As discussed in Chapter 5, brand and company reputation can be powerful marketing assets for a company.

Brand name or symbol is an indication of pedigree and a guarantee of what to expect from the product — a quality statement and a value-for-money signal. Heinz baked beans, for example, can command a premium price because of the assurance of quality the consumer gets in choosing the brand. Similarly, retailers such as Sainsbury and Marks & Spencer are able to differentiate their own branded products from other brands because of a reputation for quality that extends across their product ranges. Branding is also a highly defensible competitive advantage. Once it is registered competitors cannot use the same branding (name or symbol).

Service can be a major differentiating factor in the purchase of many products, especially durables (both consumer and industrial).

> ■ Enhanced service was a major factor in the success of Wilhelm Becker, a Swedish industrial paints company. Becker developed 'Colour Studios' as a service to its customers and potential customers to enable them to experiment with different colours and combinations. Volvo, the Swedish auto manufacturer, used the service in researching alternative colours to use on farm tractors and found that red (the colour used to date) was a poor choice as it jarred, for many farmers, with the colours of the landscape. Changing the colour scheme resulted in increased sales.
>
> In domestic paints, too, there has been an attempt to add service, this time provided by the customer him- or herself. Matchpots were introduced by a leading domestic paint supplier to allow customers, for a small outlay, to try different colours at home before selecting the final colour to use. In this case, however, unlike Becker's Colour Studios, copy by competitors was relatively easy and the advantage quickly disappeared. ■

Service need not be an addition to the product. In some circumstances a reduction can add value. The recent growth in home brewing of beers and wines is a case where a less complete product (the malt extract, hops, grape juice, yeast, etc.) is put to market but the customer is able to gain satisfaction through self-completion of the production process. Thus the customer provides the service and becomes part of the production process.

Providing superior service as a way of creating a stronger link between supplier and customer can have wide-reaching consequences. In particular, it makes it less likely that the customer will look for alternative supply sources and hence acts as a barrier to competitor entry.

To ensure and enhance customer service Peters (1988) recommends that each company regularly conduct customer satisfaction studies to gauge how well it is meeting customers' expectations and to seek ways in which it can improve on customer service.

Further elements of the augmented product that can be used to differentiate the product include installation, credit availability, delivery (speedy and on time, when promised) and warranty. All can add to the differentiation of the product from that of competitors.

Deciding on the bases for product differentiation

Each of the elements of the product can be used as a way of differentiating the product from competitive offerings. In deciding which of the possible elements to use in differentiating the product, three considerations are paramount.

First, what do the customers expect in addition to the core, generic product? In the automobile market, for example, customers in all market segments expect a minimum level of reliability in the cars they buy. In the purchase of consumer white goods (fridges, freezers, washing machines, etc.), minimum periods of warranty are expected. In the choice of toothpaste, minimum levels of protection from tooth decay and gum disease are required. These expectations, over and above the core product offering, are akin to 'hygiene factors' in Hertzberg's theory of motivation. They must be offered for the product or service to be considered by potential purchasers. Their presence does not enhance the probability of consumers choosing the products with them, but their absence will certainly deter purchase.

The second consideration is what the customers would value over and above what is expected. In identifying potential 'motivators', the marketer seeks to offer more than the competition to attract purchasers. These additions to the product beyond what is normally expected by the customers often form the most effective way of differentiating the company's offerings. Crucial, however, is the cost of offering these additions. The cost of the additions should be less than the extra benefit (value) to the customers, and hence should be reflected in a willingness to pay a premium price. Where possible an economic value should be placed on the differentiation to allow pricing to take full account of value to the customer (see Forbis and Mehta, 1981).

The third consideration in choosing a way of differentiating the product from the competition is the ease with which that differentiation can be copied. Changes in the interest rates charged by one building society, for example, can be easily copied in a matter of days or even hours. An advantage based, however, on the location of the society's outlets in the major city high streets takes longer to copy and is more costly.

Ideally, differentiation is sought where there is some (at least temporary) barrier precluding competitors following. The most successful differentiations are those that use a core skill, competence or marketing asset of the company that competitors do not possess and will find it hard to develop. In the car-hire business, for example, the extensive network of pick-up and drop-off points offered by Hertz, the market leader, enables it to offer a more convenient service to the one-way customer than the competition. Emulating that network is costly, if not impossible, for smaller followers in the market.

Peters (1988) has argued that many companies overemphasise the core product in their overall marketing thinking and strategy. He suggests that, as it becomes increasingly difficult to differentiate on the basis of core product, greater emphasis will need to be put on how to 'add service' through the augmented (and potential) product. This change in emphasis is shown in Figure 12.4, which contrasts a product focus (core product emphasis) with a service-added focus (extending the augmented and potential products in ways of value and interest to the customer).

A focus away from the core product towards the 'outer rings' is particularly useful in 'commodity' markets where competitive strategy has traditionally been based on price. Differentiation through added service offers an opportunity for breaking out of an overreliance on price in securing business.

In summary, there are a great many ways in which products and services can be differentiated from their competitors. In deciding on the type of differentiation to adopt, several factors should be borne in mind: the added value to the customer of the differentiation; the cost of differentiation in relation to the added value; the probability and speed of competitor copy; and the extent to which the differentiation exploits the marketing assets of the company.

12.2.2   Promotional differentiation

Promotional differentiation involves using different types of promotion (e.g. a wider communications mix employing advertising, public relations, direct mail, personal selling, etc.), promotions of a different intensity (e.g. particularly heavy promotions during launch and relaunch of products) or promotions of a different content (e.g. with a clearly different advertising message).

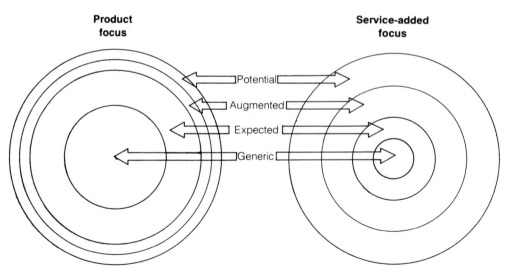

Source: Based on Peters (1988), Figure 8, p. 93.

Figure 12.4 Alternative emphases for differentiation

Many companies today make poor use of the potential of public relations. Public relations essentially consists of creating relationships with the media and using those relationships to gain positive exposure. Press releases and interviews with key executives on important topical issues can help to promote the company in a more credible way than media advertising.

■ A small-UK based electronics company brilliantly exploited a visit by Japanese scientists to its plant. The company gained wide coverage of the event, presenting it as an attempt by the Japanese to learn from this small but innovative company. The coverage was in relevant trade journals and even the national media. The result was a major increase in enquiries to the company and increasing domestic sales of its products.

The PR had two major advantages over media advertising. First, it was very cheap in relation to the exposure it achieved (the company could never have afforded to buy the exposure at normal media rates). Second, the reports appearing in the press carried more credibility because they had been written by independent journalists and were seen as 'news' rather than advertising. (From *The Marketing Mix*, a television series by Yorkshire TV.) ■

Using a different message within normal media advertising can also have a differentiating effect. When most advertisers are pursuing essentially the same market with the same message, an innovative twist is called for.

■ Most beers were promoted in the 1970s by showing gregarious groups of males in public houses having an enjoyable night out. Heineken managed to differentiate their beer by using a series of advertisements employing humour and the caption 'Heineken refreshes the parts other beers cannot reach.'

When Krona was launched by Van den Berghs into the margarine market (see Chapter 11), aimed at consumers who were increasingly sensitive to the price of butter but who still required the taste of butter, the company had a major communications problem. Legislation precluded stating that the product tasted like butter (Clark, 1986) and the slogan 'Four out of five people can't tell the difference between Stork and butter' had already been used (with mixed success) by one of the other company brands.

The solution was to use a semi-documentary advertisement featuring a respected reporter (Rene Cutforth) that majored on a rumour that had circulated around a product of identical formulation in Australia (Fairy). The rumours had been that the product was actually New Zealand butter being dumped on the Australian market disguised as margarine to overcome trade quotas. The slogan selected was 'the margarine that raised questions in the Australian parliament', and the style of the advertisement, while never actually claiming taste parity with butter, cleverly conveyed the impression that people really could not tell the difference. ■

12.2.3 Distribution differentiation

Distribution differentiation comes from using different outlets, having a different network or a different coverage of the market.

Recent developments in direct marketing are not only related to creating different ways of promoting products. They also offer new outlets for many goods. Shopping by phone through TV-based catalogues has yet to take off in any big way but there are certainly opportunities for innovative marketers.

12.2.4   Price differentiation

Lower price as a means of differentiation can be a successful basis for strategy only where the company enjoys a cost advantage, or where there are barriers to competing firms with a lower cost structure competing at a lower price. Without a cost advantage starting a price war can be a disastrous course to follow, as Laker Airways found to its cost.

Premium pricing is generally possible only where the product or service has actual or perceived advantages to the customer and therefore is often used in conjunction with and to reinforce a differentiated product.

In general, the greater the degree of product or service differentiation, the more scope there is for premium pricing. Where there is little other ground for differentiation, price competition becomes stronger and cost advantages assume greater importance.

12.2.5   Summary

Where differentiation is the route selected to competitive advantage, the key differentiating variables, those which offer the most leverage for differentiation and use the company's skills to the full, should be identified. Where possible, differentiation should be pursued on multiple fronts to enhance differentiation. In addition, value signals should be employed to enhance perceived differentiation (e.g. building on reputation, image, presence, appearance and pricing of the product). Barriers to copying should be erected, through patenting, holding key executives and creating switching costs to retain customers.

12.3   Maintaining a defensible position

It will be clear from the above that there are a variety of ways in which companies can attempt to create for themselves a competitive advantage. Some of those ways will be easier for competitors to copy than others. The most useful ways of creating defensible positions lie in exploiting the following.

12.3.1   Unique and valued products

Fundamental to creating a superior and defensible position in the market place is to have unique and valued products and services to offer to customers.

■ Dow Jones maintains high margins from unique products. The *Wall Street Journal* is a product that customers want and are willing to pay for.   ■

Central to offering unique and valued products and services is the identification of the key differentiating variables — those with the greatest potential leverage. Uniqueness may stem from employing superior, proprietary technology, utilising superior raw materials, or differentiating the tangible and augmented and potential elements of products.

Unique products do not, however, stay unique for ever. Successful products will be imitated sooner or later, so the company that wishes to retain its unique position must be willing, and even eager, to innovate continually and look for new ways of differentiating. This may mean a willingness to cannibalise its own existing products, before the competition attacks them.

12.3.2   Clear, tight definition of market targets

To enable a company to keep its products and services both unique and valued by the customers requires constant monitoring of, and dialogue with, those customers. This in turn requires a clear understanding of who they are and how to access them. The clearer the focus of the firm's activities on one or a few market targets, the more likely it is to serve those targets successfully. In the increasingly segmented markets of the 1990s, the companies that fail to focus their activities are less likely to respond to changing opportunities and threats.

12.3.3   Enhanced customer linkages

Creating closer bonds with customers through enhanced service can help establish a more defensible position in the market. As suggested above, a major advantage of JIT manufacturing systems is that they require closer links between supplier and buyer. As buyers and suppliers become more enmeshed, so it becomes more difficult for newcomers to enter.

Creating switching costs, the costs associated with moving from one supplier to another, is a further way in which customer linkages can be enhanced.

■ Loomis, writing in *Fortune* (30 April 1984), pointed to the success of Nalco in using its specialist expertise in the chemicals it markets to counsel and problem-solve for its customers. This enhancement of the linkages with its customers makes it less likely that they will shop around for other sources of supply. ■

12.3.4   Establishing brand and company credibility

Brand and company reputation are among the most defensible assets the company has, provided they are managed well and protected. Brands can take many years to build but can be destroyed overnight by a lack of attention to issues such as quality control or safety.

■ Worthington Steel in the USA has an enviable reputation for superior quality workmanship. The company also has a high reputation for customer service. Combined they make it hard for customers to go elsewhere (Peters, 1988). ■

12.4   Conclusions

While two basic approaches to creating a competitive position have been discussed, it should be clear that the first priority in marketing will be to decide on the focus of operations, industry-wide or specific target market segments. Creating a competitive advantage in the selected area of focus can be achieved either through cost leadership or differentiation. To build a strong, defensible position in the market, the initial concern should be to differentiate the company's offerings from those of its competitors on some basis of value to the customer. The second concern should then be to achieve this at the lowest possible delivered cost.

THIRTEEN

Offensive and defensive marketing strategies

Companies fail in the market-place because their strategies are ill-conceived, poorly prepared and badly executed in relation to those of their competitors.

Barrie James (1984)

Introduction

Successful strategy amounts to combining attacking and defensive moves to build a stronger position in the chosen market place. In recent years several writers, most notably Kotler and Singh (1981), James (1984) and Ries and Trout (1986), have drawn an analogy between military warfare and competitive battles in the market place. Their basic contention is that lessons for the conduct of business strategy can be learned by a study of warfare and the principles developed by military strategists. Indeed, the bookshelves of corporate strategists around the world now often contain the works of Sun Tzu (see Clavell, 1981), Mushashi (1974) and von Clausewitz (1908).

There are five basic strategies that an organisation may pursue to reach its overall objectives. It may pursue a build (or growth) strategy, a holding (or maintenance) strategy, a niching strategy, a harvesting strategy, or a deletion (divestment) strategy. Each type of strategy is discussed below. The structure of the discussion draws on both Kotler (1991) and James (1984).

13.1 Build strategies

Build strategies are most suited to growth markets. In such markets it is generally considered easy to expand, as this expansion need not be at the expense of the competition and does not necessarily provoke strong competitive retaliation. During the growth phase of markets companies should aim to grow at least as fast as the market itself.

Build strategies can also make sense in non-growth markets where there are exploitable competitor weaknesses.

■ In the UK chocolate bar market Rowntree Macintosh identified an exploitable competitor weakness. Cadbury Dairy Milk, the market leader, had responded to escalating costs of raw materials by making the product progressively smaller. One manifestation was that the product was made thinner.

Customer research carried out by Rowntree showed that a significant proportion of customers were dissatisfied with the 'thinner' bars and were prepared to pay higher prices for a chocolate bar that was thicker, or more 'chunky'. The Rowntree product 'Yorkie' which emerged was a major marketing success, capturing a large slice of the mature chocolate bar market. ■

Similarly, where there are marketing assets that can be usefully deployed, a build strategy may make sense.

■ Rank Hovis MacDougal successfully exploited the granule technology developed for its Bisto gravy product in the market for instant packet soups with the launch of the 'Welcome' range of granular soups. ■

Build strategies are often costly, particularly where they involve a direct confrontation with a major competitor. Before embarking on such strategies the potential costs must be weighed against the expected gains.

13.1.1   Market expansion

Build strategies are achieved through market expansion or taking customers from competitors (confrontation). Market expansion, in turn, comes through three main routes: new users, new uses and/or increased frequency of purchase.

New users

As products and services progress through their life cycles, different purchasers will emerge at different times. During the introductory phase, innovators may be attracted to the offering. Once the market among innovators has been exhausted, new customers must be sought. For many expensive consumer durable products, such as compact disc players or home computers, a 'trickle down' effect has been observed with the products selling first to wealthy consumers at the top end of the social scale. As the product moves more into growth, competition intensifies and prices typically begin to fall, so newer customers are attracted to purchase the product. These are less wealthy and lower down the social scale.

For products which have reached the mature phase of the life cycle, a major task is to find new markets for the product. This could involve geographic expansion of the company's activities, domestically and/or internationally. Companies seeking growth but believing their established market to be incapable of providing it roll out into new markets.

New uses

For some products the market may be expanded through introducing existing (or new) users to different uses. The recent campaign for Hellmann's mayonnaise has stressed the versatility of its mayonnaise product and the fact that it can be used as an accompaniment to a variety of dishes, not just in the traditional salad usage.

Increased frequency of use

The third route to market expansion is through encouraging existing users to use more of the product. Clearly, this route is most applicable to repeat purchase (both of consumer and industrial) products. Segmentation by volume of consumption can help to identify medium or light users who might be targeted in an attempt to increase their frequency.

When segmenting by volume purchased or consumed, the typical approach is to focus activity on the heavy users. In mature markets, however, it is probable that the heavy users are already consuming near to maximum amounts of the products or services offered, and that growth for one competitor in that segment will be only at the expense of another, initiating a confrontation strategy. Depending on their reasons for using the product or service less, medium or light users may prove an easier target.

13.1.2   Market share gain through competitor confrontation

When a build objective is pursued in a market that cannot, for one reason or another, be expanded, success must by definition be at the expense of competitors. This will inevitably lead to some degree of confrontation between the protagonists for customers. Kotler and Singh (1981) have identified five main confrontation strategies (see Figure 13.1).

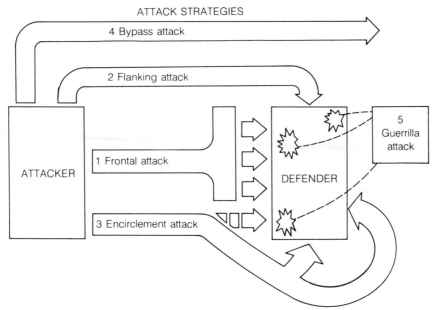

Source: Philip Kotler, *Marketing Management: Analysis, planning, implementation and control*, 7th edn © 1991, p. 388. Adapted by permission of Prentice Hall Inc., Englewood Cliffs, NJ.

Figure 13.1 Attack strategies

Frontal attack

The frontal attack is characterised by an all-out attack on the opponent's territory. It is often countered by a fortification, or position defence (see below). The outcome of the confrontation will depend on strength and endurance.

James (1984) points to the successful use of the frontal attack by Montgomery at El Alamein in 1942 when the attackers had a superiority of forces (men, guns, tanks and air support) of between two and three to one. The attackers also had the reserves to sustain the heavy casualties normally associated with a frontal attack.

The requirement of a similar three-to-one advantage to ensure success in a commercial frontal attack has been suggested (Kotler and Singh, 1981), further calibrated (Cook, 1983) and questioned (Chattopadhyay, Nedungadi and Chakravarti, 1985). All are agreed, however, that to defeat a well-entrenched competitor that has built a solid market position requires substantial superiority in at least one key area of the marketing programme.

■   IBM's attack on the PC market in the early 1980s is a classic example of the frontal attack. The market pioneer (Apple) was attacked partly as a defensive move by IBM, as the company saw the likelihood that PCs would become executive workstations and hence threaten IBM's traditional dominance of the mainframe business market. There were several aspects to IBM's attack on the market. It was spearheaded by a technological improvement (16-bit processors gave increased power and speed over the competitive 8-bit machines).

At the same time IBM made the technical specification of its machines widely available to software houses and other peripheral equipment manufacturers so that software became readily available and soon established an industry standard ('IBM compatible'). The creation of the industry standard was made possible by the use of that prime marketing asset — the IBM name and reputation. Finally, a massive promotional campaign was launched in the small business market. The results were not only a dominant share of the market for IBM, but also the further growth of the market as a whole.   ■

Frontal attacks, however, can be costly failures. The charge of the Light Brigade at Balaclava in the Crimean War of 1854 resulted in the death of 500 officers and men in the space of 30 minutes. Trench warfare in France during the First World War saw millions of casualties. In one five-month period during 1916 over 1,250,000 men died in attempts to break through enemy lines (James, 1984). In April 1915 thousands of Australian and New Zealand (ANZAC) troops lost their lives in frontal attacks on Turkish-held positions on the Gallipoli peninsula, only to abandon their beachhead a few weeks later when it became clear that the Turkish positions were unassailable.

In business, too, the frontal attack can prove suicidal. Laker Airways attacked the major airlines in the late 1970s on a low-price platform but with a matched product and service offering. When the other airlines reacted by cutting their prices, Laker was eventually forced out of business as the company's cost structure was no lower than those of competitors, and the company's reserves, badly affected by currency fluctuations in the early 1980s, were inadequate to sustain the losses.

For a frontal attack to succeed requires sufficient resources, a strength advantage over the competitor(s) being attacked, and that losses can be both predicted and sustained. For most companies, the muscle of IBM is not available and a frontal attack is not a sensible strategy to pursue.

Flanking attack

In contrast to the frontal attack, the flanking attack seeks to concentrate the aggressor's strengths against the competitor's weaknesses. In warfare, a flanking attack would seek to shift the battleground away from the enemy's strength to the unguarded or less well-defended flanks.

In business, a flanking attack is achieved either through attacking geographic regions where the defender is underrepresented or through attacking underserved competitor segments.

■ In the battle for domination of the grocery business in the UK, grocery multiple Sainsbury has identified competitor weaknesses in the north of England and recently attempted to expand into those regions.

World-wide Coca-Cola dominates the soft drinks market, but in some specific locations Pepsi Cola has exploited Coca-Cola's weaknesses and dominates. ■

Segmental flanking involves serving distinct segments that have not been adequately served by existing companies. James (1984) gives as an example the development of grocery retailing in the USA.

■ During the late 1970s and 1980s US supermarkets were getting bigger, emphasising one-stop shopping and (because of their sheer size) locating out of town. The problems for the smaller grocery stores were acute. There was, however, a limited market for convenience stores, those with a limited product range but local availability and long opening hours. Importantly, customers were prepared to pay more for convenience, and smaller chains such as 7—11 emerged. ■

The Japanese entry into the UK motor cycle market and subsequently the automobile market are classic examples of a flanking strategy. In autos especially, the Japanese took advantage of the OPEC-induced oil crisis of the early 1970s to cater to customer needs in the sub-compact car segment. The Japanese cars were cheap, reliable and offered good m.p.g. to the hard-hit motorist. Having established a toe-hold in the market, the Japanese car manufacturers have subsequently moved into other segments.

Crucial to a successful flanking strategy can be timing. The Japanese entry into the sub-compact car market was timed to take advantage of the recession and power crises of the early 1970s. The strategy requires the identification of competitor weaknesses and their inability or unwillingness to serve particular sectors of the market. In turn, identification of market gaps often requires a fresh look at the market and a more creative approach to segmenting it.

Encirclement attack

The encirclement attack, or siege, consists of enveloping the enemy, cutting him off from routes of supply to force capitulation. In warfare, the analogy would be with castle sieges of the Middle Ages where attackers would force defenders into their castles and cut the supply lines to starve the defenders into submission.

In business, there are two approaches to the encirclement attack. The first is to attempt to isolate the competitor from the supply of raw materials on which it depends and/or the customers it seeks to sell to. The second approach is to seek to offer an all-round better product or service than the competitor.

Bypass strategy

The bypass strategy is characterised by changing the battleground to avoid competitor strongholds. The Maginot line, built by France to protect itself from invasion, was simply bypassed and ignored by the invading German armies in the Second World War.

Bypass in business is often achieved through technological leap-frogging. Casio bypassed the strength of the Swiss watch industry through the development and marketing of digital watches. It similarly bypassed slide rule manufacturers with pocket calculators.

Guerrilla tactics

Where conventional warfare fails, guerrilla tactics often take over. During the Second World War the French Resistance harassed the occupying German forces. Terrorist activities in Northern Ireland, the Basque Country, Nicaragua and Sri Lanka are all designed to weaken the morale and determination of the terrorists' enemies.

In business, guerrilla or unconventional tactics can be employed primarily as 'spoiling' activities to weaken the competition. Selective price cuts, especially during a competitor's new product testing or launch, depositioning advertising (as attempted by the Butter Information Council Ltd in its campaign against Krona margarine), alliances (as used against Laker Airways), executive raids and legal manoeuvres can all be used in this regard. Guerrilla tactics are used by companies of all sizes in attempts to soften up their competitors, often before moving in for the kill. Their effectiveness lies in the difficulty the attacked has in adequately defending against them due to their unpredictability.

13.2 Hold strategies

For market leaders, especially in mature or declining markets, the major objective may be not to build but to maintain the current position against potential attackers. It could also be that, even in growing markets, the potential rewards judged to be possible from a build strategy are outweighed by the expected costs due, for example, to the strength and nature of competition.

A hold strategy may be particularly suitable for a business or product group designated as a cash generator for the company, where that cash is needed for investment elsewhere.

13.2.1   Market maintenance

The amount and type of effort required to hold position will vary depending on the degree and nature of competition encountered. When the business dominates its market, it may have cost advantages through economies of scale or experience effects that can be used as a basis for defending through selective price cutting. Alternatively, barriers to entry can be erected by the guarding of technological expertise where possible and the retention of key executive skills.

13.2.2   Defensive strategies

While in some markets competitor aggression may be low, making a holding strategy relatively easy to execute, where the potential gains for an aggressor are high, more constructive defensive strategies must be explicitly pursued. Kotler and Singh (1981) suggest six basic holding strategies (see Figure 13.2).

Fortification
Market fortification (position defence) involves erecting barriers around the company and its market offerings to shut out competition. The military analogy is the opposite side of the wall from the siege. The defender creates the largest walls and moats possible and sits tight until the aggressor gets weary, or finds other more pressing

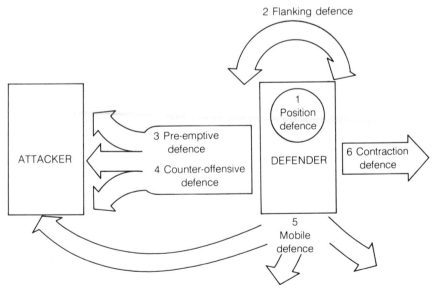

Source: Kotler (1991), Figure 14.2, p. 379.

Figure 13.2   Defend strategies

priorities, and withdraws. During the Second World War Leningrad was besieged by the German army for 900 days but never taken. Eventually, in 1944, Hitler had other preoccupations and called off the siege (James, 1984).

In business, a position defence is created through erecting barriers to copy and/or entry. This is most effectively achieved through differentiating the company's offerings from those of competitors and potential competitors. Where differentiation can be created on non-copyable grounds (e.g. by using the company's distinctive skills, competencies and marketing assets) that are of value to the customers, aggressors will find it more difficult to overrun the position defended.

For established market leaders, brand name and reputation are often used as a major way of holding position. In addition, higher quality, better delivery and service, better (more appealing or heavier) promotions and lower prices based on a cost advantage can all be used to fortify the position held against a frontal attack.

Flanking defence

The flanking defence is a suitable rejoinder to a flanking attack. Under the attack strategy (see above), the aggressor seeks to concentrate its strength against the weaknesses of the defender, often (especially in military warfare) using the element of surprise to gain the upper hand.

A flanking defence requires the company to strengthen the flanks, without providing a weaker and more vulnerable target elsewhere. It requires the prediction of competitor strategy and likely strike positions. In food marketing, for example, several leading manufacturers of branded goods, seeing the increasing threat posed by retailer own-label and generic brands, have entered into contracts to provide own-label products themselves rather than let their competitors get into their markets.

The first major concern in adopting a flanking strategy is whether the new positionings adopted for defensive reasons significantly weaken the main, core positions. In the case of retailer own labels, for example, actively co-operating could increase the trend towards own labels and lead to the eventual death of the brand. As a consequence, many leading brand manufacturers will not supply own labels and rely on the strength of their brands to see off competition (effectively a position, or fortification, defence). Kellogg is a prime example in the breakfast cereal market, where it has adopted the slogan, 'If it doesn't say Kellogg on the label it isn't Kellogg in the box.'

The second concern is whether the new position is actually tenable. Where it is not based on corporate strengths or marketing assets, it may be less defensible than the previously held position.

Pre-emptive defence

A pre-emptive defence involves striking at the potential aggressor before it can mount an attack. The objective is to strike a physical or demoralising blow that will prevent the aggressor from attacking in the first place.

In military conflict, the classic attempt at a pre-emptive strike was the attack by the Japanese on the American fleet in Pearl Harbor in 1941. In that conflict the pre-emptive strike did not deter the Americans from entering the Second World War; indeed, it may have hastened their inevitable entry (James, 1984). More successful was the Israeli strike into Lebanon in 1982 to prevent a major offensive on Israel's home ground. The NATO strategy of threatening first use of nuclear weapons in the event of Warsaw Pact aggression in northern Europe during the cold war was also a pre-emptive defence strategy signalling the threat of retaliation.

In business, the pre-emptive defence can involve actually attacking the competition (as occurs in disruption of competitor test marketing activity) or merely signalling an intention to fight on a particular front and a willingness to commit the necessary resources to defend against aggression.

> ■   When Goldenfry gravies were about to launch a major offensive on the gravy granule market in 1984, the defender, Bisto, launched a major pre-emptive strike with heavy account calling and detailed marketing research demonstrating Bisto product superiority. ■

Sun Tzu, writing around 500 BC (translated by Clavell, 1981) summed up the philosophy behind the pre-emptive defence: 'the supreme art of war is to subdue the enemy without fighting'. Unfortunately, it is not always possible to deter aggression. The second best option is to strike back quickly before the attack gains momentum, through a counter-offensive.

Counter-offensive defence

Whereas deterrence of a potential attack before it occurs may be the ideal defence, a rapid counter-attack to 'stifle at birth' the aggression can be equally effective. The essence of a counter-offensive is to identify the aggressor's vulnerable spots and to strike hard.

> ■   When Xerox attempted to break into the mainframe computer market head on against the established market leader, IBM launched a classic counter-offensive in Xerox's bread-and-butter business: copiers. The middle-range copiers were the major cash generators of Xerox operations and were, indeed, creating the funds to allow Xerox to attack in the mainframe computer market. The IBM counter was a limited range of low-priced copiers directly competing with Xerox middle-range products with leasing options that were particularly attractive to smaller customers. The counter-offensive had the effect of causing Xerox to abandon the attack on the computer market (it sold its interests to Honeywell) to concentrate on defending in copiers (James, 1984). ■

The counter-offensive defence is most effective where the aggressor has made itself vulnerable through overstretching resources. The result is a weak underbelly that can be exploited for defensive purposes.

Mobile defence

The mobile defence was much in vogue as a military strategy in the 1980s. It involves creating a 'flexible response capability' to enable the defender to shift the ground which is being defended in response to environmental or competitive threats and opportunities. The US Rapid Deployment Force is one example of flexible response.

In business, a mobile defence is achieved through a willingness continuously to update and improve the company's offerings to the market place.

> ■ Much of the success of Persil in the UK soap powder market has been due to the constant attempts to keep the product in line with changing customer requirements. The brand, a market leader for nearly half a century, has gone through many reformulations as washing habits have changed and evolved. Reformulations for top-loading washing machines, front-loaders, automatics and more recently colder washes have ensured that the brand has stayed well placed compared to its rivals.
>
> Interestingly, however, Persil went too far when it was modified to a 'biological' formula. Most other washing powders had taken this route to improve the washing ability of the powder. For a substantial segment of the population, however, a biological product was a disadvantage (these powders can cause skin irritation to some sensitive skins). The customer outcry resulted in an 'Original Persil' being reintroduced. ■

The mobile defence is an essential strategic weapon in markets where technology and/or customer wants and needs are changing rapidly. Failure to move with these changes can result in opening the company to a flanking or bypass attack.

Contraction defence

A contraction defence, or strategic withdrawal, requires giving up untenable ground to reduce overstretching and allow concentration on the core business, which can then be defended against attack.

In 1980/1 in response both to competitive pressures and to an adverse economic environment, Tunnel Cement rationalised its operations. Capacity was cut in half and the workforce substantially reduced. Operations were then concentrated into two core activities where the company had specialised and defensible capabilities: chemicals and waste disposal.

In UK retailing, Woolworth's 'Operation Focus' rationalised its operations in 1987 to six key areas where the company believed it had a defensible position. British Home Stores has recently withdrawn from food retailing to concentrate its efforts on other retail areas.

Strategic withdrawal is usually necessary where the company has diversified too far away from the core skills and distinctive competencies that gave it a competitive edge. Many of the tobacco companies diversified into totally unrelated fields in the 1970s only to find themselves in untenable positions and having to divest in the 1980s.

13.3 Market nicher strategies

Market nicher strategies, focusing on a limited sector of the total market, make particular sense for small and medium-sized companies operating in markets which are dominated by the larger operators. The strategies are especially suitable where there are distinct, profitable but underserved pockets within the total market and where the company has an existing differential advantage in serving that pocket, or can create such an advantage.

The two main aspects to the nicher strategy are, first, choosing the pockets, segments or markets on which to concentrate, and second, focusing effort exclusively on serving those targets.

13.3.1   Choosing the battleground

An important characteristic of the successful nicher is an ability to segment the market creatively to identify new and potential niches not yet exploited by major competitors. The battleground, or the niches on which to concentrate, should be chosen by consideration both of market (or niche) attractiveness and the current or potential strength of the company in serving that market.

For the nicher the second of these two considerations is often more important than the first. The major automobile manufacturers, for example, have concentrated their attentions on the large-scale segments of the car market in attempts to keep costs down, through volume production of standardised parts and components and assembly line economies of scale.

This has left many smaller, customised segments of the market, where the major manufacturers are not prepared to compete, open to nichers. In terms of the overall car market, these segments (such as the segment for small sports cars) would be rated as relatively unattractive, but to small operators such as Morgan Cars, with modest growth and return objectives, they offer an ideal niche where their skills can be exploited to the full. The Morgan order books are full and there is a high level of job security and a high degree of job satisfaction in manufacturing a high-quality, hand-crafted car.

13.3.2   Focusing effort

The essence of the nicher strategy is to focus activity on the selected targets and not to allow the company blindly to pursue just any potential customer. Pursuing a niching strategy requires a discipline to concentrate effort on the selected targets.

Hammermesh, Anderson and Harris (1978) examined a number of companies that had successfully adopted a niching strategy and concluded that they showed three main characteristics:

- An ability to segment the market creatively, focusing their activities only on areas where they had particular strengths that were especially valued. In the metal container industry (which faces competition from glass, aluminium, fibrefoil and plastic containers), Crown Cork and Seal has focused on just two segments: metal cans for hard-to-hold products such as beer and soft drinks, and aerosol cans. In both of these segments the company has built considerable marketing assets through its specialised use of technology and its superior customer service.

- Efficient use of R & D resources. Where R & D resources are necessarily more limited than among major competitors, they should be used where they can be most effective. This often means concentrating not on pioneering work but on improvements in existing technologies that are seen to provide more immediate customer benefits.
- Thinking small. Adopting a 'small is beautiful' approach to business increases the emphasis on operating more efficiently rather than chasing growth at all costs. Concentration of effort on the markets the company has chosen to compete in leads to specialisation and a stronger, more defensible position.

13.4 Harvesting strategies

The above building, holding and niching strategies are all applicable to the products and services of the company which offer some future potential either for growth or for revenue generation.

At some stage in the life of most products and services it can become clear that there is no long-term future for them. This may be because of major changes in customer requirements that the product as currently designed cannot keep pace with, or it may be due to technological changes that are making the product obsolete.

In these circumstances a harvesting (or 'milking') strategy may be pursued to obtain maximum returns from the product before its eventual death or withdrawal from the market.

Kotler (1978) defines harvesting as:

a strategic management decision to reduce the investment in a business entity in the hope of cutting costs and/or improving cash flow. The company anticipates sales volume and/or market share declines but hopes that the lost revenue will be more than offset by lowered costs. Management sees sales falling eventually to a core level of demand. The business will be divested if money cannot be made at this core level of demand or if the company's resources can produce a higher yield by being shifted elsewhere.

Candidate businesses or individual products for harvesting may be those that are losing money despite managerial and financial resources being invested in them, or they may be those that are about to be made obsolete due to company or competitor innovation.

Implementing a harvesting strategy calls for a reduction in marketing support to a minimum, cutting expenditure on advertising, sales support and further R & D. There will typically be a rationalisation of the product line to reduce production and other direct costs. In addition, prices may be increased somewhat to improve margins while anticipating a reduction in volume.

Occasionally, a harvested product can continue to produce healthy revenues for some time into the future. The John Player Special (Blacks) brand of cigarettes was effectively harvested in the 1970s when marketing support was reduced to a minimum and returns from the brand were used to support new ventures such as the relaunch of the Lambert and Butler range. The brand declined to a steady state of core, loyal customers who continued to buy the brand. More recently, with changing customer tastes and requirements from a cigarette, the brand has been revived and enjoyed increased marketing support to rebuild its market position.

13.5 Divestment/deletion strategies

Where the company decides that a policy of harvesting is not possible — for example, where despite every effort the business or product continues to lose money — attention may turn to divestment or deletion from the corporate portfolio.

Divestment, the decision to get out of a particular market or business, is never taken lightly by a company. It is crucial when considering a particular business or product for deletion to question the role of the business in the company's overall portfolio.

■ One company, operating in both consumer and industrial markets, examined its business portfolio and found that its industrial operations were at best breaking even, depending on how costs were allocated. Further analysis, however, showed that the industrial operation was a crucial spur to technological developments within the company, which were exploited in the consumer markets in which it operated. The greater immediate technical demands of the company's industrial customers acted as the impetus for the R & D department to improve on the basic technologies used by the company. These had fed through to the consumer side of the business and resulted in the current strength in those markets. Without the industrial operations it is doubtful whether the company would have been so successful in its consumer markets. Clearly, in this case, the industrial operations had a non-economic role to play, and divestment on economic grounds could have been disastrous. ■

Once a divestment decision has been taken, and all the ramifications on the company's other businesses carefully assessed, implementation involves getting out as quickly and cheaply as possible.

13.6 Matching managerial skills to strategic tasks

The above alternative strategies require quite different managerial skills to bring them to fruition. It should be apparent that a manager well suited to building a stronger position for a new product is likely to have different strengths to those of a manager suited to harvesting an ageing product. Wissema, Van der Pol and Messer (1980) have suggested the following types of manager for each of the jobs outlined above.

13.6.1   Pioneers and conquerors for build strategies

The pioneer is particularly suited to the truly innovative new product that is attempting to revolutionise the markets in which it operates. A pioneer is a divergent thinker who is flexible, creative and probably hyperactive. Many entrepreneurs would fall into this category.

A conqueror, on the other hand, would be most suited to building in an established market. The conqueror has a creative but structured approach, and is a systematic team builder who can develop a coherent and rational strategy in the face of potentially stiff competition.

13.6.2   Administrators to hold position

The administrator is stable, good at routine work and probably an introverted conformist. These traits are particularly suited to holding/maintaining position. The administrator keeps a steady hand on the helm.

13.6.3   Focused creators to niche

In many ways these are similar to the conquerors, but they have more creative flair in identifying the initial area for focus. Once that area has been defined, however, a highly focused approach is necessary at the expense of all other distractions.

13.6.4   Economisers for divestment

The diplomatic negotiator (or 'hatchet man'!) is required to divest the company of unprofitable businesses, often in the face of internal opposition.

13.7   Conclusions

A variety of strategies might be pursued once the overall objectives have been set. The strategies can be summarised under five main types: build, hold, harvest, niche, divest. To implement each type of strategy different managerial skills are required. An important task of senior management is to ensure that the managers assigned to each task have the necessary skills and characteristics.

FOURTEEN

Summary and conclusions

If you give a man a fish he will have a single meal. If you teach him how to fish he will eat all his life.

Chinese proverb

Introduction

This book has addressed the central issues in marketing strategy today: the identification of target market and the creation of a competitive edge in serving that chosen market. Taken together these decisions constitute the *competitive positioning* of the organisation. As markets become more crowded and competitive and less predictable, so the importance of clear positioning increases.

The view presented in this book is that segmentation and positioning do not just involve an off-the-peg solution or the adoption of a segmentation scheme accepted throughout an industry as a standard. That way lies competitive stalemate as all organisations view the market the same way. What competitive positioning does involve is creatively searching for a position that can be sustained and defended, and then taking the actions necessary to do so. In that respect, competitive positioning is akin to a fishing trip, skilfully netting the next meal, rather than eating a ready-prepared one.

As markets develop and evolve in response to changing customer expectations and the continuously improving offerings of the organisation and its competitors, so it is necessary to look constantly for newer, more effective ways of targeting the organisation's offerings. It is unlikely that a segmentation scheme adopted today will remain unchanged into the twenty-first century.

This final chapter summarises the main issues involved in creating a clear competitive position.

14.1 Competitive market analysis

It has been argued in previous chapters that the starting point for developing a clear positioning strategy is a thorough analysis of the competitive market in which the organisation operates. There are several strands to this analysis.

14.1.1   Definition of business purpose

Fundamental is deciding on the purpose or mission of the organisation. That requires management to define both the business that the organisation is in, and the business it wants to be in. Increasingly, organisations are finding it helpful to adopt a formal, written mission statement. Chapter 2 discussed the formation of such statements and the factors that should be taken into consideration in their construction.

14.1.2   Company analysis

As a contribution to defining what business the organisation wishes to be in (the options open to it), management need to be aware of the skills, competencies, capabilities and marketing assets of the organisation. Core competencies constitute the processes and technologies that the organisation is adept at, while capabilities include the skills to weld those competencies into the next generation of products and services. Marketing assets are those properties, such as brand name and reputation, distribution networks and internal information systems, that the organisation can bring to bear in the market place to create a stronger position.

An additional consideration for the multiproduct organisation is the overall portfolio of products and services offered. Methods for modelling portfolio balance and future prospects were discussed in Chapter 3.

14.1.3   Customer analysis

The second aspect of market analysis is to focus on customers and potential customers. Chapter 6 examined the types of information required concerning customers and the main methods of research available for collecting the data that can then be converted into information for decision making.

Critical issues include: identifying who the customers are, and who they will be in the future; identifying what gives them value, and what will give them value in the future; understanding how to bring them closer to the company, and what will bring them closer in the future. Constantly the emphasis should be on uncovering the value-adding activities of the organisation, from the customers' perspective, and seeking ways of increasing value.

14.1.4   Competitor analysis

The third side of the triangle of market analysis is competitor analysis. In Chapter 7 this was discussed in detail, from competitor identification, through strategic group analysis, to the prediction of competitor positionings and strategies. The issue of what constitutes a good competitor was also discussed.

14.2 Market target identification

Following from the analysis of company, customers and competitors (the three Cs, or strategic triangle), both the segmentation structure of the market and the current positions of the various providers can be identified. Chapters 8, 9 and 10 focused on segmentation and positioning research techniques and methods.

In addition to traditional, a priori segmentation on the basis of background customer characteristics or behavioural data, the more creative, cluster-based, post hoc methods were discussed. Post hoc segmentation offers the advantage of looking afresh at a market, and not accepting the status quo view of that market. This can often lead to new insights, uncovering hitherto unseen market niches that could offer opportunities for well-targeted offerings.

Positioning research, the subject of Chapter 10, offers a number of techniques for understanding and visually representing markets. In particular, perceptual mapping, through the use of multidimensional scaling techniques, offers a powerful approach to uncovering current positions and identifying market gaps. Recent developments in positioning research were discussed.

Finally, methods for selecting among the alternative potential market segments were discussed in Chapter 11. Two main sets of factors were considered.

The first is market attractiveness. This was seen to involve more than merely market size and growth rate. A number of other factors also need to be taken into account from economic considerations (such as margins achievable), through longer-term viability, to competitor strength and activity.

The second set of factors centre around current or potential strengths in serving the market. Essentially these boil down to the exploitable competencies and assets the organisation can bring to bear in that particular market, and their importance to the customers in that target segment.

14.3 Competitive advantage creation

Competitive success ultimately depends on creating a sustainable competitive advantage in the market place. That in turn requires tuning the organisation's activities and offerings to the requirements of the chosen segment or segments, and then offering those targets something better, in their terms, than the competition.

Two 'generic' routes to creating a competitive advantage have been suggested in the past: cost leadership and differentiation. Both are discussed in Chapter 12. It is noted, however, that cost leadership as a strategy is an internally focused, financial strategy that does not give the customers a reason to buy from the supplier. Differentiation, on the other hand, is a market-based strategy that focuses on giving customers greater value, typically through extending and augmenting the product or service offer.

In conclusion it is suggested that differentiation is the route to effectiveness (doing the right thing, offering customers products and services of value to them), while cost leadership is concerned with efficiency (making those offerings at the lowest achievable cost). Hence, for competitive success, differentiation is the starting point. Once the offer has been differentiated in a way of value to the customers, attention can then shift to offering it as economically as possible.

14.4   Putting it all together

Once the target markets have been selected, and the differentiation designed to allow the organisation to serve those targets more effectively, implementation of the competitive strategy is pursued through build, hold, niche, harvest or divest strategies. Each is considered in Chapter 13.

Build strategies attempt to expand the market (through appealing to new customers, new uses or increased frequency) or win a greater share of the existing market (through attacking competitor positions). Hold strategies attempt to defend current market positions through approaches such as pre-emptive strike, counter-offensive, flanking defence, position defence and mobile defence.

Niching strategies are designed to attack more narrowly defined sectors of the market. They can employ build or hold strategies but are characterised by the clear and specific focus they adopt.

Harvesting strategies are adopted for products and services whose role in the portfolio is to generate cash for investment in other aspects of the business. These products and services are typically in the mature or even decline stages of their life cycles, where the costs of building are judged to outweigh the potential longer-term benefits.

Finally, divestment strategies are pursued when a product or service has reached a stage where it is a drain on resources, both financial and managerial, and the prospects for turnround are low, or outweighed by the costs.

14.5   The future of positioning

Through this book a number of trends have been identified that will influence future developments in competitive positioning.

14.5.1   Increased competition

In many, if not all, markets we are likely to see an increase in competition over the coming years rather than a reduction in it. This has been brought about by a number of factors, chiefly increased international trade (both within and between trading regions) and a slowing of economic growth rates in many developed countries, suggesting increased competition for the existing market pie.

This increased competition, together with a less predictable market place, will make strategic marketing planning both more important and more difficult than it has been in the past.

14.5.2   Increasingly focused marketing activity

Partly as a result of the increasing levels of competition experienced by many companies, clearer targeting is becoming essential. Gone are the days when a standardised product could be offered to the market with a good expectation of taking the bulk of that market.

Nowadays, and into the visible future, the successful organisations are and will be those that know their customers well and tune their offerings accordingly. It is likely that markets will continue to fragment, with ever smaller niches being identified and pursued by those organisations creative enough both to recognise and serve them.

This fragmentation of markets will create many opportunities for smaller organisations, without the resources of the larger players in the market, to create their own speciality niches.

Developments in flexible manufacturing are making 'mass customisation' more possible, encouraging suppliers to take advantage of production efficiencies where possible, while at the same time ensuring that customer wants are specifically addressed.

As marketers become more adept at creatively segmenting markets and fully implementing a marketing orientation, so it will become important to look for new ways of defining and redefining markets. That is one of the central challenges of marketing for the 1990s.

14.5.3   Greater sophistication in marketing support infrastructure

Partly in response to their own customer demands, and partly through the availability of improved research methodology and more sophisticated data analysis techniques, marketing research agencies are increasingly able to offer tailor-made research to help marketers identify new niches in the market.

Developments in off-the-peg segmentation methods, such as ACORN and SAGACITY, have been matched by wider availability in a more 'user-friendly' form of software to enable marketing strategists to perform their own segmentation studies. PC-based software, in particular, has brought the power of sophisticated data analysis techniques, such as conjoint analysis, multidimensional scaling and cluster analysis, on to the desks of managers, enabling them to experiment with newer segmentation methods.

At the same time, media vehicles are becoming ever more sharply focused on specific customer targets, making the accessibility of segments, once identified and selected for targeting, that much greater. Developments in the field of direct marketing, for example, make almost pinpoint targeting possible in many consumer markets.

14.6 Conclusions

As stated at the outset of this book, marketing as an approach to business has come of age. The preoccupation of the 1970s and 1980s with getting across what constitutes a marketing orientation and how it differs from being product or sales oriented has given way to concerns over how companies can actually implement the marketing philosophy in their business.

For that implementation to succeed requires strategic management to be increasingly market led. That, in turn, requires a sharp focus on customers and their requirements. In increasingly competitive, heterogeneous and fragmented markets that focus must come from a clear identification of the organisation's customer targets and a commitment to building a superior set of customer benefits into what will be offered to those targets.

Competitive positioning lies at the heart of the successful implementation of marketing, and for many companies constitutes the key to market strategy.

References and further reading

Aaker, D.A. (1982) 'Positioning your product', *Business Horizon*, vol. 25, no. 3, pp. 56–62.

Abell, D.F. (1978) 'Strategic windows', *Journal of Marketing*, vol. 42, no. 3, pp. 21–6.

Abell, D.F., and Hammond, J.S. (1979) *Strategic Market Planning: Problems and analytical approaches*, Hemel Hempstead: Prentice Hall.

Allio, R.J., and Pennington, M.W. (1979) *Corporate Planning Techniques and Applications*, New York: AMACOM.

Alpert, M.I. (1972) 'Personality and the determinants of product choice', *Journal of Marketing Research*, vol. 9, no. 1, pp. 179–83.

Anderberg, M.R. (1973) *Cluster Analysis for Applications*, New York: Academic Press.

Ansoff, I. (1979) *Strategic Management*, London: Macmillan.

Ansoff, I. (1984) *Implanting Strategic Management*, Hemel Hempstead: Prentice Hall.

Argenti, J. (1974) *Corporate Collapse*, London: Thomas Nelson.

Arthur Young and Co., Australia (1989) *The Arthur Young Report on Brand Valuations: Practical implications for Australian business*, Arthur Young and Co., Australia.

Baumwoll, J.P. (1974) 'Segmentation research: the baker vs the cookie monster', in *Proceedings, American Marketing Association Conference*, pp. 3–20.

Bernard, K.N. (1987) 'Functional practice and conceptual function: the inherent dichotomy of marketing', *Journal of Marketing Management*, vol. 3, no. 1, pp. 73–82.

Bloom, P.N., and Kotler, P.C. (1975) 'Strategies for high market share companies', *Harvard Business Review*, vol. 53, no. 6, pp. 63–72.

Boston Consulting Group (1979) *Specialisation*, Boston, Mass.: BCG.

Bradley, U. (1987) *Applied Marketing and Social Research* (2nd edn), Chichester: Wiley.

Brandt Commission (1980) *North–South: A programme for survival*, London: Pan.

Brandt Commission (1983) *Common Crisis*, London: Pan.

Brittan, Sir Leon (1990) 'A compelling reality', *Speaking of Japan*, vol. 10, no. 110, pp. 18–24.

Broadbent, S.M. (1981) *Advertising Works*, London: Holt, Rinehart and Winston.

Broadbent, S.M. (1983) *Advertising Works 2*, London: Holt, Rinehart and Winston.

Brown, G. (1986) 'The link between advertising content and sales effects', *Admap*, pp. 151–3.

Brown, R. (1987) 'Marketing: a function and a philosophy', *Quarterly Review of Marketing*, vol. 12, nos 3 and 4, pp. 25–30.

Business Week (1972) 'Mead's technique to sort out losers', 11 March, pp. 124–30.

Business Week (1979) 'Kellogg still the cereals people', 26 November, pp. 80–93.

Buzzell, R.D., and Gale B.T. (1987) *The PIMS Principles*, New York: The Free Press.

Buzzell, R.D., and Wiersema, F.D. (1981) 'Successful share building strategies', *Harvard Business Review*, vol. 59, no. 1, pp. 135–44.

Cardozo, R.N. (1979) *Product Policy*, Reading, Mass.: Addison-Wesley.

Chang, J.J. and Carroll, J.D. (1969) 'How to use MDPREF: A computer program for multi-dimensional analysis of preference data', unpublished paper, Bell Telephone Laboratories, Murray Hill, NJ, USA.

Chang, J.J. and Carroll, J.D. (1972) 'How to use PREFMAP and PREFMAP 2: Programs which relate preference data to multidimensional scaling solutions', unpublished paper, Bell Telephone Laboratories, Murray Hill, NJ.

Chattopadhyay, A., Nedungadi, P., and Chakravarti, D. (1985) 'Marketing strategy and differential advantage: a comment', *Journal of Marketing*, vol. 49, no. 2, pp. 129–36.

Chisnall, P.M. (1985) *Strategic Industrial Marketing*, Hemel Hempstead: Prentice Hall.

Churchman, C.V., and Schainblatt, A. (1965) 'The research and manager: a dialectic of implementation', *Management Science*, vol. 11, pp. B69–87.

Clark, P. (1986) 'The marketing of margarine', *European Journal of Marketing*, vol. 20, no. 5, pp. 52–65.

Clausewitz, C. von (1908) *On War*, London: Routledge and Kegan Paul.

Clavell, J. (1981) (ed.), *The Art of War* by Sun Tzu, London: Hodder and Stoughton.

Coad, T. (1989) 'Lifestyle analysis: opportunities for early entry into Europe with effective customer targeting', *Institute of International Research Conference on Customer Segmentation and Lifestyle Marketing*, London, 11–12 December.

Cook, V.J. (1983) 'Marketing strategy and differential advantage', *Journal of Marketing*, vol. 47, no. 2, pp. 68–75.

Cooper, A.C., and Schendel, D. (1976) 'Strategic responses to technological threats', *Business Horizons*, vol. 19, no. 1, pp. 61–9.

Cravens, D.W. (1982) *Strategic Marketing*, Homewood, Ill.: Irwin.

Cravens, D.W. (1991) *Strategic Marketing* (3rd edn), Homewood, Ill.: Irwin.

Crimp, M. (1990) *The Marketing Research Process* (3rd edn), Hemel Hempstead: Prentice Hall.

Crouch, S. (1984) *Marketing Research for Managers*, London: Heinemann.

Davidson, H. (1983) 'Putting assets first', *Marketing*, 17 November.

Davidson, H. (1987) *Offensive Marketing* (2nd edn), Harmondsworth: Penguin.

Davies G., and Brooks, J. (1989) *Positioning Strategy in Retailing*, Hemel Hempstead: Prentice Hall.

Day, G.S. (1977) 'Diagnosing the product portfolio', *Journal of Marketing*, vol. 41, no. 2, pp. 29–38.

Day, G.S. (1986) *Analysis for Strategic Market Decisions*, New York: West Publishing Co.

Day, G.S., Shocker, A.D., and Srivastava, R.K. (1979) 'Customer oriented approaches to identifying product markets', *Journal of Marketing*, vol. 43, no. 4, pp. 8–19.

Dixon, N.F. (1976) *On the Psychology of Military Incompetence*, London: Jonathan Cape.

Douglas, S.P., and Le Maire, P. (1974) 'Improving the quality and efficiency of life style research', *27th ESOMAR Congress*, in *The Challenges Facing Marketing Research: How do we meet them?*, Amsterdam: ESOMAR.

Doyle, P., and Fenwick, I. (1975) 'The pitfalls of AID analysis', *Journal of Marketing Research*, vol. 12, no. 4, pp. 408–13.

Doyle, P., Saunders, J.A., and Wong, V. (1986) 'A comparative study of Japanese and British marketing strategies in the UK market', *Journal of International Business Studies*, vol. 17, no. 1, pp. 27–46.

Drucker, P. (1973) *Management: Tasks, responsibilities and practices*, London: Harper and Row.

Drucker, P. (1981) *Management in Turbulent Times*, London: Heinemann/Pan.

Duncan, W.J. (1974) 'The researcher and the manager: a comparative view of the need for mutual understanding', *Management Science*, vol. 20, pp. 1157–63.

English, J. (1989) 'Selecting and analysing your customer/market through efficient profile modelling and prospecting', *Institute of International Research Conference on Customer Segmentation and Lifestyle Marketing*, London, 11–12 December.

Evans, F.B. (1959) 'Psychological and objective factors in the prediction of brand choice', *Journal of Business*, vol. 32, no. 4, pp. 340–69.

Ferrell, O.C., and Lucas, G.H. (1987) 'An evaluation of progress in the development of a definition of marketing', *Journal of the Academy of Marketing Science*, vol. 15, no. 3, pp. 12–23.

Forbis, J.L., and Mehta, N.T. (1981) 'Value based strategies for industrial products', *Business Horizons*, vol. 24, no. 3, pp. 34–42.

Foster, R.N. (1986a) *Innovation*, New York: Summit.

Foster, R.N. (1986b) 'Attacking through innovation', *McKinsey Quarterly*, Summer, pp. 2–12.

Foster, R.N. (1986c) *Innovation: The attacker's advantage*, London: Macmillan.

Frank, R.E., Massey, W.F., and Boyd, H. (1968) 'The demographic segmentation of household products', in F.M. Bass, C.W. King and E.M. Pessemier (eds), *Applications of the Sciences in Marketing Management*, New York: Wiley.

Frank, R.E., Massey, W.F., and Wind, Y. (1972) *Market Segmentation*, Hemel Hempstead: Prentice Hall.

Franks, J.R., and Boyles, J. (1979) *Modern Managerial Finance*, Chichester: Wiley.

Frohman, A.L. (1982) 'Technology as a competitive weapon', *Harvard Business Review*, vol. 60, no. 1, pp. 97–105.

Frost, W.A.K. (1973) 'Cost effective market mapping using the "Item x Use" concept', *ESOMAR Seminar*, Brussels, June, pp. 73–89.

Fry, J.N., and Siller, F.H. (1970) 'Comparison of housewife decision making in two social classes', *Journal of Marketing Research*, vol. 7, no. 3, pp. 333–7.

Fulmer, W.E., and Goodwin, J. (1988) 'Differentiation: begin with the customer', *Business Horizons*, vol. 31, no. 5, pp. 55–63.

Gale, B.T. (1978) 'Planning for profit', *Planning Review*, vol. 6, no. 1, pp. 4–7, 30–2.

Garda, R.A. (1981) 'A strategic approach to market segmentation', *McKinsey Quarterly*, Autumn, pp. 16–29.

Gluck, F. (1986) 'Strategic planning in a new key', *McKinsey Quarterly*, Winter, pp. 173–83.

Green, P.E., Carmone, F.J., and Smith, S.M. (1989) *Multidimensional Scaling: Concepts and applications*, London: Allyn and Bacon.

Green, P.E., Tull, D.S., and Albaum, G. (1988) *Research for Marketing Decisions* (5th edn), Hemel Hempstead: Prentice Hall.

Green P.E., and Wind, Y. (1975) 'New way to measure consumers' judgements', *Harvard Business Review*, vol. 53, no. 4, pp. 107–17.

Haley, R.I. (1968) 'Benefit segmentation: a decision oriented research tool', *Journal of Marketing Research*, vol. 32, no. 3, pp. 30–5.

Haley, R.I. (1984) 'Benefit segmentation: 20 years on', *Journal of Consumer Marketing*, pp. 5–13.

Hall, W.A.K. (1980) 'Survival strategies in a hostile environment', *Harvard Business Review*, vol. 58, no. 5, pp. 75–85.

Hamel, G., and Prahalad, C.K. (1989) 'Strategic intent', *Harvard Business Review*, vol. 67, no. 3, pp. 63–76.

Hamil, S., and O'Neill, G. (1986) 'Structural changes in British society: the implications for future consumer markets', *Journal of the Market Research Society*, vol. 28, no. 4, pp. 313–24.

Hammermesh, R.G., Anderson, M.J., and Harris, J.E. (1978) 'Strategies for low market share businesses', *Harvard Business Review*, vol. 50, no. 3, pp. 95–102.

Handy, C., Gordon, C., Gow, I., and Randlesome, C. (1989) *Making Managers*, London: Pitman.

Hansen, F. (1972) 'Backwards segmentation using hierarchical clustering and Q-Factor analysis', *ESOMAR Seminar*, May.

Haspeslagh, P. (1982) 'Portfolio planning: uses and limits', *Harvard Business Review*, vol. 60, no. 1, pp. 58–73.

Hedley, B. (1977) 'Strategy and the business portfolio', *Long Range Planning*, vol. 10, no. 1, pp. 9–15.

Henderson, B.D. (1986) 'Perspectives on experience', unpublished monograph, BCG.

Henderson, B.D. (1970) *The Product Portfolio*, Boston: The Boston Consulting Group.

Hildegaard, I., and Krueger, L. (1968) 'Are there customer types?' in F.M. Bass, C.W. King and E.M. Pessemier (eds), *Applications of the Sciences in Marketing Management*, New York: Wiley.

Hill, R. (1979) 'Weak signals from the unknown', *International Management*, vol. 34, no. 10, pp. 55–60.

Hooley, G.J. (1979) 'Perceptual mapping for product positioning: a comparison of two approaches', *European Research*, vol. 7, no. 1, pp. 17–23.

Hooley, G.J. (1980) 'Multidimensional scaling of consumer perceptions and preferences', *European Journal of Marketing*, vol. 14, no. 7, pp. 436–48.

Hooley, G.J. (1982) 'Directing advertising creativity through benefit segmentation', *Journal of Advertising*, vol. 1, pp. 375–85.

Hooley, G.J., Cox, A.J., and Adams, A. (1992) 'Our five year mission: to boldly go where no man has gone before', *Journal of Marketing Management*, vol. 8, no. 1, pp. 35–48.

Hooley, G.J., Krieger, N., and Shipley, D.D. (1988) 'Country of origin effects on brand image', *International Marketing Review*, vol. 5, no. 3, pp. 67–76.

Hooley, G.J., Lynch, J.L., and Shepherd, J. (1990) 'The marketing concept: putting the theory into practice', *European Journal of Marketing*, vol. 24, no. 9, pp. 7–23.

Hughes, M. (1981) 'Portfolio analysis', *Long Range Planning*, vol. 14, no. 1, pp. 101–3.

Hunt, S.D. (1976) 'The nature and scope of marketing', *Journal of Marketing*, vol. 40, no. 3, pp. 17–28.

Imai, M. (1986) *Kaizen: The key to Japan's competitive success*, New York: McGraw-Hill.

Jain, S.C. (1985) *Marketing Planning and Strategy* (2nd edn), Cincinatti, Oh.: South Western.

Jain, S.C. (1990), *Marketing Planning and Strategy* (3rd edn), Cincinatti, Oh.: South Western.

James, B.J. (1984) *Business Wargames*, London: Abacus.

Jobber, D. (1977) 'Marketing information systems in British industry', *Management Decision*, vol. 15, no. 2, pp. 297–304.

Jobber, D., Saunders, J., Hooley, G., Guilding, B., and Hatton-Smooker, G. (1989) 'Assessing the value of a quality assurance certificate for software: an exploratory investigation', *MIS Quarterly*, vol. 13, no. 1, pp. 18–31.

Johnson, G., and Scholes, K. (1988) *Exploring Corporate Strategy* (2nd edn), Hemel Hempstead: Prentice Hall.

Kamen, J.M. (1964) 'Personality and food preferences', *Journal of Advertising Research*, vol. 4, no. 4, pp. 29–32.

King, S. (1985) 'Has marketing failed or was it never really tried?', *Journal of Marketing*

Management, vol. 1, no. 1, pp. 1—19.

Kinnear, T.C., Taylor, J.R., and Ahmed, S.A. (1974) 'Ecologically concerned consumers: who are they?', *Journal of Marketing*, vol. 38, no. 2, pp. 20—4.

Koponen, A. (1960) 'Personality characteristics of purchasers', *Journal of Advertising Research*, vol. 1, no. 4, pp. 6—12.

Kotler, P.C. (1978) 'Harvesting strategies for weak products', *Business Horizons*, vol. 21, no. 4, pp. 15—22.

Kotler, P.C. (1991) *Marketing Management: Analysis, planning, implementation and control*, Hemel Hempstead: Prentice Hall.

Kotler, P., Fahay, L., and Jatusripitak, S. (1985) *The New Competition*, Hemel Hempstead: Prentice Hall.

Kotler, P.C., Gregor, W., and Rogers, W. (1977) 'The marketing audit comes of age', *Sloan Management Review*, vol. 18, no. 2, pp. 25—44.

Kotler, P.C., and Levy, S.J. (1969) 'Broadening the concept of marketing', *Journal of Marketing*, vol. 33, no. 1, pp. 10—15.

Kotler, P.C., and Singh, R. (1981) 'Marketing warfare in the 1980s', *Journal of Business Strategy*, vol. 1, no. 3, pp. 30—41.

Kruskal, J.B., Young, F.W., and Seery, J.B. (1973) 'How to use KYST: a very flexible programme to do multidimensional scaling', Multidimensional Scaling Program Package of Bell Laboratories, Murray Hill, NJ.

Lancaster, G., and Saunders, J. (1978) 'Student choice of courses in higher education', *Journal of Business Education*, vol. 1, no. 3, pp. 7—21.

Levitt, T. (1960) 'Marketing Myopia', *Harvard Business Review*, vol. 38, no. 4, pp. 45—56.

Levitt, T. (1975) 'Marketing Myopia: retrospective commentary', *Harvard Business Review*, vol. 53, no. 5, pp. 26—39, 44, 173—81.

Levitt, T. (1986) *The Marketing Imagination*, New York: The Free Press.

Lilien, G.L., and Kotler, P. (1983) *Marketing Decision Making: A model building approach*, London: Harper and Row.

Little, J.D.C. (1970) 'Models and managers: the concept of a decision calculus', *Management Science*, vol. 16, no. 8, pp. B466—85.

Little, J.D.C. (1975) 'BRANDAID: a marketing-mix model, part 1: structure; part 2: implementation calibration and a case study', *Operations Research*, vol. 23, pp. 628—73.

Little, J.D.C. (1979) 'Decision support systems for marketing management', *Journal of Marketing*, vol. 43, no. 3, pp. 9—27.

Lusch, R.F., and Laczniak, G.R. (1987) 'The evolving marketing concept, competitive intensity and organisational performance', *Journal of the Academy of Marketing Science*, vol. 15, no. 3, pp. 1—11.

MacDonald, M. (1984) *Marketing Plans*, London: Heinemann.

McLeod, J. (1985) 'Marketing information systems: a review paper', *Quarterly Review of Marketing*, vol. 10, no. 3.

Maier, J., and Saunders, J. (1990) 'The implementation of segmentation in sales management', *Journal of Personal Selling and Sales Management*, vol. 10, no. 1, pp. 39—48.

Market Research Society, *Organisations Providing Marketing Research Services in the UK*, MRS annual publication.

Markowitz, H. (1952) 'Portfolio selection', *Journal of Finance*, vol. 7, no. 2, pp. 77—91.

Morrison, A., and Wensley, R. (1991) 'Boxing up or boxed in?: a short history of the Boston Consulting Group share/growth matrix', *Journal of Marketing Management*, vol. 7, no. 2, pp. 105—30.

Morrison, J.R., and Lee, J.G. (1979) 'The anatomy of strategic thinking', *McKinsey Quarterly*, Autumn, pp. 2–9.

Murphy, J. (1991) *Brand Valuation* (2nd edn), London: Business Books.

Murphy, P.E., and Staples, W.A. (1979) 'A modernized family life cycle', *Journal of Consumer Research*, vol. 6, no. 1, pp. 12–22.

Musashi, M. (1974 translation), *A Book of Five Rings*, Woodstock, NY: Overlook Press.

Naert, P., and Leeflang, P. (1978) *Building Implementable Marketing Models*, Leiden, Netherlands: Martinus Nijhoff.

NIESR (1990) *Productivity, Education and Training*, London: National Institute for Economic and Social Research.

O'Brien, N., and Ford, J. (1988) 'Can we at last say goodbye to social class?', *Journal of Market Research Society*, vol. 16, no. 2, pp. 43–51.

Ohmae, K. (1982) *The Mind of the Strategist*, Harmondsworth: Penguin.

O'Shaughnessy, J. (1988) *Competitive Marketing* (2nd edn), London: Unwin Hyman.

Oxx, C. (1972) 'Psychographics and life style', *Admap*, pp. 303–5.

Pagnamenta, P., and Overy, R. (1984) *All Our Working Lives*, London: BBC Publications.

Parasuraman, A., Zeithaml, V.A., and Berry, L.L. (1985) 'A conceptual model of service quality and its implications for further research', *Journal of Marketing*, vol. 49, no. 4, pp. 41–50.

Parasuraman, A., Zeithaml, V.A., and Berry, L.L. (1988) 'SERVQUAL: A multiple-item scale for measuring consumer perceptions of service quality', *Journal of Retailing*, vol. 64, no. 1, pp. 12–40.

Park, C.W., Jaworski, B.J., and MacInnis, D.J. (1986) 'Strategic brand concept–image management', *Journal of Marketing*, vol. 50, no. 4, pp. 135–45.

Patel, P., and Younger, M. (1978) 'A frame of reference for strategic development', *Long Range Planning*, vol. 11, no. 6, pp. 6–12.

Peters, T. (1986) *Thriving on Chaos*, London: Macmillan.

Piercy, N. (1991) *Market-Led Strategic Change*, London: Thorsons.

Porter, M.E. (1980) *Competitive Strategy*, New York: The Free Press.

Porter, M.E. (1985) *Competitive Advantage*, New York: The Free Press.

Porter, M.E. (1987) 'From competitive advantage to corporate strategy', *Harvard Business Review*, vol. 65, no. 3, pp. 43–59.

Prahalad, C.K., and Hamel, G. (1990) 'The core competence of the corporation', *Harvard Business Review*, vol. 68, no. 3, pp. 79–91.

Punj, G., and Stewart, D.W. (1983) 'Cluster analysis in marketing research: review and suggestions for applications', *Journal of Marketing Research*, vol. 20, no. 2, pp. 135–48.

Richards, E.A., and Sturman, S.S. (1977) 'Life-style segmentation in apparel marketing', *Journal of Marketing*, vol. 41, no. 4, pp. 89–91.

Ries, A., and Trout, J. (1981) *Positioning: The battle for your mind*, London: McGraw-Hill.

Ries, A., and Trout, J. (1986) *Marketing Warfare*, New York: McGraw-Hill.

Robinson, S.J.Q., Hitchins, R.E., and Wade, D.P. (1978) 'The directional policy matrix: tool for strategic planning', *Long Range Planning*, vol. 11, no. 3, pp. 8–15.

Rothwell, R. (1981) 'Why new products fail', *Marketing*, 29 July.

Rowe, A.J., Mason, R.D., Dickel, K.E., and Snyder, N.H. (1989) *Strategic Management: A methodological approach* (3rd edn), Reading, Mass.: Addison-Wesley.

Rubinstein, M. (1973) 'A mean-variance synthesis of corporate finance theory', *Journal of Finance*, vol. 28, no. 1, pp. 167–81.

Saunders, J. (1985) 'New product forecasting in the UK', *Quarterly Review of Marketing*, vol. 10, no. 4, pp. 1–11.

Saunders, J. (1990) 'Brands and valuations', *International Journal of Advertising*, vol. 9, no. 2, pp. 95–110.

Saunders, J., Sharp, J., and Witt, S. (1987) *Practical Business Forecasting*, Aldershot: Gower.

Saunders, J., and Watt, A. (1979), 'Do brand names differentiate identical industrial products?', *Industrial Marketing Management*, vol. 8, no. 2, pp. 114–23.

Schultz, R.L., and Henry, M.D. (1981) 'Implementing decision models' in R. Schultz and A. Zoltners (eds), *Marketing Decision Models*, New York: North-Holland.

Segmit, S., and Broadbent, S. (1973) 'Life-style research: A case history in two parts', *European Research*, January, pp. 6–13, March, pp. 62–8.

Smith, S.M. (1990) 'PC-MDS Version 5.1: multidimensional statistics package', Prova, Ut.: Brigham Young University.

Sparks, D.L., and Tucker, W.T. (1971) 'Multivariate analysis of personality and product use', *Journal of Marketing Research*, vol. 8, no. 1, pp. 67–70.

Stalk, G. (1988) 'Time: the next source of competitive advantage', *Harvard Business Review*, vol. 88, no. 4, pp. 41–51.

Stevenson, H.H. (1976) 'Defining corporate strengths and weaknesses', *Sloan Management Review*, vol. 17, no. 3, pp. 57–68.

Stonich, P.J. (1982) *Implementing Strategy*, Cambridge, Mass.: Ballinger.

Toffler, A. (1971) *Future Shock*, London: Bodley Head/Pan.

Toffler, A. (1981) *The Third Wave*, London: William Collins/Pan.

Tucker, W.T., and Painter, J.J. (1961) 'Personality and product use', *Journal of Applied Psychology*, vol. 45, no. 5, pp. 325–9.

Tull, D.S., and Hawkins, D.I. (1984) *Marketing Research* (3rd edn), London: Macmillan.

Urban, G. (1974) 'Building models for decision makers', *Interfaces*, vol. 4, no. 3, pp. 1–11.

Ward, J. (1963) 'Hierarchical grouping to optimize an objective function', *Journal of the American Statistical Association*, vol. 58, no. 2, pp 236–44.

Wells, W.D., and Gubar, G. (1966) 'Life cycle concepts in marketing research', *Journal of Marketing Research*, vol. 3, no. 4, pp. 355–63.

Wensley, R. (1981) 'Strategic marketing: boxes, betas or basics', *Journal of Marketing*, vol. 45, no. 3, pp. 173–82.

Westfall, R. (1962) 'Psychological factors in predicting product choice', *Journal of Marketing*, vol. 26, no. 2, pp. 34–40.

Wilmott, M. (1989) 'Whose lifestyle is it anyway?', *Institute of International Research Conference on Customer Segmentation and Lifestyle Marketing*, London, 11–12 December.

Wind, V. (1978) 'Issues and advances in segmentation research', *Journal of Marketing Research*, vol. 15, no. 3, pp. 317–37.

Wind, Y., and Mahajan, V. (1981) 'Designing product and business portfolios', *Harvard Business Review*, vol. 59, no. 1, pp. 155–65.

Wishart, D. (1969) *CLUSTAN IA: A FORTRAN program for numerical classification*, Computing Laboratory, St. Andrew's University, Scotland.

Wissema, J.G., Van der Pol, H.W., and Messer, H.M. (1980) 'Strategic management archetypes', *Strategic Management Journal*, vol. 1, no. 1, pp. 37–47.

Wright, L., Saunders, J., and Doyle, P. (1990) 'From the outside looking in', *American Marketing Association Educators Proceedings*, Washington, DC, pp. 338–43.

Zunin, L. (1972) *Contact: The first four minutes*, New York: Ballantine.

Index